Teaching
ENGLISH

English is still considered one of the most important school subjects and therefore beginning teachers can find the responsibility of teaching it both exciting and challenging. This handbook provides a comprehensive introduction to teaching the subject in primary and secondary schools. It brings together the latest standards with authoritative guidance, ensuring that readers feel confident about how to approach their teaching.

The book explores the context of the subject of English and brings readers up to date with key developments. It places the English curriculum in the context of whole-school Literacy issues. It introduces readers to key areas such as:

- planning and classroom management
- assessment, recording and reporting
- information and communication technology
- equal opportunities, special needs and differentiation
- English/Literacy and whole-school issues
- personal and professional early career development.

This practical and accessible book will give beginning English teachers a solid and dependable introduction to teaching the subject. Many of the contributors are practising classroom teachers with enormous experience to draw on. The book is absolutely grounded in the realities of teaching and offers practical and relevant advice, as well as plentiful ideas to stimulate thinking and teaching.

Andrew Goodwyn is Director of Teaching and Learning and is course leader for all secondary English student teachers and for the Masters in English and Language in Education at the Institute of Education, University of Reading. **Jane Branson** is Head of English at Peacehaven Community School in East Sussex.

Teaching Series

Teaching

ENGLISH

**A HANDBOOK FOR PRIMARY AND
SECONDARY SCHOOL TEACHERS**

LB1576.T3757 2005
Teaching English : a
handbook for primary and
secondary school teachers
London ; New York :
RoutledgeFalmer, 2005.

**Andrew GOODWYN &
Jane BRANSON**

Routledge
Taylor & Francis Group

LONDON AND NEW YORK

First published 2005 by RoutledgeFalmer
2 Park Square, Milton Park, Abingdon, Oxon OX14 4RN

Simultaneously published in the USA and Canada
by RoutledgeFalmer
270 Madison Ave, New York, NY 10016

RoutledgeFalmer is an imprint of the Taylor & Francis Group

Typeset in Palatino by
Florence Production Ltd, Stoodleigh, Devon EX16 9PN
Printed and bound in Great Britain by
St Edmundsbury Press Ltd, Bury St Edmunds, Suffolk

British Library Cataloguing in Publication Data
A catalogue record for this book is available from the
British Library

Library of Congress Cataloging in Publication Data
A catalog record has been applied for

ISBN 0–415–33527–2

Contents

CONTENTS

Illustrations

Figures

Tables

Abbreviations

AQA	Assessment and Qualifications Alliance
ASD	Autistic Spectrum Disorder
BFI	British Film Institute
CAME	Cognitive Acceleration through Mathematics Education
CASE	Cognitive Acceleration through Science Education
CPD	Continuing Professional Development
DART	Directed Activity Related to Text
DfEE	Department for Education and Employment
DfES	Department for Education and Skills
EAL	English as an Additional Language
EBD	Emotional and Behavioural Difficulties
GTC	General Teaching Council
GTP	Graduate Teacher Programme
HMI	Her Majesty's Inspectorate
ICT	Information and Communications Technology
IEP	Individual Educational Plan
INSET	In-service Training
ITT	Initial Teacher Training
KAL	Knowledge About Language
LEA	Local Education Authority
LINC	Language in the National Curriculum
LPU	Literacy Progress Unit
MLD	Moderate Learning Difficulties
NATE	National Association for the Teaching of English
NLS	National Literacy Strategy
NQT	Newly Qualified Teacher

ABBREVIATIONS

OHP	Overhead Projector
PGCE	Postgraduate Certificate in Education
PHSE	Personal Health and Social Education
QCA	Qualifications and Curriculum Authority
QTS	Qualified Teacher Status
SAT	Standard Attainment Task
SEN	Special Educational Needs
SENCO	Special Educational Needs Coordinator
TA	Teaching Assistant
TES	*Times Educational Supplement*
TLF	Teaching and Learning in the Foundation subjects
TTA	Teacher Training Agency

1 The subject of English: putting English in perspective

Andrew Goodwyn

Introduction

Everyone agrees that the subject 'English' is vitally important and typically it is described as the most important of all school subjects, principally because reading, writing, speaking and listening are needed to a greater or lesser degree in every other school subject, and for adult life. However, that is as far as the agreement goes; even attempting a simple, consensual definition proves extremely difficult. English is also the most consistently controversial and debated subject. It might be argued that English is the subject that many interested parties would most like to control. The history of English is simply a history of constant change. Inevitably, this makes teaching it a special kind of challenge, but it also imbues the subject with energy and excitement. All subjects have their debates and passions but English seems to have the most, and they are very often unusually public and attract plenty of media attention. As media attention is almost inevitably negative, the public perception of English nationally can be that children cannot spell, produce a decent paragraph or even conduct a reasonable conversation; at the same time parents, i.e. members of that 'public', will tell you that their children have received excellent English teaching at the local school. This issue of perception will be further discussed in the chapter dealing with professionalism. If you want a quiet life, perhaps you should teach a different subject.

This chapter will provide some more context for these opening remarks, including a brief history of the subject, and it will engage more fully with the issue of definition. There is an extensive range of books providing insights into the development of the subject and a selection of these are listed in the references at the end of the book.

'What's in a name'?

Even the word 'English' is an issue. English is, after all, essentially a language. However, it is not just spoken by the people who call themselves the English. The first confusion is that even these people may call themselves British and the second is that English is the first language of many other people. In a rapidly changing world, it is the second or third language of a vast number of people and also the basic mode of communication in many of the key discourses that the world relies on to make things work – air traffic control being a neat example. The most salient point for the teacher of English in the United Kingdom, and very particularly in England, is that the great majority of pupils (and their parents) are almost pathologically monolingual. Why should we learn a foreign language, they all say, when everyone everywhere speaks English?

For the teacher of the mother tongue this is a significant issue. Our colleagues in modern languages will tell you emphatically how hard it is to teach pupils another language, partly because of this negative attitude but also because children may lack a language with which to talk about language: this might be called grammatical vocabulary or perhaps a meta-language. We do have pupils who are bi- or even tri-lingual but in British schools they often hide this capacity. This inaccurate problematising of bilingualism has often led to children for whom English is their second language being treated as if they have special educational needs rather than special linguistic needs and abilities. English must be viewed, therefore, as to some extent a dominating language, and pupils can be encouraged by the culture they inhabit to see this as somehow natural and right. English teachers see it as fundamentally important to challenge these assumptions.

Task 1.1: Theory task

What is your linguistic capacity? Do you bring to teaching English an understanding of any other languages? Have your travels given you insights into other cultures and the way they use language, possibly including English? What about 'American English' that pupils experience so much of via the media? Write a brief evaluation of your knowledge about language.

If English has many global varieties, then this diversity is matched within regions and even districts. George Bernard Shaw famously remarked in his preface to *Pygmalion*, 'It is impossible for an Englishman to open his mouth without making another Englishman hate or despise him.' This statement was written in 1916 and neatly reveals its pre-feminism in the assumptions displayed in the confident use of 'man'; we will consider gender issues more fully later in the chapter. Shaw was getting at the notion of accent and linking it to social class and probably to regional prejudices. Despite almost a century of education since and also a far greater acceptance of accentual diversity – television and radio being the key indicators in this respect – there is still plenty of prejudice about the way people speak English. For example, what exactly is the Queen's English and who speaks it?

One purpose of the subject English therefore does fit the name – i.e. to teach the language as an entitlement to all pupils whether or not it is their first or second language. This purpose is not a narrow one, however. If it were, then it might only involve teaching the 'mechanics', i.e. spelling, grammar and punctuation. One controversy over the subject is how central this narrow purpose should be, as the history of the subject reveals (see below). However, most practising teachers are engaged in a broader purpose, as is borne out to some extent in current formal definitions of the subject, i.e. the National Curriculum and the Framework for English. These documents require pupils to have an understanding of the history of language per se, i.e. a more detailed grasp of the development of English as a national and also international language. Included within this would be the varieties of English down to the level of local accent and dialect. This local focus emphasises that language and identity are bound up inextricably. Each pupil belongs to several language communities simultaneously but retains an idiolect, i.e. a unique individual linguistic repertoire.

Task 1.2: Theory task

You will be a 'role model' when teaching English, whether or not you like that idea. What does your accent 'reveal' about your linguistic history? What has influenced the way you speak? Jot down a few key points about your language history and also reflect on your current linguistic knowledge. How ready are you to teach English as a language?

Teaching English from a linguistic perspective is an exciting and complex challenge. It suggests that all primary teachers and all secondary English teachers would do well to take linguistics at an advanced level, perhaps even as a complete degree. However, this is simply not the case. Although there has been some increase in people entering the profession with some level of linguistic qualification, the great majority of secondary teachers and primary English specialists choose English because of their love of and passion for literature; these are the emotive words constantly used by interviewees explaining their motives for wanting to teach English. Many further define themselves as having always loved reading. The possession of a degree in English can mean many different things, but for most graduates it means the almost exclusive study of literature, a great deal of it English Literature. Embedded within this study is the notion of literary criticism. One important perspective on this is that the highest form of English can be conceptualised as the interpretation of literary texts expressed in the traditional argumentative essay form. The majority of Year 12 and 13 students of English are still very much engaged in that activity. To express this deliberately simplistically, they spend most of their time reading books and discussing them, then are assessed almost exclusively in one very specialised form of writing. It is important to reflect on what a very narrow version of English this represents. Also, it is important to note here that this narrow focus helps to explain the rapid rise in popularity of advanced level English Language, Media Studies (very often taught by English teachers) and of syllabuses that combine language and literature.

These post-16 students have chosen English, so they might well be expected to have a love of reading. It is important to note here that many pupils select English as their third or fourth choice and that only a minority in most A level groups are considering taking English at university. What is more important for the beginning teacher of English, at whatever Key Stage, is to recognise that literature teaching forms a key part of the job. If this seems too obvious, it is time for a pause for thought.

All children are taught to read. A few learn easily at home even before school but most become independent readers within two or three years of primary schooling. Huge problems lie ahead for those who do not achieve this competence, and that is another story taken up elsewhere in this book. It could be argued that after this it should be up to children to decide whether they wish to read any more fiction or poetry. These texts were not intended by their authors to be studied in school, so why do we insist (because we do) that pupils will read them in class and, as they get older, study them? The rationale for including literature in study goes back at least to the Greeks and reminds us that the tradition of the classics (great works) is embedded in the name of that theme as a subject, i.e. Classics – itself the focus of the education of gentlemen in English schools for several centuries.

At this stage it is enough to say that all English teachers will teach literary texts and the definition adopted here is that a literary text has an aesthetic dimension and was typically written to be read for its own sake, i.e. not, for example, to help you mend the washing machine more efficiently. It is also vital to stress that many English teachers see this as the real heart of the subject and a source of their own satisfaction and enjoyment. There is nothing natural about including literary texts in the subject named after the mother tongue; it is a very particular choice and by no means makes sense to all pupils, some of whom detest reading fiction, and poetry in particular. They need convincing, especially as they get older.

No current English teacher is likely to argue that pupils should only read literary texts, and both the National Curriculum and Framework for English emphasise the need to encounter a broad range of texts, including all the key genres from non-fiction and media texts (see Chapter 6). Thus pupils in English can encounter almost any kind of text from a chocolate bar wrapper to *Romeo and Juliet*. One of the most enjoyable aspects of teaching English can be engaging with this great variety of text types and helping pupils to understand them and often to create their own. This focus on texts – the term 'text' being almost neutral – is probably the most consensual area of English and might lead to it being defined as 'Textual Studies' without much controversy. However, capital L, Literature, is, as suggested above, a distinctive and powerful element within English often associated with the notion of cultural heritage (discussed more fully below). Such an approach inevitably treats texts in terms of perceived value and relies on a notion of the canon – something still clearly reflected in A level syllabuses and the simple fact that every child is tested on Shakespeare at the age of 14.

Again, to many readers, all this may seem the norm. However, many practising teachers might well feel very happy with all pupils, regardless of ability, benefiting from an engagement with Shakespeare but very few want children tested in the current mode, and they strongly object to the teaching to the test style that often entraps them. In other words, most English teachers develop many strategies for teaching all kinds of texts, including some of the great texts of the canon, but they have many reservations about residual elements of elitism ossified in the assessment system.

This mention of Shakespeare leads into another key area of English. Just as most authors never wrote for school, so Shakespeare wrote for performance not for reading. Again, from the pupils' perspective, why on earth read Shakespeare, why not watch him on stage or screen? One partial answer is small 'd' drama. The subject Drama is not part of the National Curriculum and not all schools offer it as a discrete subject. The National Curriculum requires English teachers both to teach play texts and to use drama in their repertoire of teaching strategies (see Chapter 5). The simple point to make here is that English teachers need to think about using drama techniques, partly to make reading plays more like Drama, but also to make use of drama as an active and creative element in their work.

Perhaps the other consensual part of English is the general agreement about the fundamental importance of speaking and listening, although it is worth reflecting here that in historical terms this is a recent development (see below). The emphasis on drama is partly linked to the need to create speaking and listening opportunities for pupils, role play being an excellent example. Pupils can experiment with language and use their bodies to aid expression and communication. They can try out the language of Shakespeare as he intended it, as an embodiment. English teachers are therefore partly drama teachers, and it must be said that for some a lack of experience and training may make this a relative weakness.

Task 1.3: Theory task

For some, teaching Drama is a worry because it means a loss of 'class control'. There are real gains for pupils, although some do find Drama difficult. From the pupils' viewpoint, list the pros and cons of doing some Drama in English.

One positive reason you may have included is that Drama is active. This is important because English can seem very inactive as much time might be spent reading, listening to the teacher talk or read, or writing. We all know that writing is a slow, time-consuming process and, because of the concentration it requires, physically tiring. One of the consistent features of good English teachers is their use of variety, and their ability to read the classroom for signs of restiveness if a task is beginning to lose its effectiveness.

But inevitably there is a lot of sitting down in English and never more so than in the last of the four language modes, namely writing. Everyone is agreed that all adults must have good communication skills, but in the age of the phone and the text message it is perhaps harder to convince all young people that traditional writing is so fundamental. Some of these issues will be explored more fully in the chapter on Information and Communications Technology (ICT) in English. However, at this point it must be stressed that although ICT would seem to offer wonderful opportunities for English teachers and their pupils, the reality is rather different. Most schools still lack the required resources and the Framework for English is still very print-based in quite a nineteenth-century mode. As almost all assessments must be handwritten, pupils must learn to write in pen and paper mode. Many find this aspect of English the most demanding and unrewarding.

It is worth reflecting once more on what brings people into the profession – typically the love of reading, not writing. Whatever degree the beginning teacher of English has taken, it is almost a certainty that it has involved writing many, many essays and not a single other genre – no stories, poems or plays, for example. So teaching writing is also a very new and also different demand for the beginning English teacher. That teacher will be an excellent role model as a reader – fluent, confident and knowledgeable, able to read aloud with feeling and style. But what about modelling writing? If the pupils are asked to write a poem, should the teacher produce one too? This may depend somewhat on your own implicit view of writing. Is it a craft, made up of teachable skills? Or is it about inspiration, an innate ability that can be unlocked by the right opportunity? Most English teachers consider it a bit of both and teach accordingly.

This point leads us to a brief review of the subject's development, because one element that unites English teachers is the concern with the person and the personal. For example, they would certainly suggest that writing poetry is worth doing for all pupils, particularly as a means of personal expression. In working towards a description of contemporary English, this focus on the personal will form a key theme.

The origins of English

Beginning teachers are typically very enthusiastic to get on with the job, and rightly so. However, at that moment of their beginning, the subject itself is simply at a particular point in its ongoing evolution and it is vital to understand what has shaped and influenced it. The earlier point, that teaching literature is a very particular choice and not just common sense, is a helpful reminder about subject history. It can be argued that English, more than any other subject, requires teachers who have a genuine perspective on the current definition of the subject and a sense of how that definition has been derived. This particular overview will necessarily be brief and will focus on key influences that are still important. It will also be slightly more detailed from 1989, the year in which the National Curriculum was introduced.

English essentially replaced Classics during the course of the nineteenth century and by early in the twentieth century it was established as a degree subject in several major universities. This is important because it shows how recent, compared to, say, Mathematics, its appearance has been and equally because it inherited from Classics the mantle of cultural heritage. It partly explains the invention of English, capital L, Literature in the early part of the twentieth century. So English came into being at the time of the empire with all of the associated imperialistic and nationalistic baggage of that period. Its first great crisis came as a result of the traumas of the First World War, leading to the first of many reviews of the subject, the Newbolt Report of 1920. If this seems like ancient history, the report makes very intriguing reading, containing many statements that seem current as well as those that no longer pertain. It may raise a smile to know that employers were even then complaining that school leavers were deficient in writing, and spelling in particular. Newbolt is important also because it set the model for many such reviews, i.e. the setting up of a committee of selected worthies, may of whom were writers rather than educators. Newbolt himself was a very minor poet. A member of the committee, George Sansom, produced his view of the fundamental importance of the subject in his book *English for the English*, in which he made it clear that this new subject was needed absolutely to bind a war-torn country, and to unite the divided classes through their joint and glorious national heritage in their common language and literature. These kinds of argument for what English should be about are always reappearing and again are important in reminding us that many see the subject as an issue of national unity, implying therefore that appreciation, not critique, should be at its heart.

In the 1930s, the idea of the great tradition of English Literature was taken up by F.R. Leavis. He drew on the work of others, notably I.A. Richards, who had invented practical criticism as a way of reading, and Leavis reconfigured English as essentially about the study of English Literature. For Leavis and his many followers, English was a stern moral enterprise. Only by truly close reading of the great texts could we hope to be saved from the vulgarities of modern life, Hollywood in particular. He pursued this theme in books and articles and in his journal, *Scrutiny*, for over 40 years, directly influencing several generations of teachers. It was this influence that led Margaret Mathieson, writing in the early 1970s, to dub English teachers 'the preachers of culture', the evangelicals of literature. Here is a direct link to contemporary English in that much vaunted love of reading and in the selection of texts in the National Curriculum and at A level.

The 1960s and 1970s brought on a counter-revolution of equal force. Leavis' model was fundamentally elitist. He utterly despised popular culture and believed that there would only ever be a minority who could keep the flame of culture burning; this tended to exclude most of the population. In the radical and democratic times of the 1960s and 1970s, all of this was challenged. With the introduction of the comprehensive school and the raising of the school leaving age came the need for a new definition of English. A whole set of discordant elements were at work – popular music, the development of television, the space race, the Cold War, immigration and so on – a ferment of change. Inevitably, one political reaction was to suggest that 'standards are falling', so an inquiry into reading standards was commissioned (by the then Education Minister, a certain Margaret Thatcher), an inquiry that eventually produced the Bullock Report, *A Language for Life*. Unusually, this report drew heavily on the latest educational thinking of theorists such as James Britton, Douglas Barnes and Harold Rosen, all of whom challenged the elitism of the grammar school curriculum. In essence, they argued for the centrality of speaking and listening to all learning, that language was the key to understanding, and so the motto 'language across the curriculum' was born, urging all teachers to be teachers of language. They celebrated the richness and diversity of the English language, and the energy and power of 'ordinary people's' use of language, including immigrant communities.

One outcome of this was the central notion of personal growth through English. Instead of a notion of only studying the classics, it became more important for children to explore their identities through reflecting on the language of their immediate community, and speaking and writing to articulate their thoughts and feelings. Underlying all of this was the increasing influence of the work of Vygotsky, whose theories of learning propounded an essentially social model of knowledge creation, knowledge made by the learners themselves in social situations. Also influential were the theories of reader response developed by Louise Rosenblatt who argued that the interpretation of a text was produced in the interaction of the reader and the text, suggesting that any response had some validity, stemming as it must from the personal knowledge of the reader, and therefore no two readings could be exactly alike. For teachers, this meant that their own interpretation must be personal, not necessarily right, and that pupils' interpretations might actually be valuable. English teachers tend not to talk about 'reader response' but that concept is present whenever they talk about a personal response from pupils.

One outcome of this set of changes was an essential reform of assessment in English. By the mid 1980s the GCSE had been introduced, replacing the old two-tier (O levels and CSEs) system. Speaking and listening were for the first time part of the content of English and were assessed. Pupils at GCSE could be assessed by 100 per cent coursework portfolios, including a wide range of written genres; responses to literature did not have to be in the essay style but might be creative; pupils were rewarded for reading widely and for including attention to popular and media texts; there were no absolutely set texts, teachers could choose. A few of these elements currently remain in contemporary English, but many have been removed or severely diminished. Here is a key example for understanding that English might be very different from its current formation, helping to point up that it will continue to change. Another important point to note is that the elements of choice and coursework embedded in the original GCSE soon influenced A level. One particular syllabus from the now defunct Associated Examing Board (AEB) offered students the chance to undertake individual reading projects and to include creative writing; this form of assessment was very popular with English teachers and proved highly motivating for students, including those achieving the lower grades. The decision to scrap this syllabus was entirely a political one; for educational reasons it may yet be resurrected.

If the 1980s were marked by teacher autonomy, then the 1990s were a decade of prescription and control. The radicalism of the 1970s and 1980s provoked a somewhat predictable political reaction that standards were once more under threat, leading to the setting up of the Kingman Inquiry into the teaching of English language. This inquiry was fuelled by two reports from Her Majesty's Inspectorate (HMI) in 1984 and 1986 that had laid out, for the first time in England, a suggested English curriculum for ages 5–16. Both reports suggested that there was insufficient attention to explicit language teaching. These HMI documents also signalled the beginning of a shift from advice to prescription, backed up by an inspection regime summed up by the word 'Ofsted' – an organisation that dominated the 1990s.

Kingman investigated this issue and concluded that although there was no need to return to the grammar exercises of the 1950s, there was yet the potential to improve 'Knowledge About Language' (KAL), recommending that this should start with the teachers themselves and that there should be a national project to improve serving teachers' own KAL. The report was accepted and from 1989 to 1992 the Language in the National Curriculum (LINC) Project was undertaken.

However, other events must take precedence before the project is briefly described. Between 1988 and 1989 the idea for the practical reality of a National Curriculum came into being. Considered, as always, the key subject, English was the first subject for which a committee was set up to determine a National Curriculum. Even with the Kingman Report still warm on the desks, the politicians pushed ahead. The Cox Committee recommended English first for children aged five plus and then for ages 5–16. It was at this time that the whole concept of levels was created, together with that of the Key Stages, national tests, etc. The curriculum document produced was long, complex and quite progressive in tone. Cox, like Bullock, listened to well-informed people and resisted political pressure. The English curriculum maintained a strong emphasis on speaking and listening, and was very positive about multicultural literature. It did not please its political backers.

As a part of its remit it surveyed current good practice and offered an overview of English set out as five views of English, sometimes known as the Cox models:

- A 'Personal Growth' view focuses on the child, emphasising the relationship between language and learning in the individual child, and the role of literature in developing children's imaginative and aesthetic lives.
- A 'Cross-curricular' view focuses on the school, emphasising that all teachers have a responsibility to help children with the language demands of different subjects in the school curriculum, otherwise areas of the curriculum may be closed to them. In England, English is different from other school subjects, in that it is both a subject and a medium of instruction for other subjects.
- An 'Adult Needs' view focuses on communication outside the school, emphasising the responsibility of English teachers to prepare children for the language of adult life, including the workplace in a fast-changing world. Children need to learn to deal with the day-to-day demands of spoken language and of print; they also need to be able to write clearly, appropriately and effectively.
- A 'Cultural Heritage' view emphasises the responsibility of schools to lead children to an appreciation of those works of literature that have been widely regarded as among the finest in the language.
- A 'Cultural Analysis' view emphasises the role of English in helping children towards a critical understanding of the world and cultural environment in

which they live. Children should know about the processes by which meanings are conveyed, and about the ways in which print and other media carry values.

Task 1.4: Theory task

What is your immediate reaction to these models? Do any stand out for you as more appealing? Are they more like your own rationale for English? Note down whether they are equally valuable to you or put them in some kind of order. Having reflected on what you currently know about actual English teaching, would your order fit with 'typical' teaching? Would it be reflected in the current formal documents of the National Curriculum and the Framework for English?

Cox argued that these models had equal status in the profession. There has been much debate since then and it is ongoing. Research into teachers' own beliefs has consistently demonstrated that the great majority put Personal Growth as the key model, with Cultural Analysis generally second. They acknowledge the place of Cultural Heritage but feel that it has been far too dominant, especially since 1995 (after the curriculum was revised). Adult Needs is seen as an important outcome of good English teaching rather than a driving force in itself. Language across the curriculum is rejected as a model of English and it is seen as part of every teacher's brief (as Bullock suggested). This last issue has re-emerged in considering literacy across the curriculum and will be discussed below.

The first version of the English curriculum was much debated but was broadly accepted by the profession. It was more problematic for primary teachers as their approach had been to teach language in a chiefly integrated way. For example, in teaching a topic such as 'Light', pupils might read fiction or poetry in which light was a theme, perhaps producing their own texts. This is something of an oversimplification of how primary teachers worked, but it is helpful in contrasting their previous general approach with the sudden arrival of subjects into the primary curriculum. They were, for the first time, teaching a mandated subject called English, among others, and could be inspected upon it. One of the ironies of the introduction of the National Curriculum in primary schools was that in teaching English there may have been less attention to language, partly sparking the debate about literacy (see below).

So what happened to Kingman and KAL? While English teachers were getting used to the National Curriculum for English, the LINC project got underway. The basic idea was to create a set of materials to improve in-service teachers' (primary and secondary) KAL, to appoint LINC advisers in every Local Education

Authority (LEA) and, when all was ready, to disseminate the material through a series of in-service sessions to one teacher from every primary school and one representative of each secondary English Department. They in turn would train their peers. This is known as the 'cascade model', although it has other more pejorative names within the profession.

The story of LINC is profoundly symbolic and well worth noting as a beginning teacher aiming to teach a subject that constantly suffers from political interference. The team was appointed in 1990 and developed materials over about 18 months, then began the training before the materials were officially finished and published. The materials used a socio-linguistic model of language, based on the work of Michael Halliday. This approach examines language in action and takes a chiefly descriptive stance with an emphasis on meaning more than correctness. For teachers, this means helping pupils to learn about language through using it and reflecting on its use in society. Put very simply, teachers help pupils to develop an understanding of how language works, including its rules, rather than teaching the rules first and saying 'now prove you can use the rules'; this latter approach was the grammar school model of 'parsing' endless series of sentences.

Whatever the merits of the socio-linguistic approach, the government was very clear that this was not the return to formal grammar teaching that they espoused. The LINC materials were literally banned from schools just before final publication, producing a typical media frenzy about this farce. The government argued that the materials were inappropriate for secondary classrooms and tokenistically sent a simplified version to all higher education institutions that offered teacher education courses. So, by 1993 LINC had been killed off, apart from a few tatty photocopied versions of the materials left lingering in English Department cupboards. The whole affair can be seen only as an act of direct political interference and censorship, demonstrating once again just how seriously English teaching is taken.

Elements of KAL were already present in the original Cox curriculum, particularly the idea of studying language variation and change, so English teachers did have the opportunity to keep the spirit of LINC alive. However, having been publicly embarrassed by LINC, the government called for an immediate revision of the National Curriculum for English in 1993 and sought to reintroduce a more formal model of English based on grammar. The proposals even included prescriptions for teaching a 'correct' version of spoken English. These proposals were fiercely resisted alongside the introduction of the version of Key Stage 3 Standard Attainment Tasks (SATs) that now dominate Year 9. For several years English teachers boycotted the tests until the government employed external markers and resistance was broken, although there was some satisfaction in that the 1995 revised National Curriculum for English was less prescriptive than feared and was a much slimmed down and more manageable document.

In one sense, the battle for the English curriculum had been won, at least to some extent, by the politicians. Research into teachers' views demonstrated, however, that they still put the concept of Personal Growth first, and that they felt Cultural Analysis was increasingly important in a media-oriented world, now enhanced by the extraordinary development of the personal computer at home and in school. They felt the National Curriculum was far too prescriptive, dominated by a somewhat nationalistic cultural heritage model, and that assessment in English was increasingly problematic and inappropriate.

The final significant act of 17 years of right-wing government was the introduction of the National Literacy Strategy (NLS), once more triggered by a perceived fall in standards, this time in the reading scores of primary children. The NLS was only at a pilot stage when New Labour swept to power and turned the pilot into the largest single educational project of the twentieth century, bringing with it the much heralded 'literacy hour'. One analysis of the NLS is that it is a by-product of a National Curriculum dominated by traditional subjects. Where was the time and space to teach, for example, reading, when there was so much curriculum content to cover? Overall, primary teachers have adopted and adapted the literacy hour and tend to support its principles. They received a great deal of training and vast amounts of supporting material. This was the period when the training video really arrived in education. As with all such national top-down reforms, backed with resources, the test scores in reading definitely rose and, with teachers very conscious of school performance league tables, they thoroughly prepared pupils for the tests. So perhaps for three years (1998–2001) the results were good (there has been much debate about the validity of the scores). However, the phenomenon of the plateau, a predictable period in such top-down reforms, was reached in 2001.

It was always clear that the NLS would transfer to secondary schools at some point, hence the introduction of the Framework for English in 2001. Again, this initiative occurred just after another thorough revision of the National Curriculum for English. Curriculum 2000, the new National Curriculum, was a slimmer, more manageable document with one or two intriguing changes, such as the first appearance of the moving image as something that English teachers should explicitly teach. But to give some idea of the extraordinary and bewildering cacophony of initiatives in education in the early years of the twenty-first century, English teachers have also been affected by the complete revision of A level English and by the New Opportunities Fund ICT training, neither of which can be described as successful.

The Framework for English currently dominates Key Stage 3. As with the primary NLS, it has been accompanied by a training programme, LEA advisers delivering the training and lorry loads of materials. It is part of a series of Key Stage 3 strategies which are expected to transform the curriculum. Ironically, its status is advisory – the National Curriculum remains the statutory document.

Before reporting on research into the impact of the Framework for English and teachers' reactions to it, it is important first to reflect on the sudden predominance of the term 'literacy'.

Task 1.5: Theory task

Literacy has become a buzzword in education in many countries. Try defining it to your own satisfaction, perhaps by looking at some dictionary definitions and selecting one or combining them. Also, is there only one kind of literacy? Have you heard literacy applied to other modes of representation?

In education and society at large, the term 'literacy' was barely used for much of the twentieth century. Its opposite, 'illiteracy', was widely used, principally in relation to adults who had failed to learn to read or write. There was also a tacit assumption in the West that other societies that were 'illiterate' were primitive and inferior. The importance of literacy in the West was predicated on perhaps two kinds or levels of literacy: a basic level – the economy needs workers who can function and handle spoken and written instructions – and an advanced level – closer to the origin of the word itself ('letter'), a level conveyed by phrases such as 'man of letters' or 'faculty of letters' in a university, implying scholarship and having writing skills.

In the 1980s, as governments became ever more aware of global competition and began to make comparisons between education systems, they also became very focused on notions of underachievement. Although it was hard to prove, it seemed that being literate was becoming more demanding and that a significant number of children and adults never reached a high enough level to be literate enough for their everyday lives. As evidence of an increasingly complex concept of literacy, different versions began to appear, such as computer literacy, media literacy and, more recently, emotional literacy; some educationalists began to speak of 'multi-literacies' and in the last few years the growth in the use of the internet, mobile phones, etc. has given more credence to the notion of a multiplicity of literacies.

This is a huge challenge for teachers who are accountable for society's literacy levels. Even if literacy were defined simply as 'being able to read and write competently', would this actually cover the symbolic systems that we all make use of? For example, a recent call has been for cine-literacy. Is this a helpful clarification or another confusing obfuscation? It depends on who you ask.

If you ask secondary English teachers, they have deeply mixed feelings about the Framework for English. They recognise many good things in it but tend to argue that this is because they were already good practice. However, elements such as the four-part lesson derived from the literacy hour are seen as overly formulaic. The majority of training has been received as patronising. These reactions may be temporary but they are certainly powerful. Some teachers have reacted by defining English as something distinct from the functional model of Literacy in the Framework. One specific reaction has been to reinvigorate English teachers' concerns about pupils' encounters with texts; they do not want these encounters to be merely about pupils being able to define a text type, but rather about them developing a relationship with a meaningful text, leading to a personal response.

This historical review is almost concluded; it could not hope to be comprehensive. So far, it has not featured the ongoing challenge of gender. Put simply, English is generally perceived to be, in pupil terms, a girls' subject and on an evidence basis it is – girls consistently achieve better than boys. Almost all primary teachers, the great majority of secondary English teachers and the majority of students studying the subject in higher education are female. The explanation for this has a long history, going back to the initial formulation of the subject in the nineteenth century. For the current beginning teacher, it is vital to acknowledge that the subject is oriented towards the female. There are very real ironies in suggesting that boys need special support after centuries of male dominance, but the evidence is that either they do or that the subject somehow privileges girls, or possibly both. It can also be argued that English requires an emotional maturity and girls are acknowledged to develop this ahead of boys. In class, boys actively demand more attention. English teachers must consider gender issues whenever they plan an English lesson or choose a text. It is part of the content of the subject, not some educational fad.

Just as gender is part of the content of English, so are social class and ethnic issues. These areas have always received a special kind of attention in English. This partly derives from their relationship with language; for example, accent and dialect are closely linked with both domains. Equally, some texts, both literary and non-literary, foreground these issues and lead to opportunities for pupils to reflect on them and their own identities and possibly prejudices. Currently, English teachers have less opportunity than in the early days of the National Curriculum to select texts that they feel can help pupils understand issues of class and race, but this makes it all the more important that they find time and space to do so. The development of citizenship may be seen as a very positive initiative in this respect, but English teachers should always bring a very special linguistic and literary expertise to bear on these fundamental issues in English itself.

This section has attempted to put English into a perspective derived from developing an understanding of the subject's origins, influences and cycles of change. It is best to see English as in a constant state of development and as a subject where its teachers are willing to engage with change but also to resist impositions when they are clearly educationally unsound. In the shape of the

National Association for the Teaching of English (NATE), teachers have a subject association to act as a forum for debate and as a collective voice. It provides publications, resources to support English teachers (as its website (www. nate.org.uk) demonstrates) and also has a local structure for in-service teachers to get together both formally and informally.

Training to be an English teacher

All teachers need an initial training to prepare them for the profession (see Chapter 9) and for the exciting but highly demanding business of teaching. All trainees must meet the National Standards as defined currently by the Teacher Training Agency (TTA). The Standards are generic for all trainees but inevitably they take on a degree of subject inflection. These Standards are available from websites and from all the training institutions, and there will be no need to trawl through them here. The content of the rest of the book is designed to help beginning teachers with achieving them and also with becoming a good English teacher, and these are not exactly the same thing. Trainees are strongly advised to acknowledge the importance of the Standards but not to let them dominate their thinking, especially in the early stages of their preparation. The Standards tend to fragment teaching if they are not handled properly. Good teaching is very fluent, fluid and integrated by its nature. When trainees observe very good teachers, as discussed later in the book, they can miss most of what is happening because so much seems to go smoothly, with the teacher apparently making little effort. Good observation is a highly complex skill learnt quite gradually and through an interaction of teaching and observing, each enriching the other. The Standards can help with observation as examples of emphasis within a lesson or in relation to planning or assessment.

So make use of the Standards, but not slavishly. While we are putting English into perspective, there are some aspects of English generally and in relation to certain standards that deserve a mention. First and, for many trainees, foremost is the issue of subject knowledge. What subject knowledge might be required to teach Language, Literature, Drama and Media Studies? How valid is an exclusive English Literature degree as 'the' knowledge to teach English? These are very challenging questions and the first thing they demonstrate is that all beginning teachers of English need to review their subject knowledge but also to be careful not to adopt a reductive deficit model. Beginning teachers will bring some formal knowledge, gained through study, and a great deal of more informal knowledge gained through life experience; for example, time spent in other forms of employment will provide specific skills, but equally it will provide experience of the linguistic and social context of work, which is excellent material for teaching.

First, it is important to review formal and informal subject knowledge, but not to describe inadequacies and so sap self-esteem. Second, and related to this, are explicit references to helping pupils for whom English is an additional language. This, quite rightly, is the responsibility of all teachers, but there can be no doubt that teachers charged with teaching the majority of pupils their mother tongue have an additional duty to help English as an Additional Language (EAL) pupils acquire English, while being very sensitive and positive towards other languages and cultures. School contexts vary enormously, as does the range of languages spoken in some communities, so detailed discussion of this very important emphasis in the Standards is impossible here. Trainees should not let local circumstances which suggest EAL is a minimal concern for their schools limit their thinking. All need to maximise their learning opportunities during their training, regardless of whether they immediately apply their knowledge about EAL pupils.

Finally, all trainees are expected to demonstrate that they can help pupils learn from out-of-school settings and extra-curricular activities. In English, this can be a very enjoyable part of the job. Visits to the theatre, poetry readings, literary festivals, bookshops and so on enliven the English curriculum. Equally, teachers can be involved in school productions, cultural events and competitions, after-school clubs for budding writers, improving the school website, producing the school magazine and so on. Gaining some experience in a range of these areas will demonstrate the Standard but, more importantly, will introduce you to an enriching aspect of the English teacher's relationship with pupils.

This latter point brings us to our conclusion and links back to the opening statement about the importance of English. The subject is recognised as central to pupils' learning and so gives all teachers an immediate importance and potential professional respect. It is useful to remind ourselves that as a result of this status, all pupils have to study English for at least 11 years and for several hours each week, whether they like it or not. Perhaps our other duty, then, is to reflect on how we can make this importance relevant to their lives, as well as meaningful and interesting. Good teachers of English are especially skilled in this respect and this provides the real standard that trainees need to reach.

2 The English curriculum and the Literacy Strategy

Maureen Coales and Liana Coales

Introduction

To many outside teaching, English and literacy are synonymous. The majority of parents consider the teaching of English in the secondary school to be the teaching of, first and foremost, spelling, then handwriting, and if you are lucky, a few might mention punctuation. A mere handful of parents may wish to discuss the literature that their child has been studying. And here, of course, lies the biggest anomaly. You, like many teachers of English, may have graduated with a degree in English Literature, which you probably chose because you love reading and studying literature. Or you may have read Media Studies, Communication Studies or Theatre Studies and enjoyed those subjects similarly. In deciding to teach, you may be hoping to communicate your love of the subject. However, on returning to the classroom as a teacher, you will be expected to teach many aspects of English as defined in the National Curriculum and there will be little time for your own specialism – often the only time you will teach it will be at GCSE or AS/A level. The school and other subject teachers will expect you to produce pupils who are proficient at reading and writing so they can concentrate on their subject. And there will be times when you will hear other teachers complaining about the demise of grammar teaching; it is always the fault of the English teacher if pupils cannot read textbooks/examination questions or write 'proper English'. You will almost certainly find the emphasis on teaching literacy quite different from your own experience and possibly different from what you expected when you chose to teach.

Objectives

This chapter will:

- put the teaching of English into context;
- explore the NLS and the English Curriculum;
- show how these documents can be used as tools;
- show why the teaching of English language is essential, powerful and fun.

The context of teaching English

The teaching of English has gone through many phases over the years, with various methods being hailed as the solution to improving literacy levels. Some schools concentrated on reading, others on writing or literature. However, generally the trend had been to promote experimentation and creativity, and to focus less on grammar. Indeed, if you completed your own education fairly recently, it is highly unlikely that you were taught any formal grammar during your own schooling. There is a school of thought which still believes that pupils do not need to be taught the grammar of their mother tongue because grammar is absorbed through talking and reading, and that the study of grammar actually inhibits creativity.

For many years, teachers of English have been encouraging their pupils to use their imagination, to write stories, to describe their experiences and environment. Often, the unspoken expectation is that we are teaching budding novelists and poets. And how are these students helped to improve their writing? They are invariably told to read more and, as if by magic, their own writing will improve. This approach has indeed worked for many pupils.

Generally speaking, more reading does contribute to greater awareness of the use of language and this will have an impact on pupils' writing. However, this will probably be quite subtle and almost unconsciously achieved as the more sophisticated aspects of language use are adopted in much the same way as grammar is absorbed from birth. But what about those pupils who do not want

Task 2.1: Reflective task: improving writing

Take a moment now to answer this question: How did you learn to improve or vary your own writing? Can you make a list of things that helped? Reading is probably high on that list. Is this your own private reading or teacher-led reading? What kind of reading – classic literature; modern literature; poetry; newspapers; magazines? Why is reading important? And what else affects writing?

to read, or do not have the same opportunities to read, or can read at only a decoding level? How do they develop their writing skills?

Thinking about language

At this point it is important to think about how language skills, although different in the three areas, are transferred between reading, writing and speaking at all levels, with varying degrees of success. If we rely on those sophisticated skills being absorbed through reading, that not only makes reading extremely important, but it also seems to be a rather hit-and-miss affair and certainly would put many pupils at a great disadvantage.

And what about all those students who are not competent readers? How do they cope when they leave school? Well, a recent shocking statistic from the Learning Skills Council in 2001 is that there are 'Seven million adults in the UK who can't find a plumber in the Yellow Pages because their reading is so poor'.

You may or may not have studied language in your degree but it is worth thinking about the political aspects of language before you start teaching. David Crystal's book *The Cambridge Encyclopedia of Language* is very readable and presented in a friendly way. It covers all aspects of language and there is a chapter on Social Identity, which is a good starting point. When you stand in front of a class you will, whether you like it or not, be representing one form of language and within the class will be many different forms of language, some of which will be unknown to you. Language is important in any society: it defines the individual. The ability to use language effectively is an obvious advantage in our world. As teachers of English, our job is to empower our pupils by teaching them how to understand and utilise language most effectively.

> **Task** **2.2**: Reflective tasks: using and understanding language
>
> Take a moment to list the different forms of language that you use; that you understand but don't use; that you don't understand – for example, legal documents, regional dialects, rap music/lyrics. This will probably be affected by where you live, where you went to school and your age. Consider how capable you are of using language in many situations, but think also of all the situations where you are incapable of understanding language (regional teenage slang is one you are likely to come across and quickly become familiar with). Now think about all the situations where your pupils are incapable of using and understanding language. Think about the disadvantage they are at when they cannot converse/read/write in an appropriate and effective manner.

Language skills and thinking skills

There has been much debate about language and thought, and many theories have been put forward. (Again, these can be found summarised in David Crystal's book *The Cambridge Encyclopedia of Language*.) It is important to consider the relationship between language and thinking skills because, as a teacher of English, you will be dealing entirely with language, in one form or another, and with thinking. It is generally agreed that language and thought are related, although there are different opinions as to how far one affects the other.

It is interesting to see how the NLS reflects the general view of language that 'to see language and thought as inter-dependent . . . is to recognise that language is a regular part of the process of thinking, at the same time recognising that we have to think in order to understand language' (Crystal, 1987: 14). In the NLS a similar statement reads 'teachers have a genuine stake in strong language skills because language enables thought' (DfEE and QCA, 2001). As a new teacher you will soon see how important it is that your pupils are thinking, not just doing. And this is where teaching English is so rewarding.

Consider a lesson, for example, where a class is asked to read a text and then answer a series of questions, the answers to which can be found in the text. Which skills are the pupils using here? They may well be reading, but are they really being required to think? Now consider turning the task around so that the pupils read a text, then make up their own questions which they swap with a partner and answer each other's questions. Here they are still reading and answering questions, but they are forced to connect with the text on a deeper level as it is almost impossible to set questions without engaging with the text, whereas it is quite simple to answer questions by finding the relevant lines in the text. When planning lessons, seek and exploit opportunities to get the pupils thinking, even if they don't appear to like it.

Language has long been recognised as a crucial tool in the learning process. 'Language may not determine the way we think but it does influence the way we perceive and remember and it affects the ease with which we perform mental tasks' (Crystal, 1987: 15). This same point is reflected in the Framework: 'Language is the prime medium through which pupils learn and express themselves' (DfEE and QCA, 2001).

There is an obvious need to develop the language skills of pupils if they are to benefit fully from the education system. This is a great responsibility and a challenge for all teachers. Although English teachers have a leading role to play in developing pupils' language skills, it is not their sole responsibility, and, as discussed in Chapter 10, other teachers should play their part in this vital area.

There have been various attempts over the years to promote the importance of language in the curriculum, notably the Kingman Report (1988) and the

Bullock Report (1977), which you have (or will) probably come across in your studies. These reports supported the need for good language skills for pupils to make progress in learning, but have had a very limited effect. The introduction of the National Curriculum and the more recent National Literacy Strategy is a serious attempt to address this problem.

Exploring the Literacy Strategy and the English curriculum

The English curriculum

The National Curriculum sets out clear aims for the education of pupils, defining 'the content of what will be taught, and setting attainment targets for learning. It also determines how performance will be assessed and reported' (DfEE, 1999: 3). It has a particularly strong focus in that 'an entitlement to learning must be an entitlement for all pupils'. The English curriculum, a legal requirement, provides programmes of study defined in the Education Act (1996) as the 'matters, skills and processes' that should be taught to pupils of different abilities and maturities during the Key Stages. Schools then have to plan schemes of work, based on these programmes of study, which will support the entitlement to learning. The curriculum, while recognising the distinctive aspects of speaking and listening, reading and writing, emphasises 'their interrelatedness' and advocates the strengthening of these links. At the beginning of every Programme of Study this fact is highlighted: 'Teaching should ensure that work in speaking and listening, reading and writing is integrated' (DfEE, 1999: 6).

Task 2.3: Theory task: exploring the National Curriculum for English

Take some time to look at English in the National Curriculum, copies of which can be obtained from DfEE or at www.nc.uk.net, but don't just look at the Key Stage which you are aiming to teach. One of the keys to being a good teacher is to be informed. There is a danger in teaching of becoming isolated in your classroom. Watch out for this happening and remember that your classroom is only a small part of the pupils' learning experience. By showing your pupils you are aware of this, you will help them to transfer their learning from class to class.

Look at En1 Speaking at Key Stage 1 and you will see that the requirements there are valid for all Key Stages. Compare them now to En1 Speaking at Key Stage 3. What do you notice? How would you describe the difference? This kind of exercise is worth doing with Key Stage 3 and 4 pupils because all too often they do not really understand how progression can be defined.

Look at En2 Reading at Key Stage 2 and compare the sub-headings with those at Key Stages 3 and 4, as shown in Table 2.1. There are some interesting differences which will be referred to later in discussing the NLS. Try to identify how the National Curriculum plans for progression across the Key Stages. Be aware of what your pupils have already studied and what they will encounter in the future.

Table 2.1 En2 Reading sub-headings for Key Stages 2, 3 and 4

Key Stage 2	Key Stages 3 and 4
Reading strategies	Understanding texts:
Understanding texts	reading for meaning
Reading for information	understanding the author's craft
Literature	English literary heritage
Non-fiction and non-literary texts	Texts from different cultures and traditions
Language structure and variation	Printed and ICT-based information texts
	Media and moving image texts
	Language structure and variation

Source: DfEE, 1999: 25, 34

A quick mention here about the negativity you may come across among some teachers regarding the National Curriculum, particularly at Key Stages 3 and 4. It is popular and easy to dismiss something because one part may not be to your own liking. This is true of anything and this is what happens in education. Many people, not just teachers, criticise the National Curriculum because it lists the major writers and poets to be taught, as shown in Figure 2.1. Obviously, any list would be open to debate. It is a starting point; it is not a reason to dismiss the National Curriculum out of hand. Check through the rest of the requirements for reading and you will find it difficult not to agree that this is what should be taught. The list does not preclude the use of other writers: you can add other authors/poets in your own planning and make useful comparisons between writers in this way.

The National Curriculum has been statutory since 1999 and has been reflected in schools' schemes of work since then with varying degrees of success. It is this variation that has led to the development and introduction of the National Literacy Strategy, which was introduced in the primary sector in 1997 and in the secondary sector in 2001.

Major writers published before 1914

Jane Austen, Charlotte Brontë, Emily Brontë, John Bunyan, Wilkie Collins, Joseph Conrad, Daniel Defoe, Charles Dickens, Arthur Conan Doyle, George Eliot, Henry Fielding, Elizabeth Gaskell, Thomas Hardy, Henry James, Mary Shelley, Robert Louis Stevenson, Jonathan Swift, Anthony Trollope, H.G. Wells.

Major poets published before 1914

Matthew Arnold, Elizabeth Barrett Browning, William Blake, Emily Brontë, Robert Browning, Robert Burns, Lord Byron, Geoffrey Chaucer, John Clare, Samuel Taylor Coleridge, John Donne, John Dryden, Thomas Gray, George Herbert, Robert Herrick, Gerard Manley Hopkins, John Keats, Andrew Marvell, John Milton, Alexander Pope, Christina Rossetti, William Shakespeare (sonnets), Percy Bysshe Shelley, Edmund Spenser, Alfred Lord Tennyson, Henry Vaughan, William Wordsworth, Sir Thomas Wyatt.

Source: DfEE 1999: 36

Figure 2.1   Major writers and poets, as specified in the National Curriculum

The National Literacy Strategy

As stated in the National Literacy Strategy, the government recognises the importance of language skills in improving education: 'Language lies at the heart of the drive to raise standards in secondary schools' (DfEE and QCA, 2001: 5). For the first time a government has committed vast sums of money to achieve this aim, with great emphasis on the teaching and learning of literacy skills.

Task   2.4: Theory task: becoming familiar with the NLS Framework for Teaching

All teachers should spare some time to look at this important resource. If you are reading this as a secondary school teacher, it is advisable that you become familiar with the primary NLS because the secondary Framework is a continuation of it and you will benefit from having an overview. Pupils do not start their education in Year 7. Some of the topics in Year 7 will be based on revision of work done in Year 6, so you would be right to expect the pupils to be familiar with the skills and concepts. Similarly, pupils will be reassured that you know what they have done in Key Stage 2 and this is a good beginning to forging that all important relationship between teacher and learner.

Look at how the Framework is divided up. Look at the sub-headings. Notice that although grammar is mentioned in the primary objectives under 'Grammatical awareness', it is not in the secondary list of objectives. Beware those people who have decided that the NLS is just about grammar. You will also notice that literacy does not just mean the ability to read and write, but also being able to understand the author's craft and write for a variety of purposes and audiences – essential skills in school and beyond.

Why was there a need for the NLS?

The NLS Framework for Teaching was instigated because there was such variance between schools, even between classes in the same school. The aim is to promote a clearer focus on literacy instruction to make it more uniformed so that all pupils will receive the same opportunities for learning, and parents, teachers and pupils know what to expect. It provides guidelines and direction that have not been available before for teachers of English and it brings a coherence to Key Stages 2 and 3. It is not statutory and there is an expectation that it will be used with professionalism and flexibility to suit the needs of the pupils. The emphasis is on teaching that has learning as its focus. The most successful teaching is described as:

- discursive
- interactive
- well-paced
- confident
- ambitious.

See p. 8 of the NLS for further explanation and for a list of strategies advocated by the Framework.

Using the NLS and the Curriculum

When this Framework was introduced in primary schools, the literacy hour was promoted as the means of teaching the objectives. Examples of the ways in which it can be used can be found in the NLS but, with experience and confidence, teachers are beginning to adapt this model to suit their own pupils more and more. For example, some schools do not have a whole hour every day; some schools are choosing to devote more time to extended writing and so on. Try not to consider the National Curriculum and the NLS as constraints, but as tools to help you to teach effectively and to give your pupils an effective education. Observe how other teachers utilise these documents and the strategies suggested by them in order to develop your own teaching.

Task 2.5: Observation task: observing a literacy hour

Visit one, or preferably two, different primary schools and observe a literacy hour lesson. This will both inform you and enable you to talk to your own pupils with knowledge and understanding. Note the aspects that you find interesting and effective and try them out in your own teaching. Teachers, like pupils, learn better from experiencing, not from reading about something.

The idea of a literacy hour was to give a specified time for the explicit teaching of reading and writing because in many cases the teaching of English had just become part of project work and had therefore lost its status. The model has been used extensively at Key Stages 1 and 2 for about the last six years and the strategies used – such as guided and shared reading, scaffolding and modelling writing – are now being transferred to Key Stage 3. An example of a Key Stage 2 literacy hour lesson is shown in Table 2.2. Here you can see how the literacy

Table 2.2 An example of a Key Stage 2 literacy hour

Objectives		Sentence 5 – to form complex sentences. Reading 12 – to comment critically on the language, style and success of reports. Writing 15 – to develop a journalistic style.
Introduction Whole class	15 mins	Shared reading. Explore the conventions of a short newspaper report. Comment on the language and style.
Word/sentence level work Whole class	15 mins	Focused sentence level work. Identify and explore complex sentences focusing on the connecting devices used.
Development group and independent work	20 mins	Guided writing. Teacher works with one ability group on developing their report writing. Encourage pupils to use complex sentences. All other pupils work individually, composing a report using a writing frame.
Plenary Whole class	10 mins	Pupils share their work with the class. Other pupils offer constructive criticism of the work they hear.

hour is divided into whole class, group and individual work. You can also see that there are specific and explicit objectives taken from the Literacy Strategy and that the lesson incorporates interactive and explicit teaching strategies, such as shared reading and guided writing. Further details of how to use these strategies can be found in the NLS documents. This is another reason for teachers who are preparing to teach in secondary schools to become familiar with Key Stages 1 and 2 resources because it will help them to understand the terminology used in the Framework for Teaching English: Years 7, 8 and 9.

Explicit teaching of literacy

The word 'explicit' as used in the NLS is important to notice because it summarises the changes in the teaching of English. It is no longer acceptable to expect pupils to develop their skills through absorbing language. The emphasis now is on explicitly teaching those skills and organising learning so that knowledge and understanding of literacy skills is accessible to all pupils.

What is meant by literacy?

In the NLS, literacy is defined as uniting 'the important skills of reading and writing. It also involves speaking and listening . . .' and it gives a list of what literate primary pupils should be able to do, which is a very useful point of reference for teachers of all Key Stages. This list can be found on page 3 of the National Literacy Strategy: Framework for Teaching: Years 7, 8 and 9.

Why is literacy important?

In the Framework for Teaching English: Years 7, 8 and 9, the definition of literacy is developed further. The words 'language' and 'literacy' are mentioned several times in significant statements, whose relevance is not restricted to the classroom. For example, in the Foreword it states that language:

> is the key to developing in young people the capacity to express themselves with confidence, to think logically, creatively and imaginatively and to developing a deep understanding of literature and the wider culture.
>
> (DfEE and QCA, 2001: 5)

Once again, the importance of acquiring sophisticated language skills is emphasised and the breadth of its significance beyond the classroom is made clear.

Both the primary and secondary strategy documents refer to 'equipping pupils for the world in which they will live and work', and this takes us back to the question of what is the role of teachers of English. If your pupils are not all budding novelists and poets, how will they use English in their lives? Similarly, how would you want English to enrich their lives? The world is an increasingly literate one, with the growth of the internet just one example of the importance of the written word. If you can read fluently, you can save money by buying on the web. If you can't, then that is one more area that is denied to you. But, of course, it is not just reading and writing that are important – the spoken word is increasingly powerful in this visual world in which we live.

Task 2.6: Reflective tasks: considering the importance of literacy

Imagine that you cannot read or write or speak well. How would this affect one week in your life, maybe last week? How would you cope? Have you ever been abroad in a country where you could not read, write or speak the language competently, perhaps where you could only decode and use words at a slow and insecure level? How did you feel? Which of the skills did you need most? Bear in mind that some of the pupils you encounter are in a similar situation in their home country. Remember, too, that for some of them English is not their first language. A successful teacher will always try to imagine themselves in the position of their pupils.

What is expected in English lessons?

As we have seen, literacy is much more than reading and writing, and English teaching encompasses much more than reading novels or deconstructing grammar. As teachers of English, we are fortunate in that our day-to-day routines encompass so many different aspects. As you develop as a teacher you will find interesting ways of incorporating all the different aspects of English teaching into your lessons. Here, despite what you may hear about the National Curriculum and NLS being restrictive, you can see that the most effective English teachers are still highly creative in being able to use all their resources to create successful lessons. It is interesting to step back and consider what English and, more specifically, English teaching, mean to you.

Task 2.7: Reflective task: what is English?

Make a list of what you think should be taught in English.

Ask your pupils the same question. Are the lists the same? What do the differences show? Is there a difference between what is needed and what is expected? This is a good point for discussion with pupils to make them think about what they want to achieve over the term/the year and to make them become involved in their own learning. For your reference, how do these lists compare to the Framework objectives?

The following definition from the Framework for Teaching English: Years 7, 8 and 9 is worth remembering. It sums up the far-reaching goals of what an English teacher would hope to achieve with all of his or her pupils:

Literacy encompasses the ability to recognise, understand and manipulate the conventions of language and develop pupils' ability to use language imaginatively and flexibly.

(DfEE and QCA, 2001)

Whether we are reading a novel by Jane Austen or a poem by Spike Milligan, we are responding to the author's choice of words; whether we are writing a letter of complaint or filling in an application form, we are choosing appropriate words; whether we are giving a presentation or gossiping on the phone, we are using words to create effect. From a very early age a child learns how to manipulate language to achieve what they want from their family and friends, whether it is sweets, toys or watching television. Thus, as English teachers you can enjoy encouraging your pupils to develop this skill more fully and consciously; then they will begin to understand the potential of language and how they can master it.

Why language is essential, powerful and fun

Teaching language

As we have seen, pupils who are unable to read, write and speak fluently, confidently and appropriately are greatly disadvantaged both in school and beyond.

As English teachers, we are obliged to develop our pupils' understanding of language in many different aspects in order to enable them to become powerful citizens. Without language, it is almost impossible to function within society. Most tasks, on whatever level, require some understanding and manipulation of language.

A word about grammar

As you read this, you may be worrying about your inability to teach grammar due to your own lack of experience of explicit grammar teaching or a lack of confidence with the necessary terminology. However, grammar should not be viewed as a hideous dinosaur. Indeed, it is an essential and natural element of language. By the age of five, most children have picked up the rules of grammar and use them intuitively and usually unconsciously. Stephen King in his book *On Writing* refers to grammar being absorbed and he continues with this observation:

> Communication composed of . . . parts of speech must be organized by rules of grammar upon which we agree. When these rules break down, confusion and misunderstanding result. Bad grammar results in bad sentences.
> (King, 2001: 133)

'Confusion and misunderstanding' will be words and states that you come across constantly in teaching. You will be confused by what has been written or said by your pupils. Simultaneously, pupils will be confused by or misunderstand what they read or what they have been asked to do, and this can lead to all sorts of other problems, usually in the form of disruptive behaviour, until the confusion is recognised and resolved. For you, the problem will most probably be confusion arising from bad grammar and/or imprecise vocabulary or expression. For your students, the problem will arise from not being able to cope with more sophisticated language structures or unfamiliar vocabulary. For both situations there are benefits in being able to refer to the rules of grammar. A very simple example is the use of capital letters for proper nouns. A pupil who does not recognise this rule will be unnecessarily defeated by unusual names and, failing to work out what the new word means, may just give up, instead of being able to move on easily by recognising that the word is a proper noun. It is helpful to teach grammar explicitly.

The difference between speaking and writing

According to documentation, pupils must be taught the different conventions associated with speaking and writing. There are numerous studies on the acquisition of language and grammar and many debates about what is right and what is wrong. Against this you have to accept that language is a social phenomenon and is constantly being revised and adapted.

Most grammar is absorbed through speaking and reading, but there are differences between spoken and written grammar, and this is where some pupils are

Task 2.8: Theory tasks: exploring the difference between speaking and writing

You can make this into an interesting study at any level. Record and transcribe a short conversation, word for word. Now try to read what is written. You will find that it doesn't look right and is confusing when written down, yet it was perfectly understandable at the time. Why is this? You will notice in the classroom that some children write as they speak, word for word, and the result is dull, repetitive and often confusing. Refer to Figure 2.2 for an example of such a piece of work. The pupil was asked to explain who her favourite author was and why. The text is awkward to read because it has been written as it might be spoken and not how it should be written. Frequently, pupils who write like this do not understand why they have lost all the energy that was captured in speech. This indicates a lack of understanding of the difference between the written and spoken word, but it can and should be taught (Year 7; Speaking and Listening objective 2, NLS). In order to teach this important aspect of language, you will first need to ensure that you fully understand and can articulate the differences yourself. Study the example of the pupil's work. How would you help this pupil to improve her writing? How might you explain her errors to her in a way that she will understand?

R.L. Stine at first wrot books on comedy but a lot of people wondered how he got from comedy to horror? Well, after he wrote comedy an old friend told him to have a go at writing horror, so he did try and everyone gave him a better grade for horror so he stuck with it and wrote on. He was a very good writer actually and it was very good the way he wrote scary stories. I think he's the greatest writer ever because of the way he went from comedy to horror so I definetly like to read his books and to watch the films of them as well.

Figure 2.2 Example of a pupil's work

disadvantaged if they have not been exposed to forms of written grammar, through reading, early in their lives. The Standard English, which is referred to in the National Curriculum, is English which is widely understood but is not widely used in speech. It is defined by its grammar, vocabulary, spelling and punctuation, but not pronunciation. Speaking is a very different activity. A useful reference about the differences between speech and writing can be found in *Rediscover Grammar with David Crystal* (Crystal, 2001).

Grammar can seem to be perplexing because for every rule there is an exception, but that does not mean to say that it should be avoided. It will not fit into a perfect logical pattern, although clear patterns are discernible. And here is where the fascination lies. Playing around with these patterns creates many effects, one of the most important being humour. When young children begin to create jokes they are usually funny because of the mistakes they make, not because of the content. They have picked up the pattern but do not know how to use it effectively. And so, as pupils become more confident with their language, they should be encouraged not simply to recognise patterns, but to understand how to manipulate them. The study of language is beneficial, even essential, in giving pupils the power to manipulate and control language.

Making language teaching fun

Some English teachers approach the literacy/language aspects of their lessons grudgingly. There seems to be considerably less enthusiasm about exploring complex sentences with a class, for example, than discussing the inner turmoil of Dickens' characters. However, whenever we discuss literature, we are discussing language – words, sentences, grammar – the tools of the author's craft that create the fictional world and the characters. Encourage your pupils to play with language and show them that they too can write in complex sentences and thus improve their own writing. Let pupils explore tabloid headlines, identifying the grammatical and linguistic 'errors', and get them to write their own puns. Show your classes that language is fun. There is nothing in the NLS or the National Curriculum which says that grammar/literacy/language must be taught through dull lessons; indeed, quite the opposite is expected. As teachers of English and literacy, we are expected to use our creativity and to exploit the strategies suggested to us in order to engage our pupils, thus ensuring their progression.

The NLS and the National Curriculum were designed to standardise teaching and to ensure that pupils in all classes and all schools receive an appropriate, challenging and inclusive education. The two documents together provide the basic tools for your teaching: they outline what should be taught and suggest ways in which you might effectively teach. The complexity of the language has been broken down to help you teach, but it still needs your interpretation. English is rich in vocabulary, which allows for great variety and shades of meaning. It is a much more flexible language than many others, which is both an advantage and a disadvantage for the learner. It has, as Bill Bryson states, a 'deceptive complexity. Nothing in English is quite what it seems' (Bryson, 1990: 9). This is the pleasure of teaching English. By showing your pupils how they can develop their literacy skills, you can give them the confidence, knowledge and understanding to explore their language in all its various forms and enable them to become competent language users in the different areas: fluent speakers; sensitive speakers; proficient readers; competent writers. The National Curriculum and the National Literacy Strategy will guide you, but you will be the person who makes it all come to life and become meaningful for your pupils. Good luck! It's worth it.

Further reading

Bryson, B. (1990) *Mother Tongue: The English Language*, Hamish Hamilton, London.

Crystal, D. (1987) *The Cambridge Encyclopedia of Language*, Cambridge University Press, Cambridge.

Crystal, D. (2001) *Rediscover Grammar with David Crystal*, Longman, London.

Davies, C. (1996) *What is English Teaching?* Open University Press, London.

Davison, J. and J. Dawson (2003) *Learning to Teach English in the Secondary School*, RoutledgeFalmer, London.

Flemming, M. and Stevens, D. (1998) *English Teaching in the Secondary School: A Handbook for Students and Teachers*, David Fulton, London.

King, S. (2001) *On Writing: A Memoir of the Craft*, Hodder & Stoughton: New English Library, London.

Wyse, D. and Jones, R. (2000) *Teaching English, Language and Literacy*, Routledge Falmer, London.

3 Planning teaching and learning in English

Jane Branson

Introduction

Experienced teachers should make teaching look easy, especially to the unpractised eye, and new teachers watching experienced teachers at work will often comment on how smoothly things seem to go, and hopefully feel confident and inspired. Yet planning a first lesson often takes hours of work, and a trainee English teacher may well reconsider that initial judgement after their first lesson with that same class. Were they *really* just putty in the teacher's hand or a nightmare that, due to good planning and brisk organisation, didn't happen?

Of course, as an inexperienced observer, you may not be familiar with either the National Curriculum or the school's or department's schemes of work. It is likely that you won't know the students and you may be dropping in on a lesson in the middle of a unit of work or a sequence of lessons. Bearing all this in mind, it's going to be harder to unpack the plethora of invisible decisions a teacher is making throughout the lesson. This chapter will make explicit those decision-making processes, which occur at all levels of planning, and demonstrate how to turn your potential nightmare into a smooth, well-crafted lesson.

Objectives

This chapter will explore:

- the stages of planning in English;
- classroom management and the right climate for learning in English;
- how to plan an English lesson.

Stages of planning

Experience counts for a lot, but good planning combined with flexibility are the essential ingredients at all stages of the process, from long-term Key Stage and yearly outlines, to an individual teacher's lesson-by-lesson planning. At each level of planning (see below), there needs to be a focus on:

- content: what skills are to be learned; what texts and other resources will be used;

and

- process: how learning will take place; the activities students will participate in; how they will demonstrate their learning and how it will be assessed.

Long-term plans – Key Stage planning and year-by-year plans

The phrase 'long-term planning' usually refers to Key Stage and yearly outlines of course content (see Table 3.1, pp. 38–39). The National Curriculum programmes of study for English, GCSE specifications, the National Literacy Strategy and the Literacy Framework should also be included in this definition. Long-term plans may identify key areas of coverage (for example, pre-1914 poetry, media, fiction, non-fiction) and indicate when these aspects of English will be taught and to whom. Main texts and key skills to be taught are also generally named in this sort of documentation.

Medium-term plans – schemes of work for units and modules

Departmental plans are usually most detailed and useful at the medium-term level. They will typically include programmes of classroom activity for 6–8 week blocks of time (very often reflecting half-termly chunks of the school year), commonly with a text type or a theme ('Newspapers' or 'Reading the News') as a heading and a list of skills to be taught and outcomes to be achieved. In primary schools, they will be generally be created by teachers working together in year group or subject teams, led by the literacy or English coordinator, and in secondary schools by the English Department. Schemes of work should be frequently reviewed and amended to reflect new choices of text, new technologies, student need, development of classroom practice and changing personnel. Medium-term plans, which may also contain exemplar work, ensure parity of experience for different classes taught by different members of the English staff and are an important tool for monitoring purposes, as they demonstrate the practical implementation of the long-term plans and national documentation to which all teachers of English work.

Short-term plans – weekly and daily teacher planning

For the individual teacher, this is the most important planning stage, and during your training period, you will be expected to produce very detailed plans, accompanied by evaluations and filed with any observation notes made by your mentor or tutor. Tables 3.2a and b lesson plans are by a graduate trainee teacher for a Year 8 class.

To achieve planning at this level, a teacher will need ready reference to national and long-term planning documentation and the support of medium-term schemes of work. In addition, lesson planning should reflect detailed knowledge of the students in your class and their previous achievements measured by both your own marking and national testing. At this level a series of crucial decisions (listed on pp. 42–43 in alphabetical, not priority, order) are made.

Task 3.1: Observation task: timing teacher and student activity

Watch an English lesson (or preferably two or three lessons) taught by different members of staff and make a 'timing record' in two columns to identify 'Teacher Activity', including any observations about any teaching/learning assistant who is present in this column, and 'Student Activity'. Who does what? When? For how long? What happens when new activities are introduced or the focus of the lesson changes? How long is spent on the 'business' of the lesson (giving out books, finding a pen) and how long on learning activities?

Table 3.1 Long-term planning: a Year 7 course

Unit module	Focus	S&L assessment	Homework activities	Texts	
1 Identity	**Personal identity (in novels and non-fiction) Character identity**	**Role play and forum theatre** Based on extracts from different points of *Skellig*	**Personal and discursive writing** Letter to David Almond **Narrative writing** Diary of a literary character/extra passages for the novel	Prose	*Skellig* (D. Almond) Wider reading of D. Almond Non-fiction: Unit 4 The EMC Non-Fiction Book (Scott's Diary) and Anne Frank
				Poetry	William Blake (pre-1914)
				Media	Film: *Whistle Down the Wind*
				Additional	Unit 11 Happily Ever After (openings of novels) (*Language to Imagine, Explore and Entertain*)
2 Conflict	**People v. the animal kingdom**	**Improvisation/ tableaux and monologue** to create a piece of drama exploring the issues	**Persuasive writing** Letter to the editor Leaflet Poster	Prose	*Dancing Bear* (M. Morpurgo) *Zoo* (A. Brown) Extracts from *Kensuke's Kingdom*; *Harry Potter and The Philosopher's Stone* (snake episode) Non-fiction: news articles, news websites
				Poetry	Unit 2 Making a Splash ('On a Favourite Cat' – pre-1914 poetry) (*Language of Pre-1914 Literature*)
				Media	TV/magazine advertisements using animals (PG Tips; Bacardi; Andrex) Death of an Elephant (Non-fiction: *The Way People Are*)
3 Society	**Representations of the family**	**Family soundscape** **Devise and perform** an advert which uses a family setting	**Literary response** Essay on the character of Angus **Discursive writing** Representations of the family in different media	Prose	*Bumface* (M. Gleitzman) Extracts from *Goggle Eyes and Flour Babies* (A. Fine)
				Poetry	Based on the theme of the family – John Hegley (20th-century poetry)
				Media	The family on TV: The Simpsons (Unit 4 The Media Book); AOL ads
				Play	Extracts from *The Book of the*

Table 3.1 *continued*

Unit module	Focus	S&L assessment	Homework activities	Texts	
4 Change	**Childhood: children in literature and film**	**Scripted performance** of extracts from *Oliver Twist*. Adapt talk for a specific audience	**Personal writing** Reading history **Narrative writing** Children's book for Year 1 students	Prose	Short stories: 'Boys' will be Boys' and 'Equal Rights' Non-fiction: extracts from *I Know Why the Caged Bird Sings*
				Poetry	Selection of poetry on theme of childhood (Unit 4 The Poetry Book)
				Media	Children and adults in film: *Matilda; The Phantom Menace;* Unit 2 Tackling Teletubbies (media) (The Media Book)
				Play	*Oliver Twist* (script adaptation)
				Additional	**Non-fiction:** Bound Feet (The Way People Are); Unit 7 Stories to Share (children's stories) (*Language to Imagine, Explore and Entertain*)
5 Culture	**Literature from other cultures**	Present a piece of performance poetry	**Information retrieval** Poetry anthology and evaluation	Prose	Extracts from *Chandra* Non-fiction: extracts from Zlata's Diary; short stories in *Fifty-Fifty Tutti-Futti Chocolate Chip*
				Poetry	John Agard (Unit 3 The Poetry Book); Shakespeare; a selection of poetry from other cultures
				Media	A Ghanaian Funeral (BBC News online report) (*The Way People Are*)

Table 3.2a Lesson plan produced by a trainee teacher

Unit: Year 8 Unit 10: Culture (Poetry)	**Class**
Lesson number: Lesson 3 **Date** 25.06.03	8b1 English
Lesson duration: 60 minutes	
SEN students: Karen White L&N; Ben Taylor EBD	**Size 25**
Teacher: Deborah O'Donoghue **School**: Peacehaven Community	**13 B 12 G**

Areas for development identified from previous lesson
Challenge perception of poetry as requiring Standard English, regular rhyme etc.
Reinforce expectations for end-of-term presentation.

Evidence of planning
Activities planned.
Smartboard resource created and saved from last lesson.
Eminem resource created.

Learning objectives

1 EN1S&L 1g and 6c. Explore use of, and attitudes, to standard English and non-standard English.

2 EN2R 3g. Consider diversity of language use in author's craft in (8b) contemporary poetry.

3 EN3W 1a and c. Write to explore, imagine and entertain, drawing on different poetic forms and explicit choice of language and structure.

Learning outcomes
All will have participated, through speaking or listening, in class discussion recapping poem and use of SE. All will produce list of non-standard English words and start to use them in their poem.

Most will write a poem, based on Tom Leonard's 'Unrelated Incidents'.

Some will also comment on and explain own and others' language choices.

Assessment opportunities
Informal oral questioning.
Informal observation of writing.
(Building towards end-of-term formal oral assessment.)

Cross-curricular learning
Literacy
Citizenship: valuing cultural and linguistic diversity

Resources
Smartboard resource saved from last lesson
Pens and paper

Keywords
Standard English
Dialect
Accent

Table 3.2b Lesson plan produced by a trainee teacher

Time & O	Organisation and resources	Student activities	Teaching points and strategies	Evaluation
8.50	Pars Keywords	Entry to class, settling, awareness of attendance	Remind class of start routine. Take register.	
8.55 #LO1 #LO2	**Starter** Teacher leads session Smartboard	Students brainstorm, nonstandard English vocabulary.	Recap ideas from poem read yesterday. Compare with and annotate nonstandard English in Eminem lyrics. Use of ICT to engage Ben here.	
9.05 #LO3	**Main**	Using words from Starter, students observe modelled writing of version of 'Unrelated Incidents'.	Ensure two-stage modelling: out loud thinking through of own ideas; then taking contributions. Retain students' attention throughout by having them copy thought process, including crossings out.	
9.15	**Development**	Students write own version of 'Unrelated Incidents'.	Differentiation: Ben to complete work on PC if necessary.	
9.35	**Plenary**	Reading aloud and sharing ideas.	Use 'musical object' to ensure 'fair' picking of students to read out work. Praise students' writing and recapping key terms in analysis.	
9.45	**Pack away**		Wait for order before exit.	

Activities

The activities in which the students and the teacher engage in the course of the lesson are its flesh and blood. In your observations (see p. 37) you may see a range of activity types of varying lengths and different foci. You may be surprised by how long is spent on classroom management issues. A typical English lesson may begin with short, pacy activities to warm up, prepare and engage students, followed by a longer activity carried out by the whole class, led by the teacher and requiring a more intense period of concentration or by a carousel of group activities. In the final stages of the lesson there are likely to be more independent activities designed for individual students to apply what they have learned in the lesson or a communal summing up to reinforce what has been covered. When making decisions about activities, the teacher's priority is to provide enough of the right type for students to do, while also allowing for reflection, application and consolidation.

Aims and objectives

The learning objectives should be apparent in all planning documentation, but at the short-term, lesson-by-lesson stage of planning the objectives will inform all the other decisions to be made and should be shared with the students. Aims are generally broader than objectives and may relate to themes, ongoing areas of learning and cross-curricular skills, whereas objectives will be more focused on specific skills. Both will be drawn from the scheme of work and will reflect students' prior attainment and learning, as well as long-term goals as students work towards the end of a Key Stage or an examination.

Structure

The lesson structure can be regarded as its scaffolding; the teacher will need to bear in mind a number of elements which underpin other decisions, such as focus and range of activities and timing. A good English lesson will have a sense of direction, shared by teacher and students, and the structure will reflect this. External factors need to be taken into account; a lesson just after a break or in the afternoon may need to be structured differently in order to accommodate students' varying levels of concentration. Some schools operate a lunch and break-time rota, so that a lesson structure needs to be adjusted and also provide opportunities for focusing and developing activities around the break from the classroom. Good practice also suggests that a lesson structure should reflect our human weaknesses where concentration is concerned – a twenty-minute period of intense writing followed by a meaningful feedback session and an activity which requires movement around the room are more likely to combine well and sustain effective learning for longer.

Timing

Whatever the length of lesson a trainee plans for, generally far too much is planned at first. The practical necessities which are all part of classroom management (arranging the seating, taking the register, giving out books, packing away) have to be accounted for and may be overlooked by the enthusiastic beginner. Then a delicate balancing act – of teacher exposition, a range of activities, time for development and practice of student skills, summing up and, of course, the enjoyment and celebration of learning – needs to take place in order for the ideal pace to be achieved.

The areas described above represent the main areas of decision-making that will occur in the process of planning a lesson. Many of these decisions will be implicit and informed, particularly in the realms of timing and lesson structure, by experience and confidence about what works and what doesn't. Of course, the whole-school context is another enormous factor, and the classroom management procedures, the environment and resources, and other whole-school and departmental policies (relating to assessment or setting, for example) will be hugely influential at both departmental and individual planning levels. When planning an English lesson in a new school, whether you are newly qualified or as a result of a career move, you will need to be well informed about all of the whole-school factors. A more detailed approach to lesson planning is described at the end of this chapter (see pp. 52–59).

Flexibility

We mentioned above that good planning needs to be complemented by flexibility. This is another area of crucial balance; lessons planned rigidly to the last minute may provide you with that sense of security, but if things go wrong – for example, if you lose that pile of handouts, or the network crashes, an activity flops, or the school photographer turns up in the middle of your lesson – you need a back-up plan. At the very least, you need to be confident that if your lesson goes off at a tangent (or just goes off), you and your students will rise to the occasion. In such an event, it will help to have considered beforehand what other directions your lesson content might take and perhaps another way in which the same material can be delivered. In either case, good classroom management will be the key to turning the unexpected in a positive direction.

Managing the classroom and creating the right climate for learning in English

Classroom management is undoubtedly the one area that makes new teachers, as well as experienced teachers in new settings, most anxious. Lack of familiarity with school systems and, most significantly, with students, means that at first you will be trying to teach without having a relationship with anyone in your class. Relationships are what make good teaching, and especially good English teaching, so the sooner you can forge a relationship, preferably one based on mutual respect and enjoyment of learning in English, the better.

This is not easy, of course, but neither is it as difficult as it may seem. Fortunately, although no teacher training course can deliver charisma, a repertoire of strategies can be learned and put into practice, and strengthen the relationships you make with your classes. Remember that the classroom is your space and your responsibility is to share it as a learning environment with your class(es). A number of areas need to be considered in this quest.

Lesson planning

Everything that has been discussed earlier in this chapter and elsewhere is relevant to classroom management: timing and range of activities; thoughtful adaptation of schemes of work and preparation of resources to cater for everyone's needs; careful deployment of classroom assistants; relevant selection of texts and materials. The bottom line is that students are much more likely to be bored, stressed and restless, and therefore to misbehave, if they are not given meaningful, challenging and enjoyable things to do.

Class dynamics

The dynamics of the English classroom – i.e., the responses and counter-responses made by teacher and students – will determine the success of a lesson and, in the long term, how students feel about coming to your classes. Some of the key factors in creating a positive and productive learning dynamic, to which all can, and are expected to, contribute, are discussed below.

Seats of learning?

The seating and grouping arrangements of the classroom can and should be manipulated by the teacher to bring about different dynamics:

A pupil in a classroom occupies what we have come to call a 'learning zone'. This zone is fairly flexible. Most of the time it consists of the desk of the learner, plus the desks and personalities of the other one, two or three pupils in the same block or pair . . . its most enduring features will be dominated by the shape and character of the learners in the immediate vicinity. If pupils have a free rein about choosing their friends as neighbours, they will invariably choose those who share the same values. Thus an underachieving boy will choose to sit next to another underachieving boy, and the same with girls.

(Noble and Bradford, 2000: 95)

Recent research, carried out under the auspices of finding out why boys appear to underachieve in English, now suggests that both boys *and* girls make more progress if they are seated alternately (Hannan, 1999). Taking into account the caveats presented by Colin Noble and Wendy Bradford about using seating plans flexibly and communicating the reasons for them (Noble and Bradford, 2000: 98–100), it is sensible to operate a variety of seating plans. Used sensitively to enhance learning and not in order to disturb and irritate students or to punish bad behaviour, they help to prevent poor and unproductive relationships between students becoming embedded, and also reinforce the notion that students need to learn to work with a range of others in a variety of ways.

One effective strategy is to establish three alternative seating arrangements at the beginning of the academic year (although it is possible to do this at a later point, it will be easier if you do it as part of the 'establishment phase' (Rogers, 2000). For example, it will take some time to organise these three arrangements, but the payback in terms of ease of changing the seating for different English activities later makes it worthwhile. The teacher now needs to use all three alternatives on a regular basis, telling students as they arrive in class which of the seating plans will be in use on that occasion, and prompting the movement of

Seating plan A: based on a boy/girl/boy/girl pattern, perhaps arranged alphabetically.
Seating plan B: based on friendship pairs sitting together, in which students choose a friend to sit with and the teacher places them strategically in the room to facilitate seating plan C.
Seating plan C: based on groups made up of friendship pairs combined into learning groups of four or six.

tables and chairs where necessary. If you can develop a nickname or shorthand way of referring to each plan (the Bee Gees or the FPs, for example) with the class, all the better. It's a good idea to make a record of each seating plan which can be displayed in the classroom and amended whenever necessary. (See Figure 3.1 for an example which also shows the teacher's planned deployment of Teaching Assistants (TAs) during one-to-one work.) Whichever system of the

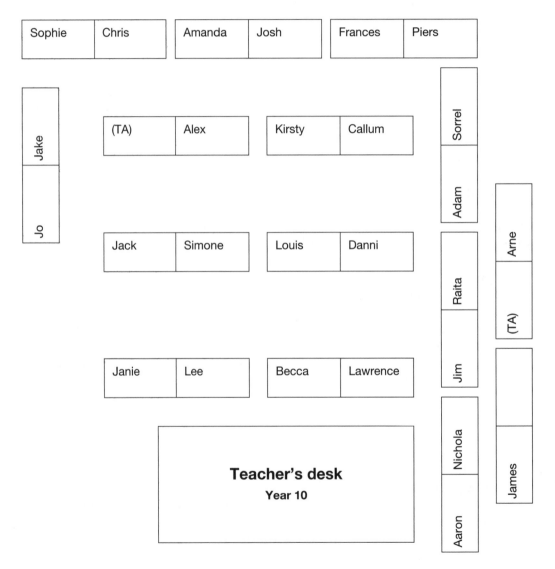

Figure 3.1 A Year 10 seating plan using boy/girl pairings

three plans you choose, it obviously needs to take into account whole-school policy (adjustments to the examples above will obviously be necessary in single-sex schools and in those schools where English is taught in single-sex groups), as well as the size and layout of the individual classroom.

A development of working this way with students in order to control and influence the classroom dynamic is expounded in the work of Alistair Smith, founder of the group 'Accelerated Learning in Training and Education' (ALITE) (for further information, see their website, www.alite.co.uk).

Communication

'I think I can be a good teacher because I like young people and I'm a good communicator.' It may be a cliché, but it's true. The challenge here is to show the young people in your care that you like and respect them, even when they haven't handed in their homework and they've just designed an intricate paper aeroplane using the worksheet you designed so carefully last night. A positive, happy and orderly atmosphere in your classroom is central to a positive dynamic.

Communicating effectively with students, not only about the content of their lessons but about the structure and design of their lessons, has a very positive impact on classroom dynamics. Students learn to see you as being in charge, but more importantly, as careful and *caring* about the experiences they are getting. Simple explanations, such as 'We're sitting like this today because . . .', and plenty of advance warning of activities changing, such as 'Now you're going to have three minutes to talk about this in pairs and then you're going to work independently, in silence, for ten minutes', are reassuring for students, indicative of a teacher's control and confidence, and show that the lesson has direction and purpose.

The modulation of voice and tone are also important, not least because your voice is precious and easily worn out by a lot of shouting. For teachers have a problem being heard; a group of them in a pub are likely to be the loudest people there! Many teachers also develop deeper voices after years of stretching their vocal cords and talking through sore throats. Ideally, the teacher's voice needs to be authoritative, but not strident. Learners are rightly sensitive to the ways they are spoken to, and shouting at your class is hardly going to get the best from them, let alone set a good example of classroom manners. A firm, brisk tone is more effective, especially when it is alternated with a repertoire of voices for other parts of the teaching performance, such as reading a sinister story aloud, demonstrating styles of speaking and listening, or putting the characters' voices into the class novel. Moving around as you talk or read can also help to modulate your voice for the listeners, as well as giving you a more complete awareness of levels of attention and response around the classroom. Sipping water through the day will help preserve your voice for all these occasions.

Task 3.2: Observation tasks: tone and volume in the classroom

This is an ideal way to use any 'pupil shadowing' or 'pupil pursuit' opportunities you may be given during induction to a school. Watch a range of lessons across the curriculum and keep a note of the way different teachers use their voice and to what effect. Compare the use of the voice in practical lessons and when students are more desk-bound, and for different parts of each lesson (arrival, introduction, one-to-one, whole-class expositions and summing up).

The use of humour in your relations with students is in some ways contentious. Some teachers are overly sarcastic, use humour against students who they feel are challenging them and make jokes at the expense of others. In English, when we might at any point wish to discuss a sensitive issue or ask for personal responses to a complex text, to alienate students like this is at best a questionable technique. Anyway, students are adept at seeing when this is going on and are unlikely to react well. On the other hand, you don't want students coming to class expecting stand-up comedy; even if you could keep it up day after day, they will soon get into the habit of expecting to sit back and be entertained. It's better that they arrive knowing they will be expected to work hard, but in a caring, friendly, good-humoured atmosphere.

So, sympathetically used, humour is an essential part of a teacher's classroom management toolkit. A joke about something that was on TV last night as students come in, seeing the funny side of the class reader, or telling a silly story at your own expense will all help to establish and promote good relationships. Knowing when and how to turn these happy dynamics to more industrious effect is also important.

Expectations and control

If you watch a good teacher at work, you will see evidence of high expectations of behaviour, attitude and application. The vast majority of students *want* to learn and look to the class teacher for guidance and leadership in this process; showing them how to conduct themselves, through example and by expecting, and praising, certain standards, is another class management strategy.

Making expectations explicit may seem like hard work at first, especially if you are taking over a class in the middle of the academic year, but, like setting up your seating plans, it is well worth it. Controlling and responding to incidents of poor behaviour is much easier if there are plenty of examples of good learning going on around you. For additional guidance, the generic text in this series (Nicholls, 1999: Chapter 6) deals thoroughly with classroom management and the list of further reading at the end of this chapter may also be useful.

Classroom climate

The word 'climate' has become a popular buzzword in recent times. The Hay Group, a London-based management consultancy with expertise in 'leadership and human motivation' (Hay Group, 2002) has carried out research, for example, into teacher effectiveness for the DfES. Their website (www.transforming learning.co.uk), which has evolved from such research, provides an evaluation service for use by both individual teachers and whole schools to test attitudes and perceptions of different aspects of their teaching. It names nine areas or 'dimensions' of teaching and learning which comprise their definition of climate:

- clarity
- order
- standards
- fairness
- participation
- support
- safety
- interest
- environment.

This is a fair summary of what students need in the classroom, and therefore what their teachers should provide, and it is also useful as a checklist of aspects to which the teacher must give some thought in planning a lesson or sequence of lessons, and creating the right climate for learning in English. Some of the categories appear to subsume others and need clarification. Of course, in an English lesson safety may not appear to be such a significant concern as in, say, Science or Food Technology. However, we should take the term in a less literal way and think about the challenge of providing learning opportunities which will take a student – with a supportive framework to scaffold learning – to the edge of the comfort zone, rather than sending him or her into unfamiliar territory where defences will be erected and minimal learning, or even engagement with the task, will take place.

> **Task** **3.3**: Theory tasks: defining and creating classroom climate
>
> Consider the nine dimensions of classroom climate identified above. Write your own definition of each, using examples from your own experience to illustrate their significance. If possible, discuss these with your mentor or a teaching colleague. When planning your next lesson, use the nine areas as headings and determine how you will provide for each in your classroom. Evaluate your success in each area using a simple 0–10 scale.

Planning teaching and learning

How planning has changed

Asked to plan a scheme of work for a Year 6 class in 1990, Robert Jeffcoate devised a list of eight units. They were a Dickens topic covering various prose, script and moving image versions of *Great Expectations* and *David Copperfield*; two units on 'language awareness'; animal poetry; group work on newspapers; story-telling; reading around the theme of 'islands', and a unit on Shakespeare. He comments on his choices:

> This scheme does, I hope you agree, have a satisfying balance and well-roundedness to it, even if it's essentially an expression of my own predilections and prejudices and limited by the arbitrariness which characterises all curriculum planning in English. Although it would, I think, go down well with a top junior class, it would be equally suitable for just about any secondary school class as well.
>
> (Jeffcoate, 1992: 70–71)

When the author was reflecting on his choices in 1992, the National Curriculum had been in place for two years (DES, 1990), but the National Literacy Strategy and the Framework for Teaching English were still to come. Let's take the main points he makes in turn:

- The 'satisfying balance and well-roundedness' ascribed to the choices of topics for this class over a year is something we should still aspire to, in the texts, authors, activities and assessments we provide for students.

- In terms of our 'own predilections and prejudices', planning now will be still essentially by personal choice, as neither the National Curriculum, the Framework nor the NLS prescribes named texts.
- However, Initial Teacher Training documents like the Career Entry Profile require new teachers to identify and rectify weaknesses and 'gaps' in their own subject knowledge and the National Curriculum and the NLS insist on certain aspects of the subject being taught.
- In addition, the kind of autonomy enjoyed by English teachers until the 1990s is likely to have been lost as English Departments and coordinators put more prescriptive schemes of work in place in order to meet the demands of national documentation and its enforcers, Ofsted.
- The 'arbitrariness' of English planning still exists, in that teachers have to make choices to suit their classes and their schools, although it has been countered to a significant extent by the statutory and non-statutory guidelines of the National Curriculum and the NLS, and their attempts to define the content and the boundaries of the subject.
- The judgement that this scheme of work is 'equally suitable' for Year 6s or another class in the lower secondary years highlights one of the most noteworthy developments in English planning in recent times. Much emphasis is now placed on academic attainment being maintained and improved as students move through the Key Stages, and one of the key aims of the Framework is to 'promote continuity and progression between Key Stage 2 and Key Stage 3' (DfEE, 2001: 9).

Here, then, is a brief demonstration of how much has changed and how much has not in the last decade or so. English teachers' experiences of planning in the early part of the twenty-first century are surely equally characterised by a desire to teach a wide range of texts and skills, suited to their own and their students' interests, but the guidelines, impositions, constraints and advice to be adhered to now are greater than ever before.

Task 3.4: Theory task: investigating lesson plans

Some sample English schemes of work and lesson plans are available on the Qualifications and Curriculum Authority website (www.qca.org.uk) and demonstrate one way in which planning can be formatted and shared. View or download these examples and contrast them with the schemes and lesson plans used by the school you are currently working in. Adapt and use the QCA material if it is relevant to you.

Planning a lesson

Like planning a scheme of work, planning an individual lesson is subject to a set of national criteria, and lesson planning templates, such as the samples illustrated in Figures 3.2a and b, reflect the necessary areas of consideration. It is likely that you will be asked to use a standard lesson planning proforma provided by your training institution or school. In addition, the following steps are offered as a general guide to lesson planning:

1 Find out about the prior learning of the class. This includes looking at their work from the previous year, term and lesson. The current scheme of work and the yearly outline or Key Stage plan will be essential here. If you have a topic or precise focus for the lesson in mind, you will need to look at previous work the students concerned have completed in this area, as well as at the references to this aspect of the curriculum in national documentation from the previous Key Stage.

2 Look at evidence of the prior attainment of the class and individual students. Various data should be available, such as your own assessment records for the group, the previous class teacher's records and the National Curriculum levels most recently attained by the class.

3 Using information about prior learning and attainment, make a decision about what the class needs to do next. This may be influenced by:

- the appropriate next stage in developing their skills in a particular area, such as progressing from writing narrative openings to exploring narrative development;
- the need to address an area of weakness noted in their previous similar work, such as evidence of lack of understanding of the layout of speech in prose texts during a unit of work on story-writing;
- the need for consolidation of a particular skill or knowledge before, for instance, continuing to apply it in a different, more complex context;
- the requirements of the scheme of work or other long-term plan – for example, leading up to an assessment or examination;
- the desirability of developing students' awareness of the area being studied – for example, to extend and deepen understanding or to make a cross-curricular link;
- the need to address an area or skill the class have not encountered before.

4 Develop the main activities of the lesson according to your aims and the needs of the class. The nature of this part of the lesson will depend on its overall length, the ability of the students, the availability of the resources and support

Session:				Week no.:

Date: Time:

Curriculum reference:

Objectives – at the end of the lesson student will be able to:

Time	Topic	Teacher activity	Learner activity	Materials/resources

Lesson evaluation:

Additional notes:

Figure 3.2a Lesson plan template

Source: BBC Skillswise (2003)

Scheme of work:	Year:
Lesson outline	Resources
	Outcomes
	Differentiation
	Follow on

Homework:

Notes:

Figure 3.2b Lesson plan template
Source: Teachit (1999)

staff and the chosen focus. There are no hard-and-fast rules, but the following points should be considered in order to help make the entire lesson constructive and enjoyable for the whole class, including the teacher.

Routines

Many schools and English Departments have established routines – for example, related to students' arrival and entry to a lesson, seating arrangements, teacher and student talk, homework setting, rewards, sanctions and praise. Your lesson plan should incorporate these as they will have been developed in order to create a common climate across a school or department. Any departure from familiar procedures, especially if you are new to the school, is likely to distract or agitate students, making them less likely to respond well to your lesson. Reproducing a familiar environment, and even imitating some of the techniques and strategies you may have observed in other lessons, will enhance the learning climate and reduce the chances of more general disturbances. Of course, later, when an orderly environment and your expectations have been established, it may be desirable to take risks – with resources, classroom arrangements, activities or simply by purposely disrupting the routine – to achieve a particular learning outcome.

Balance of activities

A balance of reading, writing, and speaking and listening activities in each lesson is one way to help students to concentrate and to vary the demands being made on them.

Structure

The literacy-hour type structure, beginning with a short starter activity, followed by two longer sections of the lesson devoted to introducing, developing and consolidating skills and then a plenary, can be applied successfully to most lessons (and lesson content) but, as with any lesson structure, it will become predictable, boring and unchallenging if used without variation.

Communicating learning objectives

Sharing learning objectives and revisiting them at the end of the lesson is considered good practice generally, but this should also be done in a range of ways to avoid repetitive structure and therefore predictability. Figure 3.3 provides a list of suggested types of plenary activities.

Learning styles

Students learn in different ways and the success of a lesson will be improved if it can offer something to these different types of learners. Learning styles have been the subject of much research recently, and three main types have been

- Students make a brief written note of three things they remember from the lesson. These notes can be used for reference at the beginning of the following lesson to aid continuity.

- A short spelling and definition test of key words used in the lesson.

- A whole-class question-and-answer session.

- 'Pass the parcel': an infinitely flexible and engaging way to end the lesson, especially suitable when asking students to share work or to make sure you hear from students who often opt out of oral plenaries. An object is passed from student to student in time to music; when the music stops, the pupil holding the object contributes in the specified way. The students themselves may be keen to take turns controlling the music. Another variation gives students the chance to 'answer or nominate', which handily avoids undue pressure being put on a single member of the class.

- Working in pairs, students have two minutes to tell each other the 'story of the lesson'.

- Using mini-whiteboards, students hold up the answers to key questions, focusing on the lesson content.

- Learning is consolidated by repeating or rehearsing an earlier activity in an abbreviated form. For example, after a lesson in which sentence structure for specific effects has been explored, all students are required to write a sentence in which the main action of the sentence is withheld until the final clause. These can form the starting point for a follow-up lesson.

- Students formulate questions to ask another member of the class to 'test' them on the lesson content. This can be used with the pass-the-parcel technique.

- Representatives from different groups in the class are required to recap different parts of the lesson 'as if you are telling mum or dad what we learned about today' or to inform an absentee of what was missed.

Figure 3.3   A range of plenary activities

identified – visual, kinaesthetic and auditory – which it would be worthwhile catering for in your lesson, if at all possible. Ideally, your lesson should contain something for everyone, as students rarely learn exclusively in one way. You might, for example, explore the idea of writing for different non-fiction purposes first by reading and sorting a selection of leaflets into different categories (campaign material, information, persuasion, instruction), appealing to the mainly visual learners. Then pairs of students could role-play a conversation in the same categories, kinaesthetically drawing attention to the different modes of language each requires. Finally, to practise their auditory skills further, one role-play in each category could be presented to the class, and tone, non-verbal communication and sentence structures could be analysed.

Movement and brain activity

It takes a lot of effort and concentration for a class to sit still for the duration of a lesson. Building in some opportunities for movement, preferably pertinent to the tasks they are engaged in, may appear to be momentarily disruptive, but research into brain activity suggests that even the simple act of standing up sends a spurt of oxygen to the brain, and some practitioners recommend 'brain breaks', 'simple exercises designed to . . . manage the physiology and attention of the class', of one or two minutes in order to extend periods of concentration (ALITE, 2003).

Talk

Most teachers talk too much. It can be a way of covering up lack of preparation, acquiring and retaining control over the class or even showing off. Although it is said that about 30 per cent of the population are auditory learners, this actually means that those individuals learn best from *interactive* speaking and listening. Get your students talking in structured, purposeful ways to you and to each other in pairs and groups of different sizes at different points in the lesson.

Differentiation

Differentiation is essential. Even in a set or banded class, students' abilities will range across a wide spectrum. Your analysis of prior learning and attainment will have highlighted students with particular difficulties or talents in English. You should also have access to the school's register of students with Special Educational Needs (SEN). However, often the best way to learn about how best to cater for and develop the learning of students at both ends of the ability range is to discuss them with your colleagues. The Special Educational Needs Coordinator (SENCO), the Learning Support staff, your head of department and the students' previous teachers will all have a wealth of experience to offer. The issues surrounding differentiation are discussed in more detail in Chapter 8.

Behaviour

We have already discussed classroom dynamics and management in general terms. When planning a specific lesson, it is worthwhile giving consideration to behaviour issues that you already know about and, if you have not taught a class before, you should certainly ask what to expect. This may be regarded as differentiation for behaviour reasons, and indeed, some of the information you need will come from the SEN register which lists students with Emotional and Behavioural Difficulties (EBD) as well as those with academic special needs.

There is a fine line between planning for the worst and being prepared. As has been stated, having high expectations is one of the best classroom management strategies and will often instil good class discipline, as well as pre-empt any individual lapses. On the other hand, if you know that a student has a record of challenging behaviour, it would be irresponsible not to take this into account in your planning. Seating arrangements, special resources, joint plans with any learning support assistants working in your class and the use of any strategies that have been shared in staff or departmental meetings should all appear in your lesson plan.

Resources
All the resources used in support of the lesson need to be thoroughly prepared or adapted in advance. Make sure that everything you need is to hand, and in your planning, think about how they are to be distributed and collected. You may have a rota system organised within the class for giving out books and equipment. Alternatively, you may wish to set out all the lesson resources on desks before the students arrive, although this isn't always feasible when one lesson follows hot on the heels of the next. A range of media, including audio and video tapes, printed worksheets, websites, textbooks, CD-ROMs and other software should be at your disposal. It is wise not to try to use too many resources in a single lesson, but be sure to use all available resources over the course of a sequence of lessons.

5   Decide on how time will be used in the lesson, incorporating all its 'ingredients', from the students' arrival, giving out resources, introducing the lesson, the activities and the end of the lesson with all its associated routines. Allow time for regrouping or any other movement around the room, as well as for setting, collecting and returning marked work if this is necessary (this is usually done best at the beginning or in the middle of a lesson to ensure it is orderly and meaningful).

6   You will probably be required to keep records of your planning. In any case, this is a good idea because it will save you time and effort in future when you are likely to teach similar content or classes, or need similar materials. After teaching, lessons should ideally be evaluated. Evaluation can be done at various levels and most teachers will at least reflect mentally on a lesson as it passes and make adjustments to their next lesson as a result. Written lesson plans with notes added about how students responded, what went well and possible modifications for next time make excellent evidence for a portfolio for your training course, threshold assessment and interview purposes. Portfolios for the Postgraduate Certificate in Education (PGCE), Graduate Teacher Programme (GTP) and Newly Qualified Teacher (NQT) must include evidence of lesson plans, self-evaluation by the trainee and a minimum number of evaluations (together with records of feedback and targets) by a mentor or class teacher in the observer role.

In time, these planning processes will become automatic. You will be able to plan a lesson in a few minutes, especially if you are supported by detailed, well-resourced schemes of work and if you store your previously successful materials somewhere close at hand. Once you have observed a selection of lessons, and planned and taught a few of your own, it is a good idea to return to the principles outlined here. If you have the opportunity, observe your classes being taught by another member of the department, as your ability to identify the essential components and decisions within the lessons will have been finely honed. Remember above all that, although good teaching and effective learning come about through thorough planning, a spontaneous decision to follow up a student comment or abandon the plan in favour of something more immediate, more risky, more *fun*, can be equally rewarding for all concerned, if not more so. It is the hallmark of a well-organised and creative planner that such moments are pursued with relish when they occur.

Further reading

Smith, A. and Call, N. (1999) *The ALPS Approach, Accelerated Learning in Primary Schools*, Network Educational Press, Stafford.

4　Assessment, recording and reporting

Jane Branson

From the one-to-one informal feedback given to a student in a lesson, to the publication of your school's exam results, all teachers are involved in assessment, recording and reporting of learning and attainment at a number of levels. This is the point at which your teaching and students' learning 'goes public', to parents, the local community and in the national education arena, which is why it is such a potentially contentious area. However, on a more intimate scale, well-managed assessment and relevant feedback is at the heart of the teacher–student relationship.

Objectives

In this chapter, we will deal with the following aspects of assessment, recording and reporting:

- initial Teacher Training standards relating to assessment and monitoring;
- external testing arrangements for English and their influence on the curriculum;
- setting and marking English homework;
- feedback for learning in English.

Teacher training standards relating to assessment and monitoring

For those working towards Qualified Teacher Status (QTS), the set of standards relating to monitoring and assessment (TTA, 2003: 11) is often the most difficult to achieve. This is perhaps due to the relatively short period spent in each school on a traditional teaching practice placement, which does not always provide opportunities to observe and evaluate students' progress over a period of time. In addition, there is the difficulty of getting to grips with the assessment criteria, from Early Learning Goals to National Curriculum descriptors and the grading systems of awarding bodies. Also, lack of experience and confidence can mean that marking takes a long time for trainees and new teachers. Watching experienced teachers marking or moderating is sometimes like witnessing some sort of mystical process; after years of scrutinising students' work, applying assessment criteria and justifying their decisions, they make it look easy.

Task 4.1: Observation task: applying assessment criteria

Arrange to observe a teacher marking. Ask them to let you watch them mark two or three pieces of student work and talk though the decisions and judgements they are making as part of the process, with reference to the assessment criteria (e.g. National Curriculum levels) being used.

Ongoing assessment and monitoring

We must remember that arguably the most important of the monitoring and assessment standards are those relating to the assessment that goes on in the classroom context, when teachers give 'immediate and constructive feedback to support pupils as they learn' and 'involve pupils in reflecting on, evaluating and improving their own performance' (Standard 3.2.2). To demonstrate and gain experience in this area, there are plenty of opportunities on a daily basis. The range of strategies available for evaluating learning in the classroom is wide. They include:

- teacher observation of writing;
- one-to-one questioning;
- teacher-led whole-class question and answer;

- quick testing techniques (for example, using mini-whiteboards held up to give a spot-check diagnosis);
- one-to-one redrafting;
- peer review with teacher observing;
- self-assessment;
- student oral presentation, both individual and in groups;
- formal diagnostic assessment (such as of reading or spelling);
- whole-class interaction (for example, students contributing to board work);
- formal end-of-unit or end-of-year (summative) assessment.

These kinds of assessment are virtually continuous and form part of the everyday routine of English lessons. The way that such observations and diagnoses are recorded varies and teachers need to develop their own notation systems for making brief but valuable records while a lesson is in progress.

Record keeping

Post-lesson evaluation, even if only in the form of a quick comment recording the general progress of the lesson, the strengths and weaknesses of individual students or a 'note to self' about an aspect of a student's learning which needs to be reinforced or returned to at a later date, is an important part of record keeping. Such data should be used to inform and, where necessary, amend future planning, as well as providing a record of class and individual progress that can be referred to when reporting to parents and giving feed-back to students:

Qualifying to Teach: Standard 3.2.6

They record pupils' progress and achievements systematically to provide evidence of the range of their work, progress and attainment over time. They use this to help pupils review their own progress and to inform planning.

(TTA, 2003: 11)

It is increasingly likely that you will be expected to use some sort of electronic record of data and marks awarded for your classes, and there are electronic school management systems into which such data can be entered, monitored and manipulated with ease. In most schools these systems are updated and administered centrally, but in any case it is essential that classroom teachers maintain their own records, in a traditional mark book or electronically using a data-handling application such as MS Excel. An exemplar is provided in Figure 4.1. Additional information will also need to be maintained, including, for example, Individual Educational Plans (IEPs) (for students on the SEN register), learning targets, records of parental contacts, baseline and other data (such as the results of reading tests, SATs and Cognitive Abilities' Tests, if they are used in your school). Each teacher develops his or her own systems for these records, but at the very least your records should contain the date and main focus for each assessment, a level or grade for each student and any relevant supplementary information, such as details about the support given to a particular individual, student absence or failure to complete homework on time.

Task 4.2: Observation task: using data to inform planning

Look at your own records or the sample mark book page provided in Table 4.1. Compare the Year 9 target level to the levels achieved in March and April of Year 8. Use three colours to highlight (a) students on target, (b) students unlikely to meet their target and (c) students on course to exceed their target.

Reporting

Although parents are the most obvious audience for teachers' reports, similar information is likely to be called upon for a range of other purposes in the course of a typical year, not least when giving feedback to students. Internally, the SENCO may seek information, for example when compiling an IEP, and your head of department will need access to your records as part of the monitoring and target-setting process. Outside agencies such as behaviour support services and the school educational psychologist are also likely to need the kind of information held by classroom teachers.

What do parents want to know?
As a core subject, parents rightly accord high importance to English and the progress of their children in this subject, and, as an English teacher, you are likely to be in demand at parents' consultation meetings. On these occasions and in reports, most parents simply want to know how well their child is doing in relation to national and personal expectations, and in terms of both effort and performance. Some parents, no doubt thinking back to their own school experiences or even reflecting their own anxieties, put undue emphasis on basic skills like spelling and handwriting. Sensitive and careful people management skills

Year	No.	Forename	Surname	Sex	KS2 SATs			Av.	CATs			Y9 Target	11.3.03 Reading Reading journal	17.3.03 S&L PPT Pres.	1.4.03 Writing News report
					Eng.	Ma.	Sci.		V	Q	NV				
8	1	Tariq	AZAD	M	3	5	4	4.00	2	5	4	4	ABS	4.40	4.40
8	2	Carlie	BEWSLEY	F	4	4	4	4.00	5	5	6	5	4.40	4.40	4.4 (S)
8	3	Louisa	BRIGGS	F	4	4	4	4.00	5	5	5	5	4.70	4.40	4.40
8	4	Michael	CARSON	M	5	4	5	4.67	5	6	6	6	3.70	4.70	4.40
8	5	Leila	CHARLWOOD	F	5	3	4	4.00	4	2	3	6	5.40	4.70	5.00
8	6	Emily	HARVEY	F	4	3	4	3.67	6	4	6	5	5.70	4.40	5.40
8	7	Jamie	HENRY	M	3	3	4	3.33	4	4	5	4	4.00	3.40	4.00
8	8	Craig	HUCKLE	M	5	4	5	4.67	6	6	4	6	6.00	6.70	5.40
8	9	Jack	LAVER	M	5	4	5	4.67	6	7	7	6	4.40	ABS	5.40
8	10	Gregory	LEE	M	5	5	5	5.00	8	8	8	6	ABS	6.00	5.40
8	11	Sara	MURRAY	F	5	5	5	5.00	7	8	8	6	6.00	5.40	5.70
8	12	Billie	NORBY	F	4	4	4	4.00	4	5	4	5	4.40	5.40	4.70
8	13	John	PHILLIPS	M	5	5	5	5.00	7	9	7	6	4.4 L	4.70	5.00
8	14	Connor	READ	M	3	3	4	3.33	3	4	3	4	4.00	ABS	4.00
8	15	Serena	SINGH	F	3	4	4	3.67	3	5	6	4	4.40	ABS	4.00
8	16	Rachel	SHILTON	F	4	3	4	3.67	3	4	5	5	5.40	L 4.7	5.00
8	17	Danni	TANNER	F	4	5	4	4.33	5	6	4	5	4.70	4.40	4.40
8	18	Charles	TERRY	M	3	3	4	3.33	3	3	4	4	5.00	4.70	4.40
8	19	Jennifer	WEBB	F	5	5	5	5.00	A	A	A	6	3.40	4.70	4.70
8	20	Robbie	WEBSTER	M	3	3	4	3.33	3	4	4	4	4.40	4.00	4.70
8	21	Siobhan	WESTON	F	4	4	4	4.00	5	6	7	5	5.00	4.40	4.70
8	22	Holly	WILSON	F	4	3	4	3.67	A	A	3	5	2.70	3.70	4.00
8	23	Louis	YOUNG	M	3	3	4	3.33	2	5	4	4	5.40	4.40	4.70

S = scribed by TA

L = homework overdue

Figure 4.1 A page from a class teacher's records using MS Excel

are often needed to explain that, at a time of huge technological development, we have to maintain a balance between teaching traditional skills and equipping learners to take a full part in whatever the future holds.

Written reports

Following government guidelines on reporting to parents, all schools have their own systems, which may vary from tick-box reports to statement banks to reports in full prose. In reality, a combination of different types of report during a school year provides parents with a range of information. Most demanding for the teacher are reports that require a prose comment. Writing these, you will probably find that your vocabulary dries up, you forget which student is which and, despite your painstaking record-keeping, you still can't think of anything to say about little Johnny! At such times, it helps to have a ready formula (see Table 4.1) which can be adapted as necessary and which usually creates a personalised, informative report with a warm tone, even when critical comments are necessary.

Testing arrangements in English

Table 4.2 shows all the assessments a student will experience during their compulsory and optional years of English study. These assessment points inevitably have an effect on the English curriculum, requiring students to be both schooled in examination skills – how long to spend on each question, how to read the question, how to judge whether to answer in bullets or prose – and prepared for the content and demands of the tests. For many English teachers, the design of schemes of work and lesson plans can feel like a constant and taut balancing act between 'teaching to the test' and providing enjoyable English lessons which promote students' interest, engagement and success in the subject.

Task **4.3**: Theory task: how are students assessed in English?

Ask your head of department, mentor or the Key Stage 2 literacy coordinator for a copy of the most recent Key Stages 2 and 3 assessment papers. Complete the tests in exam conditions and, if the mark schemes published by QCA are available, use them to mark your work. In discussion with your mentor, highlight the challenges of preparing students for the assessment.

Table 4.1 Writing reports: a model with illustrations

Make a general statement summarising the student's learning skills.	Jack works willingly and takes a responsible attitude towards his own learning.	Sarah is capable of remaining on task for parts of each lesson and sometimes works independently.
Make a second statement, focusing on achievement in English.	He has a good vocabulary and a thoughtful approach to his reading, so that he is able to articulate well-developed points of view.	She usually makes good use of support and enjoys being able to contribute to discussions.
Refer to one or two particular and recent pieces of work which demonstrate strengths and/or weaknesses.	He takes his studies seriously, as illustrated in the telephone conversation he worked on last half-term. This was a sustained piece of role-play which drew sensitively on the characters from the text we are reading. In his written interview, he showed a grasp of some of the main conventions of this genre, but these were not used consistently, which spoiled the overall effect of his work.	She recently worked well on the performance of a conversation between two fictional characters, and was able to use voice and some gestures to show character. In her written interview, she selected vocabulary from an inappropriate informal register and her writing was too short.
Set a target.	Jack needs to work on the clarity of his writing, focusing particularly on sentence punctuation by using a full stop to indicate the end of a sentence.	Sarah must focus on writing at greater length so that her work can be fully assessed. She should always check the minimum length required with the teacher.

Table 4.2 Assessments in English Key Stages 1–5

Assessment point	Age (approx.)	Type of assessment
End of Key Stage 1	7	Statutory tests and tasks to assess reading, writing, spelling and handwriting
During Key Stage 2	8, 9, 10	Optional reading, writing and spelling tests
End of Key Stage 2	11	Statutory tests and tasks to assess reading, writing, spelling and handwriting
End of Year 7	12	Optional progress tests (for those who did not achieve level 4 at end of Key Stage 2)
During Key Stage 3	12, 13	Optional reading, writing and spelling tests
End of Key Stage 3	14	Statutory tests and tasks to assess reading, writing (including spelling)
End of Key Stage 4	16	GCSE English and/or English Literature
End of Year 12	17	AS level English
End of Key Stage 5	18	A level English

Statutory and public examinations

Standard Attainment Tasks (SATs)

SATs, taken at the end of Key Stages 1, 2 and 3, were reformed in 2003 to 'provide a more coherent approach to assessment across all Key Stages and incorporate the teaching objectives outlined in the English strand of the Key Stage 3 national strategy's *Framework for Teaching English*' (QCA, 2002: 2). A set of 'assessment focuses' which reflect the National Curriculum and the National Literacy Strategy are now assessed at the end of each Key Stage. With school SATs results and government league tables meaning so much at a local, regional and national level, it is perhaps unavoidable that some of the pressure teachers feel is passed on to children in their classes. For example, it is not unusual for Year 6 and Year 9 students to spend much of the term preceding the SATs – and sometimes more – practising answering SATs questions, taking booster lessons and doing extra homework in readiness for the tests.

The tests are constructed around reading and writing tasks, with marks for handwriting (at Key Stages 1 and 2), spelling, composition and effect, sentence structure and punctuation, and text organisation. At Key Stage 3, students' understanding and response to a Shakespeare play (in 2003 either *Macbeth*, *Twelfth Night* or *Henry V*) is also assessed. Marks in each of these areas are translated into National Curriculum levels published for each student.

Task 4.4: Theory task: the use of SATs data in the classroom

Using a copy of the most recent SATs data for one of your classes, work out the percentage of students achieving at each level. Compare these levels to those gained by the class in their most recent teacher assessment and pinpoint any inconsistencies. Are there any students whose SATs results you mistrust, based on their day-to-day performance? Are there any students who, according to the baseline data, are underperforming?

GCSEs and AS/A levels

At GCSE and AS/A level, courses and standards are monitored by the Qualifications and Curriculum Authority (QCA) and, in the case of Key Stage 4 courses, based on the National Curriculum. As a result, variations in content and design between the main awarding bodies are limited, and the main components of all GCSE English courses (in England) are listed in Table 4.3. Aiming to attract teachers and departments whose students and needs are diverse, the awarding bodies can only adapt their courses within the constraints imposed. For example, all awarding bodies must abide by the rules which state that the proportion of marks for internally assessed coursework must not exceed 40 per cent of the total, although they design different GCSE specifications in which reading, writing or speaking and listening tasks are given prominence in the coursework assessment.

Table 4.3 The components and weighting of assessment for English GCSE

Component	Range assessed	Weighting
Speaking and listening	A variety of formal and informal contexts, including: • explain, describe, narrate; • explore, analyse, imagine; • discuss, argue, persuade.	20 per cent
Reading	Prose, poetry and drama, including: • a play by Shakespeare; • work from the English literary heritage by at least one major writer with a well-established critical reputation (para 8a of the reading programme of study); • texts from different cultures and traditions.	40 per cent
Writing	A variety of forms and genres, including: • explore, imagine, entertain; • inform, explain, describe; • argue, persuade, advise; • analyse, review, comment.	40 per cent
Key skills	Application of number Communication Information technology Improving own learning and performance Problem solving Working with others	N/A

Source: GCSE Criteria for English, QCA, 2001

Task 4.5: Theory task: teaching to the GCSE specifications

Obtain a copy of the GCSE English and English Literature specifications taught at your teaching practice schools. These can usually be downloaded from the websites of the awarding bodies if spare copies are not available in the schools. Review the Key Stage 4 schemes of work in the school and draw up a rough outline of a typical GCSE English or English Literature course.

Setting and marking homework

You've probably already heard from your colleagues, in a confidential whisper of course, that 'English teachers have the most marking to do'. Marking writing does take a long time, and in English, students do a lot of writing. As a result, English teachers need to develop quick reading skills and the ability to mark anywhere, any time (at the bus stop, on the beach or in bed!) or, alternatively, a manageable homework and marking strategy, which means that you can spend at least as much time planning and delivering as assessing.

Task **4.6**: Observation task: investigating students' views on homework

Interview a group of five or six students in different year groups (e.g. Year 6, Year 8 and Year 10) about their views on English homework. Ask them to show you their homework diaries or organisers, and discuss how much homework they are given; how much time is spent on it; what they enjoy and think is valuable; when and where they complete their homework, and what feedback they receive.

Principles of setting homework

Amount
The amount of homework an individual English teacher sets should be guided by the school or department homework policy. Most schools feel under pressure to meet government guidelines relating to the amount of overall homework to be set (see Figure 4.2), and homework – both setting and marking – is likely to be monitored across the school. As a guide, most English Departments set homework twice a week, with the expectation that students at Key Stage 3, studying English for, say, three hours a week, will work on English for between one and two hours a week at home.

Relevance and quality
The setting of homework needs to be planned as part of a lesson or sequence of lessons to ensure that it is relevant and meaningful, and will enhance students' learning and understanding. Some schools and departments will have clear

Schools will consider how much time is appropriate for pupils at each stage and can use the following recommendations:

Years 1 and 2	1 hour per week
Years 3 and 4	1.5 hours per week
Years 5 and 6	30 minutes per day

At secondary level, the Government recommends that the time spent on homework or GCSE coursework should fall within the following ranges:

Years 7 and 8	45 to 90 minutes per day
Year 9	1 to 2 hours per day
Years 10 and 11	1.5 to 2.5 hours per day

In Years 12 and 13 the amount will depend on the pupils' individual programmes. However, they will need guidance, as will parents, on what has to be achieved and how much time it might take to achieve the required standard. Most schools set out course requirements in manuals at the beginning of the courses, with flow charts stating what has to be submitted and when.

Source: DfES, 2002

Figure 4.2   Extract from DfES sample homework policy

policies about the type and range of homework tasks. However, some homework is set for its own sake, and there is little that is more demoralising for students or teachers. Quality homework tasks should ideally:

- arise from and be integral to the lesson or scheme of work;
- focus on specific criteria which are shared with students;
- be targeted and differentiated according to student need and ability;
- revise, extend or develop students' knowledge and skills.

This does not mean that every homework task needs to be a full-length essay or a thousand-word story. Short, focused tasks are easier to set and allow for more frequent and worthwhile feedback. Longer pieces and more challenging work should be broken down into a sequence of manageable chunks leading up to the whole. Table 4.4 shows how some simple English homework tasks can be made more purposeful by setting the context of the activity, outlining specific criteria and providing appropriate support and resources.

Table 4.4 Some typical English homeworks and how not to set them

Don't set	Do set
Private reading – 30 minutes.	15 minutes reading – own choice of fiction. Spend 15 minutes responding in your reading journal (see Figure 4.2).
Write a side about yourself.	Write three paragraphs about yourself and underline the topic sentence in each paragraph.
Prepare a talk to be given to the class on a hobby of your choice.	Make a spider-gram plan of your talk and write an opening sentence that will grab the listeners' attention, ready for planning the rest of your talk next lesson.
Write a story about a time you were scared.	Using the ideas from today's lesson, write a first-person account of a time you were scared in a way which helps the reader to share the experience.
Find out everything you can about William Shakespeare.	Using the headings on the planning sheet you have been given, make notes on William Shakespeare that you will use to do a piece of information writing in the next lesson.

Variety

Homework tasks need to be varied for the sake of both students' learning and English teachers' sanity. For trainee teachers, the trap to be avoided at all costs is consistently setting writing tasks as homework, which may seem attractive as it appears to test students' skills and understanding easily, satisfy parents' desire to monitor their children's English work, and require the least work in advance on the part of the teacher. In the end, though, you will end up frustrated and disappointed, spending hours marking over-long, poor quality responses. Instead, plan a range of homework opportunities for each class. Table 4.5 provides a list of possible homework activities and how they can be used for different learning purposes.

Clear expectations

All English teachers have to set homework and setting homework that you will enjoy responding to when it is handed in or shared in class is a skill. The key here is to have in mind what the outcome of the homework will be and to make these expectations explicit. Most schools now provide a homework diary or planner for each student and time must be allowed for homework to be recorded, so that students, and parents, can refer to it later. This is especially true when you are setting major tasks, such as coursework or end-of-unit assessments, and it may even be that whole lessons will be given over to setting up homework or independent tasks at some points in the year. For such important tasks you

Table 4.5 A sample range of homework activities for English students

Homework tasks	Possible learning focuses
Carry out a survey, e.g. about class reading preferences.	Numeracy link; preparation for class discussion; speaking and listening; making notes; designing and using open and closed questions.
Brainstorm of ideas on a topic or theme.	Preparation for a new unit of work; recording ideas from a group discussion.
Evaluate an internet site according to agreed criteria.	Developing reading skills; making judgements about different text types and their conventions; formulating and justifying opinions.
Respond to class or own reading in a reading journal.	Reading between the lines; re-reading; using textual evidence.
Reduce a script to notes for a presentation.	Identifying important content; summarising; rehearsing for presentation.
Interview family members for views to contribute to a piece of non-fiction writing.	Researching a range of opinions; collecting examples to justify different viewpoints; speaking and listening in a familiar context.
Draw a spider-diagram to plan sections of a leaflet or other piece of writing.	Planning independent writing; organising writing types according to purpose and audience.
Design a mind-map.	Recording knowledge or understanding at the beginning of a topic or before starting to read a novel.
Read and highlight key words in a research document provided by the teacher.	Active, independent reading; recognising vocabulary in context.
Write a draft of a story for younger readers to be edited and redrafted in a future lesson.	Moving on from planning to drafting; choosing structure and vocabulary to suit audience needs.
Watch two TV news programmes and contrast them under headings, such as formality, number of items, range of stories.	Learning about news gate-keeping; increasing awareness of language and codes of different media texts.
Write in role (e.g. a letter/diary) as a character being studied.	Practising writing in a specific genre; empathising and developing understanding of character.
Draw a cartoon strip to show events in a chapter or key episodes in a novel.	Summarising key moments of plot; understanding structure and pace in a novel.
Collect advertising slogans from magazines and TV advertisements and categorise them.	Recognising rhetorical and figurative language; identifying uses of rhyme, alliteration, puns, etc.
Respond to a poem using a writing frame.	Structuring literary responses; developing personal response; using poetry terminology.

will probably need to produce a written document for students' reference, which can then be published on the school or department website and shared with parents as necessary. You will need to identify:

- the nature of the task and how it should be presented;
- the recommended time to be spent on it (including planning and drafting time, if applicable) and a deadline;
- the assessment criteria.

Figure 4.3 provides an example of this kind of task-setting for Key Stage 3 students. In this case, students had already been given a set of student-friendly National Curriculum criteria.

Year 7 Module 4 'Childhood' Project

Your assessment for Module 4 consists of three tasks. Look at the NC levels and aim high.

- *Task 1 should be started immediately and should be completed by Friday 19 April so that you have plenty of time to work on the other tasks.* Your teacher will tell you when you should start work on the other tasks and give you a deadline for them.

- Remember to look regularly on the 'English' pages of the school website for help relating to all these tasks.

- All the tasks for Module 4 will be assessed for writing. Your speaking and listening skills and your reading skills will be assessed in class.

IMPORTANT: At least one of the pieces of work should be handwritten.

Task 1: Design and produce A LEAFLET *or* A POSTER *or* A POWERPOINT PRESENTATION to promote the work of the National Society for the Prevention of Cruelty to Children. Use the displays in school, books in the library and the internet to research the information you will need. Think about the last time you produced work of this type and make sure you put your learning from last time into practice.

Task 2 : Plan and write A SCRIPT which shows what you think life will be like for the average child in 100 years from now, in 2102. Show that you know how to set out a script and use your imagination! Your teacher will provide a model for your work.

Task 3: Plan, draft and write A STORYBOOK for children aged 7–8. You will find out more about this task in class.

Figure 4.3   Task setting for Year 7 students

Marking

The terminology here is unhelpful. The word 'marking' has become synonymous with the final stage in the life of a piece of student work: the student labours to produce something and hands it in to be subjected to the teacher's application of various criteria. Actually, this summative assessment is only one type of feedback and is in many ways the least valuable – for both students and teachers. When the work is handed back, the student will glance at the mark given, read the accompanying comment if you are lucky and the work will be relegated to a folder or taken home, perhaps to be celebrated, probably to be lost.

As with most teacher tasks, marking is a great deal more manageable if it is part of an established set of routines:

- Referring to the scheme of work you are working to, plan ahead so that you know what you are setting for each class and when.
- Set a range of homework activities (writing, reading, planning, researching) during a given period, say, each half-term.
- Setting no more than one significant piece of written work set every six to eight weeks for each class (a full-time NQT will probably be teaching the equivalent of one class in every year group in the school) is realistic and builds in time for writing to be discussed, planned, drafted and for proper feedback to be given.
- Show that you value students' homework by asking them to spend more time on it; review and drafting routines help to make students take responsibility for their work and will mean that work is of a better quality.
- When marking a final draft, avoid the temptation to correct every error. At this stage in the assessment cycle, students will only be demoralised if they receive their work back with corrections indicated on every line. Marking is not a proofreading exercise!
- Make students aware of specific assessment criteria during the drafting process and refer to these in your marking.
- Adhere to the school marking policy and, if there is no set of school marking codes (see Table 4.6), consider designing your own to share with the class. Their awareness of assessment criteria and the importance of accuracy will only improve if they use the same set of abbreviations when reviewing their own or others' work.

Table 4.6 A sample set of cross-curricular marking codes

Writing error	Teacher response
Spelling (e.g. favorite)	Sp.
Register (e.g. inappropriate informality)	Reg.
Grammar (e.g. she don't)	Gr.
Homophone (e.g. confusion over too/to or their/they're)	Hom.
Apostrophe (e.g. say's, it's/its)	Ap.
Capitalisation (e.g. i rather than I)	Cap.
Other punctuation (e.g. use of , instead of .)	P.

Feedback for learning in English

Perhaps the most important audience for assessment information, too often over-looked, is the student. Tempting though it is to heap praise on students, in the form of 'well done!', gold stars, merits, credits or certificates, there is more valu-able feedback we should be giving them, and the systems we create in an effort to encourage students can work to opposite effect:

> Where the classroom culture focuses on rewards, 'gold stars', grades or place-in-the-class ranking, then pupils look for the ways to obtain the best marks rather than at the needs of their learning which these marks ought to reflect. One reported consequence is that where they have any choice, pupils avoid difficult tasks. They also spend time and energy looking for clues to the 'right answer'. Many are reluctant to ask questions out of fear of failure. Pupils who encounter difficulties and poor results are led to believe that they lack ability, and this belief leads them to attribute their difficulties to a defect in themselves about which they cannot do a great deal. So they 'retire hurt', avoid investing effort in learning which could only lead to disappointment, and try to build up their self-esteem in other ways.
>
> (Black and Wiliam, 1998)

In English, a subject in which we rarely want students to reach a 'right answer', it is essential that we focus on promoting learning instead of encouraging students to seek the easiest way to get the best results. In addition, because of the constant demands being made on students' literacy skills, the risk is great that they will resort to 'other ways', through disruption, poor behaviour and choosing not even to try, to avoid being exposed. Many disaffected learners, particularly boys, think of themselves as 'bad spellers', tell you that 'I can't read' and will sooner say they can't – or won't – do something than be seen to have a go and do it badly. This self-perception is only reinforced by summative assessment in which the teacher repeatedly underlines mistakes and corrects spelling. If we are to persuade learners that difficulties can be overcome, that English skills can be learned, that they are responsible for their learning, we need to focus on our use of formative assessment and feedback, and show students how they can improve, build on past successes and make further progress. According to Black and Wiliam, effective formative assessment depends on the use of 'the quality of teacher–pupil interactions' and provides:

> the stimulus and help for pupils to take active responsibility for their own learning, the particular help needed to move pupils out of the 'low-attainment' trap, and the development thereby of the habits needed by all if they are to become capable of life-long learning.
>
> (Black and Wiliam, 1998)

To create effective feedback for learning systems that provide opportunities for high-level teacher–student discussion of learning and the benefits it brings, as illustrated in Figure 4.4, we must teach less and talk about learning more. This has been referred to as 'meta-learning':

> Meta-learning capability mediates the quality of learning outcome, and may also impact on what counts as learning. Those who are advanced in meta-learning realise that what is learned (the outcome or the result) and how it is learned (the act or the process) are two inseparable aspects of learning.
>
> (Watkins, 2001)

Imagine an English classroom where students regularly practise their speaking and listening skills by carrying out peer review; evaluate their own achievements; apply the assessment criteria displayed around them to their own and others' work; seek the teacher's input during the drafting process; comment critically on their own skills and achievements; remember what they have learned in recent weeks and months and look for ways to demonstrate these new skills, and take pleasure in recognising their own progress in English.

Creating such an environment might require the support of whole-school policy redesign, as well as a national move away from a skills-based, test-driven

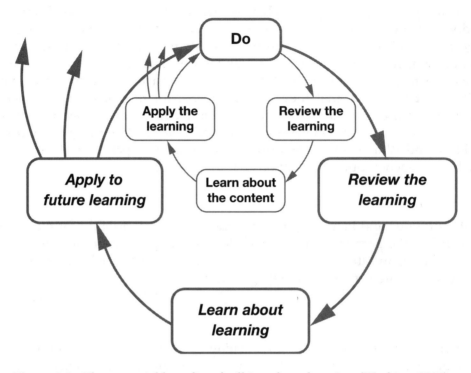

Figure 4.4 The potential benefits of talking about learning (Watkins, 2001)

curriculum towards one in which the discourse of learning is more highly valued. However, there are practices we can put in place immediately to help foster effective feedback for learning:

- Devote time on a regular basis to structured self-assessment and peer review.
- Provide opportunities for the teacher and student to discuss work in progress.
- Prompt students to talk about their learning by providing prompts and appropriate vocabulary.
- Share assessment data with students while there is still time for them to act on it.
- Encourage students to set their own targets for improvement, and while they are learning to do this, show that you value teacher-set targets by referring to them.
- Make marking meaningful by giving time for students to absorb teacher comments.

Further reading

Askew, Susan (2000) (ed.) *Feedback for Learning*, RoutledgeFalmer, London.

Black, Paul and Wiliam, Dylan (2002) *Working Inside the Black Box*, King's College, London.

Clarke, Shirley (2001) *Unlocking Formative Assessment*, Hodder & Stoughton Educational, London.

Headington, Rita (2000) *Monitoring, Assessment, Recording, Reporting and Accountability: Meeting the Standards*, David Fulton, London.

Nicholls, Gill (1999) *Learning to Teach* (Chapter 7), Kogan Page, London.

Torrance, Harry and Pryor, John (1998) *Investigating Formative Assessment: Teaching, Learning and Assessment in the Classroom*, Open University Press, Buckingham.

5 The role of Drama

Joanna Struthers

An introduction to Drama

Drama, whether it is within English or as a discrete subject, can seem the most liberating and creative or the most exhausting and terrifying subject in the entire curriculum. Either you feel excited and challenged as you walk into your designated Drama space, which may of course be doubling up as an art exhibition area, common room or assembly hall, or you wonder with an all-consuming dread where the chairs are and what stops it all turning into a riotous romp.

Drama has a clear role within the English curriculum in that scripts form a regular part of textual analysis at every Key Stage. Within the Framework for Teaching English in Years 7 to 9 there are specific requirements to explore aspects of texts in role and to develop and reflect upon performance skills through active participation and evaluation. Being able to discuss a character's motivation and the dramatic tensions that exist on stage with the live performance and staging in mind is clearly advantageous. Likewise, incorporating the vocabulary of Drama into responses to English texts is becoming more and more an expected skill. The directing of a scene in *Macbeth*, the tracking of a key character's development in a GCSE text such as *The Glass Menagerie*, the close analysis of a short exchange of dialogue all demand a working knowledge of the skill of the dramatist, and where better to realise this than through the practical application of Drama. Using Drama activities in the classroom is discussed in more detail later in this chapter.

The provision for Drama within the curriculum can vary dramatically from school to school: from regular weekly lessons in Key Stage 3 to GCSE and AS/A2 level to a haphazard provision within PHSE or the English curriculum, or perhaps once fortnightly lessons for Key Stage 3 pupils. This chapter takes the regular Key Stage 3 Drama lesson as its starting point and includes ideas and strategies for Drama within the English classroom and connections with other Key Stages as appropriate. The related tasks refer, of course, to either the ITT provider's resources, schemes of work and school systems, or those of the NQT's immediate working environment.

Drama has appeared within the school curriculum, at the very least in the form of the annual school play, since the early part of the sixteenth century. While the teaching of Drama as a route to becoming an actor has long been the preserve of specialist training at places such as RADA and LAMDA and the stage schools such as the Italia Conti, the seeds are sown within the school provision for Drama. Successful actors often cite a chance casting in a school play or the liberty and creativity of Drama lessons as the key to their professional ambition. Even for the vast majority of students who will not go on to seek fame on the stage, however, Drama can be the one lesson where raw creativity and a real love and talent for performing can be nurtured and celebrated.

There are numerous opportunities in the teaching of Drama to attain many of the required TTA/DfEE Standards as signposted by the tasks included in this chapter. Perhaps the most important factor for your professional development and attainment of QTS is to be enthusiastic and willing to involve yourself. Having the initiative to create for yourself opportunities to improve your practice will go a long way to establishing an additional and marketable identity for yourself: the English teacher who can teach Drama too.

Objectives

This chapter will:

- explore the act and art of teaching Drama;
- consider the social context of Drama and wider issues;
- give advice on the development of your Drama teaching as you move from student to professional teacher.

Exploring the act and art of teaching Drama

Drama is a dynamic and crucially active way of learning. Personal skills are developed symbiotically with an increased understanding of the structures and performance skills of drama. A new language of Drama develops as students learn to evaluate their own and others' performances. For many teachers, it represents freedom from the constraints of the classroom: in what other lesson do you have the opportunity to get a class to move around the room as baboons, walk around blindfolded, or mime the climbing of a mountain to a suitably chilling soundtrack? The rewards in Drama for both teacher and student are immediate: applause signifies success; huge leaps of a child's confidence can occur in a single task in a single lesson. You can witness those magical spine-tingling moments when real dramatic tension is realised and the participants are transported beyond their physical environment, their school uniform and, without planning to, find themselves 'in the moment', discovering a truth of action that suspends belief and inspires the audience.

Good Drama is inclusive and there should be credit for the quieter observer whose keen listening skills make them the linchpin of creativity in devising work, as there is for the showy performer. The student who is able to compromise during the devising process and see ways forward rather than cling sulkily to the superiority of their idea will be rewarded for this in GCSE and AS/A2 level work. 'Cooperation' is one of the crucial words that underpin initial drama lessons, as is 'control'. Until you have established a safe, trusting and controlled environment for learning, no effective Drama teaching can take place.

It is crucial to effective learning that students feel able to share their work without excessive criticism from their peers and, of course, their teacher. There is much work to do on constructive criticism as a part of the essential process of evaluation in the initial stages of Drama teaching. Table 5.1 provides an example of a Year 7 evaluation prompt card. Students learn from themselves and others; they should be encouraged to develop reflective skills, be able to learn from and share work in progress and, crucially, be able to act safely and respectfully in the Drama space. You will facilitate this learning through careful planning, enthusiastic and well-paced lessons and the insistence of high standards of behaviour.

Table 5.1 Evaluation prompt card

What I want to say	Drama words to help me
We worked well together as a group because . . .	Cooperation, listening skills
I enjoyed making up the story of . . .	Devising, plot, scenes
I liked playing the part of . . .	Character
X was good at the part they played because . . .	Credible, convincing
They acted really well. They did this by . . .	Movement, gestures, voice, facial expressions
I kept looking at X because they had good . . .	Focus, concentration

Planning

A strong department will have a varied programme of study for each Key Stage that provides clear links with skills needed at GCSE and beyond. It will build on existing skills and knowledge and may be based around myths and legends, modern scripts, historical events or interesting places. Although situation-based drama that explores citizenship issues and personal development clearly has its place in the Drama curriculum, students need variety, and schemes of work based almost entirely on this naturalistic, problem-solving drama will do little to develop skills in movement, mime and physical theatre.

Even if your department has detailed schemes of work that seem to 'teach themselves', you will need to develop your time-management skills and be able to judge how to pace your lesson. Sometimes you will need to deviate from the plan and you will need to be able to judge when a task is not working with a group. Flexibility is of key importance, and this is explored in more detail with other planning requirements in Chapter 3.

Structuring a lesson

A good Drama lesson has pace and variety, and a keen awareness of time is vital. The tendency to over-plan in the initial stages of teaching motivated by the sheer fear of having nothing to do is advantageous to the trainee Drama teacher. It helps to gradually instil the confidence to stop the lesson in plenty of time to provide a calm, reflective plenary session and to give younger pupils especially time to put on shoes, straighten ties and wait in an orderly way to leave for their next lesson. No one will thank you if your Drama group arrives in their lesson late, breathless with excitement, uniform awry and still in creative mode.

The parts to your lesson plan will, of course, depend on your subject matter. Aim to offer pupils the opportunity to work individually, in pairs, in small groups and as a whole group over the course of two lessons. This can then become a vital part of your stated learning objective. Similarly, you will need to establish the skills you are working on, as well as the subject matter through which this learning will take place.

A suggested structure for a one-hour lesson could be:

- Students ready themselves for Drama; change into suitable footwear etc., sit in a circle and listen in silence for register. *3 minutes*
- A recap on previous lesson's content and learning objective. Introduction of learning objective and key skill to be focused on. Explanation of intended ways of learning: whole group, small group, paired, individual. *3 minutes*

- An individual warm-up that builds on the required skills. Second paired warm-up that offers a different approach to subject matter. *5 minutes*
- Split into small groups and explain task. *2 minutes*
- Creative devising time. *15 minutes*
- Recap on expectations. *2 minutes*
- Polishing of devised work. *5 minutes*
- Share work and evaluate after each performance. *15 minutes*
- Plenary. *5 minutes*

This gives you a total of 55 minutes with 5 invisible minutes that will disappear somewhere when you're not looking.

Task 5.1: Theory task: time management

Plan the timings for a lesson that requires one whole group warm-up that usually lasts five minutes and two small group devising tasks, at the end of which students are asked to decide which would be the best one to perform. Allow five minutes on average for each group's performance. You have five groups, all of whom want to share their work.

Keeping timings explicit gives students focus and it is wise to vary these. As a general rule-of-thumb, younger students will lose direction after 20 minutes. Even if you want them to spend that amount of time on their work, it is useful to demand a couple of minutes of quiet while you recap on the expectations of the task and remind them of the skills focus. At Key Stage 4 much can be gained from the occasional long devising period of 40 minutes or so and at Key Stage 5 this can often be the only effective way to work when involved in the creative process.

Schemes and units of work

Why a scheme?

There are many great practitioners of Drama within the secondary school who sail from lesson to lesson with a wealth of creative ideas, yet never seem to commit themselves to constructing a scheme of work so that others can share in their wisdom. This, of course, is not the key to a healthy department. Sharing ideas is crucial to the combined strength of a department, whether through a practical session in a department meeting or on an In-service Training (INSET) day or through the scheme.

Within the schemes of work available, there should be opportunities to develop a range of skills. Within each Key Stage there should be opportunities to build on the skills taught and achieved in the previous year. Skills such as mime could be introduced in a discrete scheme of work in Year 7, incorporated into a scheme on physical theatre in Year 8, then utilised further in Year 9 with mask work. Table 5.2 is a brief illustration of part of a scheme of work showing how this might be documented for the teacher's purposes. The content of each scheme of work could be based on the exploration of an existing text (crucial at GCSE and Key Stage 5), a particular skill such as mime, a form of theatre such as melodrama or a historical event. Or it could be issue-based and therefore also introduce Forum Theatre. It could offer opportunities for cross-curricular work: a joint exploration of the *Canterbury Tales* with History and English, with Drama adding physicality and life to the characters in the tales, while developing related skills such as narration. Practitioners such as Bertolt Brecht, Augusto Boal and Constantin Stanislavski are perhaps best explored in Key Stages 4 and 5, but their ideas can be adapted and used in Key Stage 3. See the suggestions for further reading at the end of the chapter.

The very phrase 'scheme of work' can strike a note of dread within the trainee or NQT, loaded as it is with connotations of a heavy time commitment. A simple way of getting started is to take an existing script and look at ways of exploring it practically without simply reading it and 'getting up and doing it'. Figure 5.1 suggests some alternative approaches to text as a starting point. Once it is

Table 5.2 Suggested outline for a scheme of work

Unit title: Mime
Year: 7
Approximate duration: 4 weeks

Teaching objectives
- Understand the concept and effectiveness of mime
- Understand the need for cooperation and control
- Be able to perform a convincing mime and cooperate with others

Key words and skills	Activities
Mime	
Imagination	Session 1: What is mime?
Facial	
expressions	**Warm-up: whole class/physical**
	Walk around the drama space as neutrally as possible.
	Imagine you are walking in a very muddy field – adapt your walk. Freeze!
	Now walk as if you are skating on ice, on a catwalk, tiptoeing on a creaky landing. Freeze and make sure your facial expression is reacting to the situation.

formalised in a scheme, not only are you able to revisit your work and cut down significantly on planning, but you can pass it on to your head of department and know that you have contributed something valuable to the department. This is essential to your continuing professional development once QTS has been achieved.

> ### Task 5.2: Theory task: investigating play scripts
>
> Investigate the play scripts available for use at each Key Stage in your school. Focus on three for each Key Stage taught and note your findings under the headings themes, genre, and number and nature of characters. Do these plays offer cultural diversity (Standard 3.3.6) and equal opportunities for girls and boys?

How to start

Start with the same approach that you would have with your individual lesson planning: an objective (Standard 3.1.1). This will be your overarching super objective and, as such, should be simple: 'To gain a better understanding of the plot and characters of *Our Day Out* by Willy Russell.' Think then about the skills

---

Read through the first scene and decide on five key moments to turn into tableaux to summarise the opening of the play. Show these to other groups. Has everyone chosen the same moments?

Concentrate on a short section of dialogue involving just two or three characters. For each line of dialogue write down the characters' 'wants', e.g. I want you to listen to me, I want to finish this conversation. Try the dialogue again showing these wants in the tone of your voice, facial expressions, and movements and gestures.

If rehearsing a script to perform, prior to the performance run through just the actions and movements. It's easier if someone else reads the dialogue.

Run through a short piece of dialogue as if in fast/slow motion.

Once familiar with the script, decide on a status number for each character based on how much power you think they have. They could be numbered from one to ten. Play the scene with these numbers in mind. Experiment by swapping status numbers so that a 'number one' (low) gets to play the scene as a 'number ten'. What does this tell us about these characters in this situation?

Figure 5.1 Suggestions for script activities

you will want to focus on: 'characterisation, mime, building tableaux'. Within those skills is a further subset of skills that enables the student to achieve these objectives: 'voice, movement, gesture'. These can form your related skills that serve as a reference point, running concurrently with the description of the activity. This is also an opportunity for you to signpost opportunities to introduce and improve literacy, numeracy and ICT.

> **Task 5.3**: Theory task: a proforma for cross-referencing skills
>
> Design a format for a scheme that gives the teacher an opportunity to cross-reference skills and signposts the opportunities as outlined above. Ensure that there is room for the activities to be explained and for the lesson objectives to be outlined as appropriate.

Resources

The general truism that babies and dogs are more interested in the box that their present arrives in than the present itself can extend in some way to the universal enthusiasm for the most basic prop or costume. I have seen Year 7 students almost come to blows over a piece of red material. Costume fuels the imagination and a few well-chosen items can transport the most unconfident student into the realms of creativity. A box of thought-provoking props and some basic costumes provides a basic yet effective resource base, while additional resources will be generic to the scheme of work. These may include: short stories, short extracts from Shakespeare on laminated card and perhaps even masks. The useful Drama resource box for the peripatetic teacher whose department is a long way from being adequately resourced could include the following:

- Three beanbags of different colours for concentration games (see the next task).
- A pack of cards and/or thirty laminated numbers (one to ten) for status games. Each student takes one and, without looking, places it on their head. Students circulate around and react with appropriate disdain or respect to others. Finally, they place themselves in a line based on how high they judge their status to be.
- A range of objects to improvise around a clock, a hat, a bucket and spade, a handbag, a bunch of plastic flowers and a torch all work well.
- Pieces of material big enough to become cloaks or to hide under. These are good for work on magic or fantasy themes.

You may also want to back up your longer group or paired tasks with instruction sheets that reinforce the stages that the group needs to go through or that summarise the suggested events in a set of scenes.

Lastly, don't forget your most dynamic resource: the students themselves. Whether you are explaining the complicated love quadrangle of *A Midsummer Night's Dream* or demonstrating how to conduct a paired improvisation game, they can be the most compelling resources you could hope for. Get them to hold up signs with character names on them while you summarise part of a plot, or use a volunteer to be your partner as you explain a warm-up activity. Always ask for volunteers first, never ridicule, and give them a round of applause and a 'thank you'.

Ways in with warm-ups

Even A2 level students who have the ability to work independently and run their own workshops often insist on a warm-up which should serve as a way of channelling concentration and physically preparing the students for Drama. Ideally and most effectively, the warm-up should connect with the skill that is part of your learning objective, i.e. a lesson developing improvisation skills will be more successful if your warm-up activity concentrates on a bite-size version of the content of the lesson. More physical lessons, such as those depending on mime or physical theatre, should have a stretching, blood-flow boosting start. Initially, however, your warm-ups should be a chance for you to create a positive and purposeful atmosphere and, controversially, they should be fun. This is where you launch your lesson with energy. It's the starter of the Drama curriculum and, like a successful starter, it should not ramble on for 20 minutes while all possible permutations of the activity are explored or everyone has a go: pace is the essence. While some activities will seem more appropriate to a particular age group, a focused Year 7 group can often be more adept at an activity than a Year 9 group. The key is to think about what you want your learning outcome to be and tailor your initial activities as appropriate. It could be as simple as: 'I want this group to work well in pairs today as they only work well in friendship groups; therefore I'd like to get them mixing and moving on quickly to work with others.'

Some suggestions
For whole groups: focus and concentration.

One-, two-, three-word stories   Sitting in a circle, each student in turn offers one word to tell a story. It should make some sort of sense and contributions should be audible. Speed them up to three words when the story has gone round the circle at least once and perhaps come to a natural end.

Getting to know each other Standing in a circle, each student offers their first name prefaced by an adjective and an action, e.g. 'jolly Joanna' with a star jump. Once everyone is introduced, start swapping places in the circle by simply looking, saying a name and swapping places. Get really clever by looking at someone and saying your own name instead and finish with a silent place swapping. This time, using only eye contact, the person being alerted should try to start walking before their place is taken. Endless variations exist, but unless these are the first few lessons in Year 7, move on.

> **Task** **5.4**: Theory task: devising a warm-up
>
> You have three beanbags available: one red, one yellow and one green. Devise a warm-up game for a whole group that aims to get the group concentrating and thinking quickly, and builds on the skills outlined above.

For pairs: improvisation and cooperation Create an inner circle and outer circle of seated students who should be facing each other. Those in the outer circle start a story about anything they like until you signal to swap. The partner must add to the story, not change it, until you signal to swap again. After a couple of minutes ask all those on the outer circle to move one place to the left. Continue the game with variations. Try one-word stories in pairs and 'no you didn't'. One person starts a story about what they did on their holidays. The partner must interrupt with 'no you didn't' and the storyteller has to agree and change their tale. Keep them moving around, ideally varying how many places to keep it unpredictable.

Individual warm-ups can focus on mime skills: waking up in the morning and getting ready for a specified occasion with a specified motivation or emotion, or on physical stretching exercises: arm swinging, stretching up, warming up voice and regulating breathing.

Assessment

Assessment in Drama will focus on the attainment of skills outlined in the schemes of work discussed. By making these explicit to students, especially before an assessed performance or devising session, you are giving them an opportunity to achieve. Reflective and evaluative thinking are key, by encouraging students to discuss their progress and achievements, whether they are in devising or performance. Assessment in Drama should not just focus on performance. This is not a helpful way of preparing students for the next Key Stage and does not give students an accurate idea as to what Drama is. Creative direction and cooperative devising work should be rewarded. Some of the strongest performers can be the most didactic and inflexible group workers, inhibiting the creative process of the group. The more observational students can offer incisive evaluations of performances and they too should be praised and rewarded.

As a non-core subject, it is up to departments as to how they qualify skills attained. A simple A–D grade system may be in place with guidelines, with the words 'excellent', 'good', 'satisfactory' and 'needs improvement' denoting each grade. However assessment is worded, it should be done regularly to give students a sense of progression and an opportunity to succeed. Target setting is important and self-assessment is an excellent way of encouraging reflection and evaluation. Written evaluation is useful not only as a way of formalising these thoughts but in providing a record of progress. Looking back on a written assessment produced in the autumn term at the end of the year gives students a real feeling of progression and perspective. It can also highlight problems such as lack of confidence and difficult group combinations to the classroom teacher. An encouraging comment or an acknowledgement of such difficulties when marking these written records can engender a stronger feeling of mutual trust and interest.

Literacy in Drama

By scaffolding these written responses (see Figure 5.2 for an example) and discussing the group's progress in whole-class discussion, your students will be in a strong position to reflect on their skills and the good work of others.

It is, of course, useful to have these writing frames available as part of the assessment process. If you are teaching in a room without a whiteboard, this is especially useful and students with specific literacy difficulties can use their time more constructively. Bear in mind also that the spelling of character names, plays or playwrights may need reinforcing. Laminated cards could also be helpful, particularly when assessing the exploration of a Shakespeare play. Key terms in Drama can be reinforced on the board or perhaps again on laminated card and displayed around the room.

Moderation – a practical exercise (Standard 3.2.6)

Assessment at GCSE and AS/A2 is largely done internally and, by the very nature of Drama, judgements can be clouded by the fact that a teacher sees that student regularly and knows them well. It can be hard to be objective. At these

This term we have studied

The skills we have focused on are

I particularly enjoyed working on

Our group/pair worked well because

A character I particularly enjoyed was

I brought them to life by

A performance I really enjoyed was

This is because

I have learnt

My target for the next unit of work is

KEY WORDS

Mime
Tableau/tableaux
Levels
Gestures
Movement

Figure 5.2 A writing frame for self-evaluation

levels moderation is part of the practical assessment process. Teachers may rank a performance group in order before they attribute marks and find the best fit from the criteria available. Try this approach in an observation of any group. Look carefully at the available criteria for grading and arrange to observe a lesson where there will be at least two performances. Remember to ask the class teacher to identify each student and then rank the group in order. It may be that the group are concentrating on one skill, i.e. use of voice. If so, just mark them on this skill. Share your results with the normal class teacher. Can you justify your assessment? Are you able to point out something that they didn't spot?

Often, just having the confidence to apply the full range of available marks can be an important step professionally. Not doing so eventually devalues the system and trivialises progress.

Health and safety as part of good classroom management (Standard 3.3.8)

Stage fighting is a highly disciplined art and rugby belongs on the playing field. Sadly, this can be dismissed by the over-excited novice Drama student in a big space and be forgotten by the inexperienced Drama teacher. As a Drama teacher, you will need to remind students of the need for a safe working environment You have a legal responsibility for their physical well-being and it will take just one frightening head or back injury or scream of pain to instil this fact into your professional consciousness forever. Drama can be physical and noisy, and injuries can occur when over-excitement leads to carelessness and rough behaviour. Look also at your resources: props and even laminated card can be turned into 'weapons'.

As your cast-iron rule, let it be known that anyone acting in an unsafe way will not take part in Drama until they can behave with control and restraint. Ask over-zealous students who pounce on, drag around or attempt to beat up their fellow students to sit out immediately. Remove persistent offenders from the next lesson.

Task 5.5: Theory task: responding to disruption in Drama

Find out the procedure for severely disruptive, unsafe behaviour. Does your school operate a 'bolthole' system whereby the student spends the next lesson with another member of the department? Should the student be removed by a senior member of staff? If neither of these systems exists, what, as a classroom teacher, can you do?

Remove potential hazards such as poorly stacked chairs before the lesson starts. Build into your getting ready for Drama routine the removal of chairs, anything studded or potentially hazardous. Remember also your duty to any whole-school approach on jewellery and dress codes, and reinforce the code of conduct. High-heeled shoes and heavy boots are definitely 'not Drama'. Allow the students to wear trainers, let them take off their jumpers or change into jogging bottoms if your school allows this; just ensure that you build in time for them to restore themselves to their former attire. Bare feet can be an invitation to splinters and self-consciousness generally; socks worn on a slippery floor can spell disaster. If your students are physically comfortable, they are ready for Drama.

Classroom management

A positive and orderly start to a lesson is vital. In fact, in a recent plenary when encouraging Year 7 students to reflect on their generally poor behaviour during that lesson and ways of improving, one suggested with little prompting that they should stand quietly girl, boy, girl, boy in a line before they entered the room. Insisting on a seating plan establishes a purposeful learning environment (Standard 2.7) and in co-educational schools in the lower year groups, sitting in a circle girl/boy can be a productive start, especially if departmental codes of behaviour have been instilled. The conviction that you're in charge and the phrase 'if the class are not ready for Drama then Drama won't happen' will serve you well.

Your classroom management in a Drama space needs to focus primarily on safety, as discussed. A simple signal such as raising one hand in the air to request silence, which is then copied by each student, saves your voice and gives you ample opportunity for praise and thanks to those who notice first. To be effective, this method must be repeated every lesson and be accompanied by your own silence and stillness for as long as possible.

Problems occur when students are focused on each other rather than on you during warm-up activities. A degree of this is natural, but if all your students are walking around the Drama space engaged in private conversations rather than silently and continue to do so after you have asked them not to, it is time to stop. Asking students to sit down in silence is a more effective way of repeating your message. They then have another chance. When they get up again to resume their activity, this time they will be silent. Calmly asking persistent offenders to sit out and wait until they judge themselves ready to join in can then be possible.

Your other objective is to establish another type of safety: a learning environment where students do not feel ridiculed, rejected or undermined. In some groups this happens almost as a matter of course, but it is useful to acknowledge and praise this blessed natural phenomenon. Be extremely aware of surreptitious bullying. Insist on total silence when performances are taking place even if the dominant culture of the group is to involve themselves vocally in what they see as a positive endorsement. Positivity needs to be a key part of group evaluation. Consider 'How could they improve?' rather than 'What was bad/wrong with that performance?' By making cooperation a key skill in Drama you help to foster a positive learning environment. Try to vary your groupings by arranging set groups and observe them closely during the devising process. Experiment with groupings and keep a careful note of pastoral information from tutors and year heads. You also have a duty to inform them of problems that occur within your classroom.

Task 5.6: Observation task: compare Drama teaching styles

Ask your mentor or head of department to recommend two teachers with different yet effective teaching styles. What do they do to instil their authority? Do they use a signal for quiet and how do they deal with disruptive behaviour? Discuss your findings and reflect on your own approach. Could you incorporate the strengths of both these teachers into your classroom management?

Drama in the English classroom

is the only opportunity for using Drama to
ments of the benefits of active learning will
students as reason enough to incorporate a
Thinking skills, a very current approach to
ma warm-ups for focusing activities which
t students physically ready to learn in the

confines of the classroom and the civilising
only learning environment in which they
pproach. Of course, it is perfectly possible
youth work, environmental education or
e classroom thing a bit of a bind and the
s possible in most schools to try to secure
course, must be done well in advance of

e the clearing of a space and the stacking
member to build in time for the restora-
on't forget your health and safety mantra.
airs on desks can be easily knocked onto

hot-seating Best planned in advance, this can prove to be a memorable and insightful way of exploring character motivation and development in any form of writing. Choose three students who will be able to speak confidently and prime them as to who they will be. Give them time to establish a character profile or recap for the whole class the relationships to be explored or the crisis point faced by the characters. Spontaneity is key here, so it's best not to over-prepare and you can allow them some deviance from the known plot if it helps them to answer a question. Ask the rest of your students to write down at least one question they want to ask each character. Your character students should sit at the front and answer each question individually in character as if the others aren't there.

Thought-tracking   Similarly valuable in terms of insight but with less onus on an individual's ability to improvise, this activity gives voice to the internal monologue of a character and can be a useful reminder of the restrictions of the first person narrative. If working with a script, find a part where there is underlying tension and a disparity between the true feelings of a character and the content of the dialogue. For each character, have a student voicing their true feelings. Read the script but after each line or at another point to be decided by the students, the 'voice' reveals what they really think. This needs to be prepared in groups and works best when the focus is only on two or three characters. For characters in a novel, ask the students to improvise or script the part to be explored, in itself a valuable activity.

Tableaux   Singularly a tableau, this can be a useful way of freezing a moment and looking at the way an individual character feels at certain points of the narrative. It can be an excellent way into a Shakespearean text, particularly a scene that needs to be understood in terms of power relations and hidden motivations. A group or even a pair should freeze the moment, concentrating on proxemics, facial expression, gesture and levels. The rest of the class should be able to read the image, so there must be no shifting about and giggling. Consider the value of this approach to Act I, Scene ii of *A Midsummer Night's Dream* as Hermia pleads her case; or Act III, Scene ii of *Romeo and Juliet* as Lord Capulet disowns Juliet; or perhaps the banquet scene in *Macbeth* as Banquo's ghost appears.

What are they doing this for?

There are numerous opportunities for Drama activities within English, but what could the learning objectives be? Leaving out for a moment the clear advantages of exploring an extract of a drama text in a practical way in terms of making it more dynamic and seeing it as a text to be performed, other aspects of English can be given the Drama treatment.

Task **5.7**: Theory task: borrowing Drama strategies

For each of the teaching topics listed on the following pages add your own suggestion as to how you could incorporate Drama or simply an active approach, and evaluate the desired learning outcome of each activity.

Poetry

Ask students to break up a long narrative poem into a set number of signifi-cant tableaux, synthesising the plot and giving students an opportunity to explore the key moments in an active way.

Media

Improvise the meeting of a newspaper editorial team as they decide what news stories to prioritise on their front page.

Shakespeare

Take a soliloquy by a key character. Walk around, individually reading in role, and change direction when you come to a full stop. You could have other ideas for other forms of punctuation.

The social context of Drama and wider issues

Equal opportunities

The requirements of the trainee to 'recognise and respond effectively to equal opportunities issues as they arise' are part of the standards of professional values and practice (Standard 3.3.14). Although much of this seems common sense, in reality the massive diversity of individual students' needs may seem impossible to deal with. There will be times when you will be challenging stereotypes and assumptions as part of issue-based Drama, perhaps through Forum Theatre or by asking students to respond to a series of statements by placing themselves somewhere on a scale of agreement or disagreement (ten chairs work well for this: read out a statement and let them stand behind the appropriate chair).

As part of creating a safe environment in which good Drama can take place, you will be listening closely for name-calling during activities or derogatory com-ments during evaluation that portend to gender, ethnicity, sexuality or class. These need to be challenged; the difficulty is when and how. Perhaps if a word such as 'gay' is being trumpeted out as general term for 'not very good' in eval-uation, this could be dealt with as a whole-class discussion on positive ways of evaluating and more constructive terms to use when criticising. If in a warm-up activity or during devising you hear derogatory language, it may be better to challenge the student individually and remove them from their immediate group to do so. Remember, if you are teaching in an area that has a different dialect from your own, it is best to familiarise yourself with the local terms of abuse.

Task **5.8**: Theory task: challenging harassment

Consider this scenario and devise and discuss a solution that challenges harassment. (Standard 3.3.14). You have asked for groups of four. One girl who is socially isolated asks to join a group of four to make what will be the only group of five. The group becomes aggressive in its rejection of her. You need to intervene. What strategies can you employ to resolve the situation without further humiliation for the girl involved? Further discussion: what factors cause peer group rejection? Are they all equally serious in terms of how the classroom teacher should deal with the situation?

SEN issues in Drama and the use of ICT

Much of what is good about Drama teaching is sensitivity to individuals. Often in Drama all students are required to do an activity together. You will want to give everyone the opportunity to take part but, equally, you need to be less than evangelical about the wonders of Drama. Although not everyone loves Drama, most do, and among those will be many with severe learning difficulties, physical difficulties and sensory deprivation. But the good teacher will know when not to push, and when to let go and allow that student to sit out of the activity.

Your instructions can help the wheelchair user to feel included. Instead of asking students to walk around the space, ask them to move or travel. Demonstrate activities physically so that students with severe learning difficulties can copy you. Group sensitively so that those students feel supported, and always prime and actively involve your classroom or learning support assistant.

It is useful to have a battery of alternative tasks in Drama for those very few for whom the process of devising and performing is overwhelming. See Table 5.3 for some suggestions.

Table 5.3 Suggested alternative Drama tasks

Task	Skills/learning outcomes
Directing a scene	Use of stage space, voice, characterisation
Filming groups at work or in performance	Process of devising, cooperation Helping others with self-evaluation
Travelling director: reports back progress of each group to the class teacher	Observation and feedback. Speaking and listening skills

Task **5.9**: Observation task: teaching students with SEN in Drama

Interview a teacher who has at least one student with SEN and prepare five questions that cover issues such as group work, dealing with performance, issues of inclusion and academic progression. If possible, augment this by observing an appropriate lesson.

Further ideas for the use of ICT (Standard 3.3.10)

The use of ICT in Drama does not need to rely solely on the use of computers. Generally, the role of ICT in Drama is to plan, record and review work. Devising and directing can now be done using specially designed software which, thanks to recent Arts Council and DfES funding, is now free to network in every secondary school. Training is also available to use Kar2ouche; both their titles for Shakespeare in the English package and the newly launched Rehearsal Room give students an opportunity to structure and devise performances via a storyboard.

The use of the video camera in Drama is written into GCSE requirements and can serve any level well in terms of students having a formal performance experience and an opportunity to review their work. Similarly, a digital camera can record tableaux work with precision and students who are encouraged to consider the production process of staging a play can make use of ICT to produce publicity and programmes.

Citizenship

Drama is rich with opportunities to explore issues of citizenship, particularly at the end of Key Stage 3 and at GCSE level. Plays studied can give rise to discussion, particularly those written in a more naturalistic style. Social concerns form much of the thematic interest in Willy Russell's plays and the 'kitchen-sink' dramas of the late 1950s and early 1960s offer an interesting historical context to issues such as poor housing, teenage disaffection and representations of race, gender and sexuality. Drama Outreach work by Arts Council subsidised Theatre-in-Education companies using Drama to deliver their message is often incorporated into the Personal Health and Social Education (PHSE) programme but could be equally valuable as a piece of theatre in itself. Techniques such as hot-seating and the use of Forum Theatre explore human rights issues, homelessness and parenting, to name but a few.

Out-of-school learning

Valuable as the visit from a theatre company can be, the experience of going to the theatre and experiencing a live performance on stage brings the real vitality of Drama to the fore. For schools that teach Drama beyond Key Stage 3, such visits are crucial to students' success at these levels and are almost mandatory. Where Drama is very much part of English, there may well be trips to see productions of SAT-relevant Shakespeare plays or other set texts. While film versions give a taste of the text in performance, the experience of seeing an adaptation or straight performance of a studied text is always illuminating, even if the quality of the production is not the highest. Students can then become empowered critics and their understanding of staging and characterisation is greatly enhanced.

Task **5.10**: Theory task: planning a Drama trip

(Standard 3.1.5): Write up a stage-by-stage guide as to how to arrange a trip for a group of 40 Year 7 and 8 students to a production of a play that their Drama group is to perform as an extra-curricular production. It is an evening performance. Consider the role of whole-school communication systems, health and safety and the role of administration staff. Consider also current teaching union guidelines on designated tasks such as collecting money. Discuss with your mentor what would need to be done if a whole year group were to attend a matinee production of a set Shakespeare text.

Developing your teaching: from student to professional teacher

As a trainee, you will have been given the opportunity to try out some basic ideas, games and warm-ups that you have observed and maybe even taught a whole scheme of work. Development into one of those teachers who seem to have the ability to move seamlessly from one activity to another while wielding cast-iron discipline and maintaining a positive and creative atmosphere is now your goal. How do they do it and, more importantly, how will you?

First, observe, observe, observe. Ensure that, as part of your second placement and your Continuing Professional Development (CPD) in your first school, you still observe experienced teachers using different styles and approaches. Note down the way in which they use their non-verbal and verbal communication to exert control. Look at how they use the space and listen to the volume and quality of their voice. Note down their timings: how do they judge when to move on, and how do they maintain pace and secure the engagement of their students? Note how they explain tasks. What are their students doing when they do so? How is the drama space used? Compare and contrast, reflect and ask questions.

It is important also that you develop your own teacher identity. There are textbooks that can help you with ideas for the content of your lessons, of course, but seeking INSET is vital to your own CPD. Find out whether your Local Education Authority provides day schools or evening workshops on Drama skills. Essentially, teaching Drama successfully boils down to having a wealth of ideas and, even if a workshop on Stanislavski seems to be too advanced because you haven't got a clue who he was, this is very probably not the case. Go along and write copious notes. Try the ideas out as soon as you can and then write it all up for the department. Not only are you advancing your own CPD and possibly working towards the targets negotiated with your new mentor, you can incorporate them into your teaching and own them yourself.

Extra-curricular commitments are all part of the Drama teaching experience. The most obvious way to raise your profile with your new department, whether English or Drama, is to involve yourself in productions. Try your hand at publicity; sit in on rehearsals and maybe even volunteer to direct a scene. There are endless opportunities to immerse yourself into the life of the school in this way, as well as to pick up new ideas and approaches to Drama. There may be a Drama Club that you could attend to observe and volunteer your help, but if not, start one up and throw yourself into the proverbial deep end. If you do this, perhaps consider restricted numbers: it can be a little daunting when 40 eager Year 7s turn up to your club. The onus on performance at GCSE and AS/A2 level means that Drama teachers who teach the whole range of year groups can end up short of time and energy for Key Stage 3. This can be an excellent opportunity for the ambitious would-be Drama teacher extraordinaire to 'get in there' and make him- or herself indispensable.

Drama as a discrete subject is always in danger of being marginalised, as the attainment of targets in core subjects increases in importance and subjects such as ICT draw in more students at GCSE level. There are still misperceptions among some parents about the validity of the subject and its intellectual rigour. In the face of changes to at least one examination board's GCSE and AS/A2 level courses, this seems as farcical as an Alan Ayckbourn play. Well-worn jokes about 'being a tree' aside, most parents and guardians accept that it is (a) 'a good thing for their confidence' and (b) fun. It is immensely valuable to partner yourself with an experienced teacher of Drama at a Year 9 parents evening when options are being discussed and listen to the ways in which he or she advises parents as to the suitability of their children's choices. Tact and diplomacy also extend to the promotion of 'their' subject over another. Poaching talented students from one department to another is not good for staff morale or inter-departmental relations.

Facilities and space are key to the strength of Drama in the secondary school. Often the designated space doubles as a space to eat, have assemblies and sit exams, causing very real disruption to the curriculum. The acoustics may be poor and the space may lack atmosphere and intimacy. You may, of course, be lucky enough to train or work in a school with excellent facilities. The creation of specialist schools and the granting of Arts Status confers huge amounts of money to fund the creation of new and specific Drama spaces. It also requires the buying in of expertise on certain genres of theatre and particular Drama skills. This is immensely beneficial to all and something to consider perhaps when job-hunting.

The identities, issues and concerns of the English Department as a core subject can be very different from that of Drama. Where two departments do exist, there can be conflicts of priorities and loyalties if teachers are teaching both subjects. More positively, the two subjects complement and illuminate each other, and may provide the teacher with a varied timetable. At primary level, the ability to incorporate Drama activities into the curriculum provides variety and literally active learning. At all levels and wherever its place, Drama is a valuable and vital subject. Long may it inspire and challenge teachers and students alike.

Further reading

For ideas and basic drama terms (in the first case aimed at students themselves):

McGuire, Brian (1998) *The Student Handbook for Drama*, Pearson Publishing, Cambridge.
Scher, Anna and Verrall, Charles (1987) *Another 100+ Ideas for Drama*, Heinemann Educational Books, London.
Shiach, Don (1987) *From Page to Performance*, Cambridge University Press, Cambridge.

For a more advanced and theoretical approach:

Benedetti, Jean (1982) *Stanislavski: An Introduction*, Metheun Drama. Stanislavski himself wrote teaching books such as *An Actor Prepares, Building a Character* and *Creating a Role* which are all published by Metheun Drama, London.
Boal, Augusto (1992) *Games for Actors and Non-Actors*, Routledge, London.
Johnstone, Keith (1981, reprinted 1994) *Impro*, Metheun Drama, London.
Mitter, Shomit (1992) *Systems of Rehearsal: Stanislavsky, Brecht, Grotowski and Peter Brook*, Routledge, London.

6 The role of Media Education

Andrew Goodwyn

English teachers have been formally required to teach about aspects of the media as part of the National Curriculum since 1989, making it sound as though such work is firmly established in the English classroom. In fact, this element is still somewhat controversial and the extent to which it is taught is still chiefly dependent in the secondary school on the leadership of the head of department and the enthusiasm of individual teachers. Yet, paradoxically, Media Studies remains one of the fastest growing subjects at GCSE and A level, and is almost entirely taught by English teachers. In the primary school, Media Education has never really developed in any significant way and the National Literacy Strategy, especially the literacy hour, has, if anything, diminished its presence. Given the central importance of the media in young children's lives (see Livingstone, 2002; Kenway and Bullen, 2001) this remains a greatly missed opportunity. This chapter, somewhat regrettably, therefore places much more emphasis on the secondary classroom.

Objectives

The aims of this chapter are:

- to make a brief but clear case for teaching about the media in English;
- to identify the requirements of the National Curriculum and the Framework for English in relation to media texts;
- to provide a brief look at GCSE and Media Studies A level;
- to give some idea of what media teaching looks like, including some practical work.

English and Media Education

Chapter 1 made it clear that English is always subject both to change and controversy. The debate about whether to include media teaching within the brief of English has been ongoing since Leavis' battle cry to 'discriminate and resist' when it comes to popular culture (Leavis and Thompson, 1933). It is true that, at a simple level, the debate is over as media teaching is a requirement of English teachers. This formal requirement does elide a much more genuine and often passionate debate about the extent and nature of such teaching. Research about the views of English teachers (Goodwyn, 1997a, 1997b, 1997c) has made it clear that the great majority do support Media Education in English and consider it as a very important part of their work.

Task 6.1: Theory task

At this stage, where do you stand on this issue? Note down some pros and cons of including media in English and also consider whether Media Studies should be a compulsory subject at Key Stage 3.

As a way in to outlining the case for media teaching in English, it is important to reflect briefly on the emergence and identity of Media Studies, which has only existed in schools for about 20 years. Certainly, one simple reason for gaining this perspective is that, as a beginning English teacher, you may well find yourself teaching it in the near future. In higher education, Media Studies has become firmly established as a very popular degree programme, attracting a huge number of applicants each year from a diverse range of backgrounds. The nature of such degrees is extremely varied. A minority is essentially technical and vocational, preparing people for work in the industry, but far more are essentially theoretical, involving close study and analysis of the media. Some are a mixture, and may include placements in the industry or practical work in which students create their own media texts. Noting this range is important because all of these aspects can be introduced in English. However, a salutory point is that popularity is not status. Politicians' favourite subject to bash is Media Studies and the epithet attached is almost always (and without any clever irony) a 'Mickey Mouse subject'. These dismissive attitudes can also be found among both parents and teachers in relation to Media Studies in secondary schools. Yet, as mentioned above, it is principally English teachers who introduce the subject to a school and become its advocates (Goodwyn, 1997b, 1998; Goodwyn and Findlay, 2001).

But English and Media Studies are very different, seen by some as almost antagonistic to each other (Buckingham, 1993a). For simplicity's sake, these differences at A level might be summed up as relating to the disciplinary base of each subject. Media Studies draws heavily on sociological and psychological concepts, whereas English remains rooted in the traditions of literary criticism. The study of English Language is, of course, rooted in linguistics, giving it in some ways more affinity with Media Studies.

Task 6.2: Practical task

Compare the English and Media Studies specifications of one examination board (try Assessment and Qualifications Alliance (AQA) as an example) and reflect on the experience of a student taking both. Will they find the subjects complementary or in any way oppositional?

What is clear is that Media Studies, at GCSE and A level, is an option for an increasing number of students and is devoted to the study of the media based on a framework of concepts – typically, audience, institutions, representations, media languages and so on – often with some practical work involved. English at Key Stage 4 is a much broader subject encompassing a whole range of practices and it is compulsory, as it is at Key Stage 3. In other words, the only subject that requires students to study the media is English. This form of study is more often called Media Education, with the implication that this is not an introduction to media study but a rather more general consideration of the media. This difference will become more distinct later in the chapter.

The case for placing media teaching within English might then be explained as a rather feeble default mechanism. It might be expressed in this way: 'As there is some kind of consensus that the media are hugely important so it should be taught about somewhere, why not English which no one can define anyway?' In fact, media teaching in English has developed gradually and with a sound rationale. There are three strands to this that also reflect historical phases; for more detail, read Goodwyn (1992a and 2004) or Hart and Hicks (2002).

The first strand stems from the emergent recognition about the media's influence and importance, and some tension with the anxiety that this often generates. It has become a cliché to talk about the media's importance as we live in an age often described as media-saturated. All the research evidence shows (see Livingstone 2002 for a summary) that young people, almost from birth, are exposed to the media, principally television, in vast quantities. To a lesser extent, they also consume film, radio, print-based texts such as magazines, music, and the new bogeyman, the internet. A simple comparison of the domestic setting of the 1950s and the first decade of the twenty-first century demonstrates that in two to three generations our media consumption has increased hugely and changed dramatically. With each technological shift come new concerns; the comics and magazines of the 1950s worried the parents of that decade, as subsequently parents worried about pop music and radio, then television, then the video, so now the internet. All of these fears have grounds, but they need to be set into this patterned historical perspective.

So, strand one is a combination of taking the media and its influence very seriously and a tendency towards anxiety about its potentially negative effects; hence Leavis' concern to discriminate and resist – it is often categorised as 'inoculation theory'. For example, it is still a very common element of English to study advertising (as Leavis recommended) and to help pupils develop an appreciation of its sophistication, but also to make sure that pupils can see through its seductions and commercialism. In other words, a small dose of nasty media makes you immune for the rest of your life. Of course, such an approach is also a start in creating critical citizens (see strand three below). The element of suspicion here partly derives from the notion of mass media, i.e. that a huge audience might be manipulated by a single message – again, a genuine feature of the media that makes it appear quite different, for example, from reading a book. Generations brought up on print tend to place a much higher value on a good book and on the act of reading than on anything else. English teachers, of all teachers the most concerned about reading and the notion of valuable texts, are almost bound to inherit some anxieties, therefore, about notions of the mass media. In English, strand one can be aligned with the Cultural Heritage model (see p. 10) which tends towards selecting the traditionally agreed 'best' texts and, therefore, to be antagonistic towards popular culture, preferring the safety of retrospective critical judgement.

However, a second strand is more concerned with approaching the media differently because of its valuable differences from other forms of communication, such as print. To some extent, Media Studies developed from this recognition but so did a much more positive attitude to the media. This strand, originating in the 1960s principally because of the rapid development of television, recognises the media as popular art and information forms that have their own conventions and traditions, and as essentially providing for consumer interests and needs. In this mode teachers are concerned to explore how actual media forms work, to help pupils understand them and gain more from such forms as a result. This approach, which at least in part looks at the benefits to the consumer of media forms and conceptualises media as a valuable component in everyday life and culture, is aligned with the Personal Growth model (see p. 10).

The third strand has emerged in the last two decades. The critics of the mass element of the media have constantly sought to prove its ill effects, e.g. that violence on television and film produce violent citizens (see Buckingham, 2002 for an excellent overview). They have wanted also to prove that more means less quality rather than consumer choice. Whatever the merits of this viewpoint, it is usually predicated on a simple notion of the audience as essentially an undifferentiated and somewhat gullible mass. Media research from the 1970s onwards has demonstrated again and again that although we like being part of a mass audience, we are very capable of interpreting media messages as individuals or in peer and family-type groups. The research also shows that each generation tends to be more sophisticated, more media 'savvy' than the previous one. These trends have led teachers to conceptualise media consumers as much more active and interpretive and so to see Media Education as a critical enterprise. In this approach we study the media to understand how it works on society and on ourselves and to develop a perspective that is critical in the true sense, i.e. looking to make informed judgements that may be positive or negative. This strand then aligns with Cultural Analysis (see pp. 10–11) which partly combines strands one and two, but also treats consumers as interpretive agents with considerable implicit media knowledge.

Task 6.3: Practical task

Observe an English lesson in which an aspect of the media is important. Try to capture the teacher's approach. What attitude do they encourage pupils to take towards the media? If you can, listen to pupils talking. What do you note about their media knowledge? Would you say it is challenged and developed through the lesson?

So English incorporates Media Education not as a substitute for Media Studies but as part of its broad and comprehensive domain, although it certainly helps to promote Media Studies to many pupils. English also has a special role with media in the way that it has with language. For example, teachers of every subject use language which should help pupils to acquire the vocabulary and concepts of their subject. However, for English teachers the language is part of the content of the subject. So with media – almost all teachers make use of it in their teaching – for example, the historian showing a propaganda film, the scientist using a recent documentary. But typically, if the historian is illustrating a concept like 'bias', it will be because this is part of what historians analyse. Again, in English the teacher will be teaching about how the media can be biased so that pupils can apply this understanding in any context, including History.

A final, rather different, point about media teaching relates to the assessment regime. In both the SATs and GCSE assessments, media texts are regularly used as the basis for reading comprehension, and some questions ask pupils to engage in an analysis that treats the text as a media text, e.g. comment on layout, or compare and contrast two newspaper articles on the same topic. Equally, writing tasks frequently include writing an article of some kind, producing text for a leaflet or pamphlet, designing an advert and so on (see Hart and Hicks, 2002 for a helpful and comprehensive review). These kinds of texts, being short and complete with distinctive textual features, make good examination material and English teachers will see the benefits of giving pupils plenty of opportunities to work with them. It is also true to say that these English tests are possibly based on an unconscious assumption of the examiners that 'kids know about the media' so let's use media texts. There may be some validity in such a view, but it is never stated that pupils will be tested on their media knowledge in this way. The key point that emerges is not that English teachers should turn media study into comprehension exercises, but that they have even more reason to incorporate media texts into the full range of their teaching.

Media teaching: current requirements

This section has four elements:

1   The statements in the National Curriculum that are explicit about the media.
2   Some examples of where teachers can make use of more general statements to develop media teaching.
3   The relevant objectives in the Framework.
4   Opportunities at GCSE.

The National Curriculum

As outlined earlier, Media Education has consistently had a presence in the National Curriculum but with varying degrees of emphasis, and in no sense has it had a steady increase in attention. The most significant shift of the revised 2000 Curriculum was to include explicit teaching of the moving image; this inclusion has its own intriguing history (see Goodwyn, 2004). The convergence of technologies driven by global communication networks and the proliferation of personal computers now mean that many references to ICT have an immediate relevance to media work. Current explicit requirements are:

Media and moving image texts

5 Pupils should be taught:
   a) how meaning is conveyed in texts that include print, images and sometimes sounds;
   b) how choice of form, layout and presentation contribute to effect (for example, font, caption, illustration in printed text, sequencing, framing, soundtrack in moving image text);

> c) how the nature and purpose of media products influence content and meaning (for example, selection of stories for a front page or news broadcast);
> d) how audiences and readers choose and respond to media.
>
> 9 The range of texts should include:
> b) print and ICT-based information and reference texts;
> c) media and moving image texts (for example newspapers, magazines, advertisements, television, films, videos).
>
> (DfEE, 2000)

The final section will illustrate how these requirements may be addressed. What is clear is that these brief statements open up a huge range of possibilities, especially for a beginning teacher with enthusiasm for media teaching.

Developing media teaching

English teachers can also base their work on many more statements from the National Curriculum where media are not explicitly mentioned but where they would be equally valid as the object of study, e.g. in the Reading section for Key Stages 3 and 4 (DfEE, 2000, p. 34):

> To develop an understanding and appreciation of texts, pupils should be taught:
> a) to extract meaning beyond the literal, explaining how the choice of language and style affects implied and explicit meanings.

This statement could be applied to many media texts but it is strikingly relevant to the study of advertising. Statement 'e' is actually explicit:

> to consider how meanings are changed when texts are adapted to different media.

Statement 'k' is not explicit but its potential is clear:

> to compare texts, looking at style, theme and language and identifying connections and contrasts.

It could be used as the basis for analysing the front page of two newspapers or two mainstream soap operas.

It has to be said that the writing section is far more directly related to producing print and that there is relatively little scope for making media texts. In the 'Breadth of Study' section about writing (DfEE, 2000, p. 39), references are made to various media texts such as screenplays, information leaflets, brochures, advertisements and editorials. This is useful, but in the digital age it barely recognises the capacity that pupils have to be powerfully creative with multi-media texts. Here lies one exciting challenge for the creative and innovative English teacher.

The Framework

A close reading of the Framework makes it abundantly clear that the authors are almost always referring to written and spoken language as the relentless stress on word, sentence and text level make clear. Hunting for direct references to the media in the opening, justificatory sections reveals very little that is explicit. In the entire 'Rationale' (DfEE, 2001, p. 10) the statement that independent readers should be 'reflective, critical and discriminating in response to a wide range of printed and visual texts' is the only direct mention of the visual text and this is rather ambiguous; it might simply mean picture books. The ghost of Leavis is strongly evident in the key word 'discriminating'. The absence of any real thinking about media is made strikingly clear in throw-away comments such as the example in the section 'Covering the National Curriculum', where, in exhorting teachers not to spend too long on whole texts, they are advised to use 'priority passages, support tapes, abridgement, *television extracts* and recapitulation' (DfEE, 2001, p. 15, my emphasis). This is a very narrow view of what makes studying an adaptation so valuable.

However, and with no apparent irony, there are direct media objectives in the Framework, e.g. in the 'Reading for Meaning' section, Year 7: 10: 'identify how media texts are tailored to suit their audience and recognise that audience responses vary e.g. popular websites', and, 11: 'recognise how print, sounds and still or moving images combine to create meaning' (DfEE, 2001, p. 24). The 'Reading for Meaning' sections for Years 8 and 9 have equally explicit objectives. In fact, throughout the objectives there are explicit references and many more instances where the examples suggested come from media texts. Overall, the emphasis is very much on reading and analysis rather than on making or producing media meanings in any practical way, but what this brief review demonstrates is that media teaching in English is actually embedded in the Framework objectives themselves.

GCSE

This clear direction to teach pupils about the media can be partly explained by a similar set of objectives within GCSE specifications. For example, Task 3 in one AQA specification 'should enable the candidate to demonstrate their ability to analyse, review and comment on features of media texts such as television programmes, film, radio programmes, newspapers, advertisements and magazines – and to use an appropriate critical vocabulary' (AQA, GCSE English A specification, 2004, p. 35). In Edexcel, English A, 2004, one key assessment objective is 'This paper will assess students' responses to one or more unprepared media texts' (p. 12). In practice, this typically means that students must first analyse one or more such texts and then produce their own written media text.

Essentially, all this means that at GCSE level English teachers will be teaching at least one dedicated unit about the media and potentially more, and this work needs to build on a solid foundation developed through the Framework at Key Stage 3. Some issues about progression are discussed below.

Advanced level

In teaching English Literature at A level, teachers generally ignore the media as they have a crowded specification to cover and very little time to be creative about what kinds of texts to include. So, apart from showing the occasional screen version of Shakespeare or adaptation of some classic novel, the focus is very often exclusively on literary texts. Current specifications are very tight and the heavy weight of assessment means that teachers feel they have no time for experiment or breadth. The English Language specifications, by contrast, provide a wealth of opportunities to use media texts, although not for their own sake, as it were. There is no space here to explore Media Studies at A level in any depth, but NQTs are increasingly teaching A level in their first year and in many departments an ability to teach A level Media Studies, as well as or rather than Literature, is highly valued. It may well be to your advantage to develop yourself as a media specialist during your training. This implies teaching as much media as you can within Key Stages 3 and 4, but also looking for opportunities at least to see Key Stage 5 Media teaching and, where possible, undertake some teaching. You can develop a knowledge of the Key Stage 5 curriculum by looking at the QCA requirements and the examination boards' current specifications.

Teaching about the media in English

This section considers:

- the most commonly taught aspects of media;
- some examples where there is more developing innovation;
- the potential of practical work;
- some issues about progression.

Traditional media teaching in English

A beginning teacher is likely to find that almost any English Department will have expertise and useful resources in what might be termed the traditional areas of media teaching. One common aspect involves teaching about newspapers, which neatly illustrates the strengths and weaknesses of current media teaching in English. A typical unit of work often introduces simple concepts such as tabloid and broadsheet, examines aspects of layout and design, and analyses audiences and the point of view of the paper. Pupils often have a chance to undertake a form of practical work – designing a front page, writing stories and articles – and increasingly this is undertaken on a computer, sometimes using a publishing package. Such an approach is a good introduction to the study of newspapers and, if it makes use of ICT, a good example to pupils of how technology genuinely improves creative potential. However, this initial work rarely leads to either reinforcement or genuine progression. For example, pupils are frequently asked to 'write a newspaper article' or to produce a news story about the death of characters such as Romeo and Juliet or Macbeth – good activities in themselves but the emphasis is likely to be on the literary knowledge demonstrated. The media understandings are often left largely implicit and underused. The issue of progression is considered below.

As mentioned earlier in the chapter, English teachers generally retain a love–hate relationship with advertising, particularly television advertising. British advertising is a remarkably sophisticated industry and, at its best, is unquestionably imaginative and powerful, providing excellent opportunities for pupils to deepen their understanding of the media. Teachers frequently approach the topic via print advertisements from the glossier magazines or Sunday supplements – this allows them to build up a set of resources over time that can be constantly renewed. Each example can offer the opportunity to teach about the use of persuasive language, typography, layout and general design and, perhaps most importantly, the semiotic codes embedded in the relationship created between text and image. Pupils can then seek out examples themselves and collect them by theme, or by looking for certain kinds of implied audience and so on. This can lead to them writing an analysis of how such material works and to designing their own example, perhaps writing a commentary to articulate their thinking. This latter element can be seen as the beginning of Media Studies where creative work has almost always to be accompanied by a rationale (see Buckingham *et al.*, 1995, for a detailed examination of practical work in Media Studies).

Teachers frequently devote some of their time in such a scheme to an analysis of television advertising, ignoring radio which offers its own insights and remains an underused area in English in relation to media education. What is very valuable about moving from the static advertisements is that the moving image can become the key focus. Having gained insights into advertising more generally, pupils can develop analytical skills related to the nature of the moving image per se. More innovative teachers will draw on a wide range of such texts, including film trailers, music videos, product placements in films and so on. As they do so, they can introduce some of the technical vocabulary that helps pupils to make explicit their insights (see Goodwyn, 2004 for more detail) and especially to grasp the concept of editing that could lead to their own practical work. A different but highly effective approach asks pupils, perhaps in groups, to think up a new product and to design a wide-ranging marketing campaign involving a number of media. This approach also provides opportunities for insights into the economics of the advertising industry and, most challengingly, the notion of media institutions. This latter concept is a common feature of Media Studies specifications and, it has been argued (Buckingham, 2003), is one clear indicator of how different Media Studies is from English. Certainly, English teachers tend to shy away from a concept such as 'the advertising industry' or 'the press', focusing much more on the linguistic and semiotic features of media texts. Those English teachers who have pioneered Media Studies find this conceptual shift a genuine intellectual challenge.

The other established area is the use of media texts, especially film, to support the teaching of a literary text. For example, first Zeffirelli's and then Luhrmann's adaptation of *Romeo and Juliet* became standard video texts in almost all English Departments. There is no doubt that such visual texts offer enormous stimulus to pupils and have a generally productive impact on the study of the play or novel in question. Generally, teachers tend to conceptualise their approach as simply using the visual text to engage pupils with the 'original'. Given the pressures of assessment regimes and other external factors, this is understandable. However, it does reinforce simplistic notions about film being easy and a kind of reward for slogging through the difficult language of the print text. With Luhrmann's film, it is easy to see how his text offers many other opportunities to teach about cinema and film. The prologue is delivered as a contemporary news broadcast and offers an excellent opportunity for pupils to consider how this genre is employed to dramatic, cinematic effect, requiring pupils to analyse what the conventions of news broadcasting are and how we recognise them. Equally, his opening shots are clearly within the genre of the spaghetti Western, employing accompanying music to emphasise this genre. Having used only a few moments of film, a class now has opportunities to consider the notions of film genre and the role the soundtrack plays in directing our interpretations. For more ideas, see Goodwyn 2004. English Departments usually have plenty of video, and increasingly DVD, resources and there is always great scope for making an adaptation part of teaching about the media, not just literature.

More innovative approaches

In some countries, notably Australia, New Zealand and Canada, the notion of viewing has for many years been given status alongside reading and writing, speaking and listening. This formal recognition has led to the development of much more expertise in English teachers and a wealth of excellent resources. For example, in some Australian states, film texts are studied in English as texts entirely in their own right. This point is worth making, first because teaching the moving image is now statutory in England, and second because the National Curriculum and A level specifications may yet introduce much more emphasis on moving image and other media texts; curriculum always changes, sometimes for the better.

However, the introduction of the statements about moving image texts has had little real effect on everyday English teaching. This, then, may be the point of departure for the more innovative beginning teacher. English offers huge scope for media work and, as illustrated in earlier sections, such work is fully endorsed by the National Curriculum and the Framework etc. What it requires is imaginative teaching.

A simple step would involve developing a scheme of work around a film and treating it as a text entirely in its own right. Again, given the pressures of time, there has been a supportive attempt by organisations such as the British Film Institute (BFI) to make short films more available to teachers. Work based around short films has been valued especially for helping with literacy skills, and so has some special value at Key Stage 3 (see BFI, 1999, 2000; Higgins, 2002). However, the study of a normal length film is not problematic; at a simply practical level pupils may well be happy to give up their own time to view a film if it really is impossible to fit it into ordinary class time. Having seen a complete film, pupils can then view short sections to develop an understanding of film language. An extract of one minute can typically contain a number and variety of shots, such as close-up, long shot and so on, and a number of sound effects. One of the most simple techniques for grabbing pupils' attention is to show them the film with no sound or to let them listen to the sound without the film. In either case they can concentrate on the contribution of each medium and begin to see how editing constructs the meaning. Such attention to detail can easily lead on to the analysis of a single shot and to the *mise-en-scène*, the literal analysis of exactly what is 'in the scene'. All these activities begin to build pupils' capacity to appreciate the complexity of the moving image and to give them access to their implicit knowledge.

Another area which offers huge scope to the teacher, but is currently under-utilised, is television. In the 1980s, subsequent to the enthusiasm generated by Len Masterman's pioneering work (see Masterman, 1980), there was considerable classroom use of recorded television. Such work has all but disappeared.

Pupils still watch a great deal of television and many now have their own sets for their exclusive use. However, it is more important for the English teacher to approach television as a subject for study than to be overly concerned with trying to identify what pupils are currently watching, interesting though that may be. It is very productive to select something of clear significance within the culture such as soap opera and to ask pupils to consider what makes it so important and what function it performs in society. This kind of approach depersonalises the soaps, helping pupils to put aside favourites or the idea that 'all soaps are rubbish'. Pupils can be asked to collect the titles of all the soaps that they know, derive a definition and then, working as a class, test out the definition on a range of programmes to see which fit and which do not. They will soon discover that within soaps there are sub-categories such as docu-soaps etc. The key factor is for them to engage with the soap as a text initially and to develop an understanding of how settings work – the pub, the home, the shop, etc., and how sets of characters interact with each other and with the settings. They can then look at storylines and characterisations in particular soaps and look for more archetypal characters. Another dimension to such work is the constant reference to soaps in the popular media, which provides lots of additional media perspectives. Such work, as with film, can lead pupils to feel very powerful about their ability to comprehend and interpret the media.

The future scope of work involving the internet, computer games, multi-media software and other components of the digital revolution offers enormous and exciting possibilities (see Burn and Reed, 1999; Goodwyn, 2000; Beavis, 2001; Burn, 2003; Goodwyn 2004).

The potential of practical work

There will always be something of a debate about the value of practical work and the difficulties of assessing it, but that debate is well considered elsewhere (see Buckingham *et al.*, 1995; Buckingham, 2003; Goodwyn, 2004). The evidence is that practical work is highly engaging for pupils and the teacher, and can be both enjoyable and highly developmental. In simple terms, it is definitely worth trying out. For this book, it is important to focus more on the fact that practical work in media education may sound very technical and daunting to many beginning teachers. There are two immediate responses to that concern. First, it can be simple and straightforward, and second the rapid development of technology means that what might have been unimaginably sophisticated a few years ago is now relatively uncomplicated.

All departments make use of word processing software that allows pupils to create a range of documents, using a variety of layouts and importing images.

This combination provides a media-rich environment in which to consider newspapers, magazines, leaflets and posters. Many schools have access to more sophisticated software such as Publisher, which is specifically designed to enable greater attention to detail in the production of texts and images. Powerpoint offers considerable potential for pupils to present ideas about the media. A digital camera can capture images from a number of media sources and, with the right interface, even film on DVD, allowing teacher and pupils to examine stills and pictures to analyse them in depth and detail. As Powerpoint also allows multiple images on screen simultaneously, pupils can look at a series of shots and rearrange them. This is 'practical work' as the pupils are essentially making editing decisions. Almost all PCs now come with Moviemaker software and Apple Macs have Imovie. These packages are easy to use and enormously powerful; it is beyond the scope of this short chapter to describe their detailed workings.

Fundamentally, the digital revolution may be over-hyped in many ways, but for the teacher interested in developing pupils' understanding of the media, it is beginning to offer really exciting possibilities. The digital camera, both still and video, makes the visual material remarkably accessible and capable of manipulation. Current software is opening up practical and creative opportunities that were unthinkable even a few years ago. The internet provides an extraordinary source of material and a creative interface for pupils to create websites and a host of related artefacts. All of these developments should be considered in relation to domestic as well as educational use. There may be dangers in assuming too readily that most pupils have domestic access to such hardware and software, but there is far more danger in ignoring the fact that many do and that they are capable of great sophistication in using it. Such resources should be of great value to a teacher and his or her class if they are used wisely. Currently, it is most unfortunate that the great majority of teacher training courses have no time to provide teachers with some of these practical skills.

Conclusions and some issues about progression

There is now a reasonable amount of formal, specific attention to media education in the curriculum of English, and there is ample opportunity for imaginative teachers to do far more than this minimum. There is also little to suggest that further curricular revisions will dramatically reduce this attention, so developing this kind of expertise, particularly the practical skills involved, is a sound investment in professional development. Considered in this way, the future of media in English should be an exciting one as long as new members of the profession feel a commitment to engaging with the media-rich lives of their pupils in a genuine way.

If they do, there is one more area to consider that they may be best placed to reflect upon and then influence over time – progression. Current assessment emphases on levels, scores and added value all suggest that pupil progress is being measured and the information gained used to promote further progression. There is some truth in this, but it also obscures in its factual obsession some of the more important notions of progression that are less measurable. It is reasonable to say that we know a great deal about, for example, writing development – enough to have identified many typical things about how pupils become fluent writers, and also the kinds of problems and issues they face. Both of these understandings can inform good teaching and formative assessment. If we compare this carefully developed knowledge to what we understand about pupils' acquisition of media knowledge, then we must recognise that we have a great deal to learn in order to improve our teaching and pupils' own learning.

Take, for an example, the need for all English teachers to teach about the moving image and how meaning is conveyed. What level of understanding is a typical 10-year-old capable of when it comes to articulating his knowledge of how the moving image works? Once we know that, then how much further should a typical 16-year-old have progressed? Equally, what difference does some practical work make to the development of his media knowledge?

The current situation in many English Departments is such that there is little attention to planned progression. Newspaper articles are often studied and written in Year 7 and this continues into Year 11; pupils do make progress and produce more sophisticated work, but this seems mostly to come from maturation, their own engagements with media texts and their improving competence in traditional literacy. A further factor here is that the production of newspaper articles is treated almost entirely as a writing task. At first sight this seems perfectly reasonable, especially given the assessment pressures on teachers. However, it also keeps the newspaper article in a limited configuration in which the visual elements, images, fonts, layout and so on are marginalised. If departments looked at how the written form operates within the media environment, they would be challenged to look at a far greater range of increasingly sophisticated writing tasks for their students. It is only fair to say that the spirit of the current assessment regime does not foster such thinking.

In conclusion, then, one of the real challenges for the beginning teacher is to help take on the teaching of media in English and really move it forward. There is much good practice to learn from, but there is also much that needs to change and is capable of improvement. For the future of the pupils we teach, there can be few things more significant than to enable them to operate critically and creatively in the media-rich environment of the twenty-first century.

7 Information and Communications Technology

Chris Warren

Access

If you ask English teachers why they do not use ICT routinely as part of their lessons, most do not reply that they feel technically incompetent. Instead, they cite inadequate access to equipment. With access restricted, sporadic or inadequate, it seems difficult to get the most out of such a resource.

If you have the chance to visit a range of schools, you will see widely differing levels of provision. Some lucky English Departments have a suite of computers all to themselves; other departments are in schools where whole classes are provided with laptops.

Such schools can be rare, however. The general rule is that there are computer rooms in some remote part of the building, and if you want to teach using ICT you need to book the facility in advance. To make matters worse, you will find yourself competing for the room with every other department. Some communities in the school are specially privileged, such as students actually studying on GCSE ICT courses. They seem to have the rooms block-booked. Business Studies groups have a divine right to computers, as everyone knows.

Before you retire in defeat and despair, it is worth thinking about what you actually want to derive from an English lesson that incorporates ICT. How do you want the use of ICT to impact on the class? There are direct and indirect ways to use ICT.

All the approaches listed in Table 7.1 use ICT as a tool:

- for preparation
- for whole-class presentation
- for on-screen work, either singly or in collaborative groups.

119

Table 7.1 Uses of ICT and their class impact

ICT use	Impact on class
Use ICT to prepare high-quality conventional resources in advance of the lesson.	Students don't use computers and there isn't one in the class, but everyone benefits indirectly from professional presentation.
Use the special facilities of ICT to prepare innovative resources in advance of the lesson.	Again, students don't use computers, but you have made something for them that would be impossible without the intervention of technology (a classic example is the use of collapsed texts to introduce poems).
Employ one shared computer to run a lesson or make a powerful learning point.	Before the arrival of affordable digital projectors and interactive whiteboards, such techniques were seen as somewhat offbeat. English Departments (perhaps out of necessity) pioneered many one-computer-in-the-class approaches, including role-play simulation and the use of a computer monitor turned to face the class. Interactive whiteboards are increasingly common now. You still need to recognise that students may not use computers directly as individuals, but the quality of the lessons they receive can be substantially improved, especially if you know how to get the best out of such equipment.
Use a small cluster of computers in the class.	English teachers are enthusiastic advocates of collaboration, and encouraging three or four students to share an editing task is demonstrably powerful. If you only have a small number of machines at your disposal, you can make good use of them by setting up one computer per group. The shared screen allows cooperative writing; everyone can read the product; no one objects to suggested changes because such emendations are easy to make; there isn't the self-consciousness that is associated with handwriting; talk is often of a high quality and very task-focused. Where you have a severely restricted number of computers, you can try lessons that invite students to move around between tasks (techniques such as Jigsaw come in useful here). Thus everyone gets their 'turn', albeit a rather short one.
Use a suite of computers, enough for one computer each.	At first glance, this might appear to be the ideal scenario. However, if your intention is to emphasise collaboration, you will notice an atmosphere of quiet sterility in the class as each student labours at their own screen. Even if you have enough computers for one each, you may find yourself asking students to share.

How you actually employ the equipment for each of these tasks can vary immensely in complexity. The key point is to allow what you want to do as an English teacher to rule absolutely over the demands of the ICT curriculum. The subject comes first. If students derive some form of technical benefit because they have used a word processor, for instance, that should be secondary to the benefit they gain from learning how to edit language or to understand and manipulate the structure of a text.

So for most of us, access to equipment is, and will continue to be, an issue. It should not prevent you using ICT to boost the quality of your lessons. Exercise imagination and work with the limitations or freedoms of the school you are in. If you show yourself keen to advance, you will discover that there are more colleagues who will want to help than those who put restrictions in your path.

Geography

The way computer equipment and other furniture is arranged in the classroom often influences powerfully the way a lesson can be run. One glance at the classroom frequently reveals the philosophy of computer-use in favour when the room was organised. You may not be able to change room layouts; the furniture may be fixed by screws and bolts. However, it is useful to have an understanding of how the room layout enables or disables a lesson. And if you *can* influence the geography of the classroom, knowing what you want from the physical arrangement of tables and machines will be invaluable.

Let's look at some examples.

In the layout shown in Figure 7.1, computers are typically fixed on benches, all facing the front. There is no room for any activity other than using the computer screens. The classroom layout emphasises instruction or training – someone at the front telling everyone what to do. There is no expectation that students might collaborate on work; they each have a machine and the idea is that they work in silence on their own. Very often with this layout, the cabling of the room (power-supply to the machines and network connections) means that moving any equipment or desks is impossible. It is cramped, often hot – the priority seems to be to pack as many computers as possible into the room, so that every student can have one. Sometimes the isolation of students from each other is reinforced by small booths, putting a baffle or screen around each workspace. Moving people around in this classroom would be a nightmare.

Figure 7.2 shows another layout. Note the baffles around each workstation. Layouts like this one are fairly common because arranging computers around the walls solves the practical difficulty of supplying cabling to machines – it can be delivered from sockets in cabling plumbed into the walls and running in a circuit right around the classroom.

The philosophy of computer use here emphasises isolation while students are working at their screens, although there is an understanding perhaps that there may be plenary sessions where the class gathers around the tables provided in the centre of the room. Every student in this classroom looks outward and away from his/her peers. The booths around each machine make collaborative work

Figure 7.1 Classroom layout 1

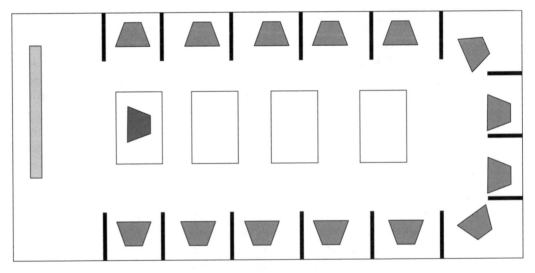

Figure 7.2 Classroom layout 2

especially difficult – see how the room geography enforces one view of classroom use – doing anything else means running against the grain of the geography.

This layout also doesn't pack as many computers into the space, so you will find that the central desks are sometimes used for more equipment (the philosophy, remember, dictating that each student has access to his/her own machine).

If we take the same layout once more but this time remove the booths around each workspace and supply two swivelling chairs for each machine, a useful degree of flexibility is achieved, as shown in Figure 7.3. (The circles represent swivelling stools or chairs – the swivelling allowing everyone to turn and face the front, or inwards towards the centre, with the minimum of disruption. The novelty of swivelling chairs is a cause for gaiety enough on its own, however.)

Now it is possible to have a plenary session, to run collaborative tasks, and to mix the activity with some work reading/talking/handwriting at the central desks. The technical convenience of arranging computers around the walls is still maintained. Asking students to move from machine to machine (a powerful technique in English but almost beyond the imagination of some ICT specialists) is enabled.

In the layout shown in Figure 7.4, computers are arranged in clusters or pods around a circular station or desk. The unspoken philosophy here is one of collaboration. The arrangement allows proper person-to-person eye contact, and it is implied that the collaborating group can, in fact, use a number of computers, not just one.

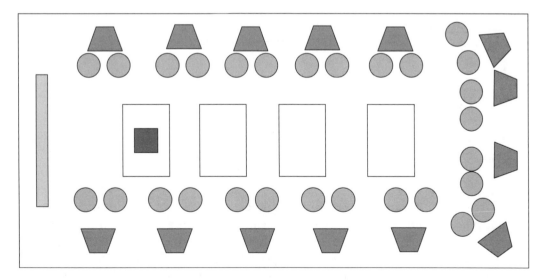

Figure 7.3 Classroom layout 3

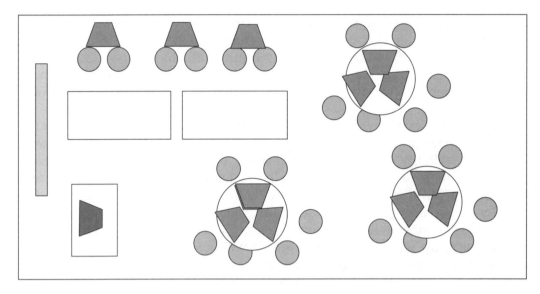

Figure 7.4 Classroom layout 4

The power and network cabling is delivered up through the centre of the pod or down from the ceiling. Some very modern computer rooms have adopted this form of layout. The modern flat (TFT) screens also consume much less space than their predecessors, again allowing easier interaction around a group without too many physical barriers between speakers. Because this layout needs generous amounts of space and cabling cannot easily use existing channels, it is more common in brand-new, purpose-built rooms. On the positive side, the room offers considerable flexibility in its use, and the way that the layout encourages collaboration makes it especially useful for English.

Other arrangements

Wireless networks, increasingly common in schools, remove the need for some of the cabling (the physical network), but all machines require power to function. You can sometimes see laptops kept in special powered cabinets where their batteries are recharged overnight, but this is an insecure strategy in the long term. If you want to be sure that the computers won't let you down at a crucial point in the lesson, there's no substitute for plugging the things in.

Some companies have recognised the inherent difficulties illustrated above and have designed special desks for the purpose, power supply included. Naturally, such desks assume solitary computer use, so usually we're still saddled with this self-centred philosophy.

Tablets and laptop computers allow for much more flexibility, especially used in conjunction with a wireless-linked whiteboard. The picture isn't all bleak.

The key point to remember is that English classrooms using ICT thrive best through collaborative work – argue for it, insist on it and, if you can, don't let the design of the classroom thwart your plans. Aim to have versatility built into the design – tables in the middle, whiteboard, two chairs to a machine – these are all ways to inject the necessary collaboration into what you do.

Networks

School computer networks have a number of advantages:

- software can be shared easily (application sharing);
- students and staff can each have their own files area to store work safely;
- files created within the school can be shared easily;
- individual students can reach the internet via the network when they need access;
- network managers can maintain a level of security (protecting the school computers from viruses and managing student access to the internet, while monitoring its use);
- expensive hardware such as scanners and printers can be shared;
- with certain types of network, the teacher at the front of the class can control every individual machine, see what's happening on it and intervene in a task if necessary.

However, networks also have disadvantages, in parallel with the above positive features:

- you need a password to log on – not a major issue but sometimes a drag;
- there is sometimes a log jam when the whole class tries to print;
- if the network goes down, the entire class is put out of action;
- problems with the network can't generally be fixed by the average teacher (apart from anything else, you require special access rights and the appropriate password) so if anything plays up, you *have* to 'call Mr Jones';
- networks can occasionally slow up;
- restrictions designed to protect young people from the horrors (imagined and real) of the internet can be frustratingly limiting, impeding serious use of the web for searching and information retrieval;
- when the network goes down, so does email and access to the internet.

The general rule is simple – get to know the network manager well and then understand the quirks of your school network by asking lots of questions. Using a networked room to teach a group of students takes patience and practice, and it's best to have assistance the first few times, until you feel you can safely 'fly solo'. Have an alternative plan up your sleeve in case the dreaded crash occurs.

How would you use a good network for English? Well, there are a number of possibilities. The most fruitful might be to focus on collaborative writing. The following suggestions are intended merely as a template. Adapt them in any way you feel is appropriate. This set of ideas explores the use of word processors attached to an efficient network, with a common area set up for files to be stored. (The principle works even if you do not have a network. Save material to a floppy disc passed from machine to machine at the end of the lesson – this is very cumbersome but still possible.)

Because word processors are also efficient 'blenders', they can be used to assemble the work of several authors. The handwriting differences disappear, the connections between sections can be edited carefully to smooth out discontinuities of style, and the order of sections can be juggled for effect. This post-writing task demands a high level of editing skills, exploits the technology very efficiently and would be difficult without a computer.

A suggested routine might follow this pattern:

- The class discusses an overall framework.
- The class decides on, and names, the sections.
- The class divides into groups of two or three.
- Groups create each section on computer.
- Each section is saved to a common area of the network with the prearranged file name.
- An editorial group is formed to connect the sections together.
- Each original group is consulted about the result, their opinions noted and adjustments made to the assembled text.
- The resultant text is printed out and copied for each group to read.

A worked example

Applying this technique to the study of *Under Milk Wood*, for instance, might lead to a version created by the class based on a day in the life of the school.

Read the play with the class as a communal reading (it helps with Year 9/10 pupils if they are told to watch out for the hidden jokes). The structure of the original should be explored – e.g. a cycle through one day, First Voice, Second Voice, the focus on the subconscious, the qualities of the language, the subversive humour and so on.

As a class, decide on a name for the new play – Under High School Wood? – and draw up a list of the characters in the play. These can be based on real people but their names must be heavily disguised. Exclude members of the group from the dramatis personae to avoid cruel laughter.

Divide the class into groups based on times of the day so that one whole day is covered. Now each group writes its section using the computers and the play is assembled as suggested above.

Voilà – a whole new play, filled with in-jokes and communally owned by the class. *Under Milk Wood* will be enjoyed in new ways after this.

A similar technique can be used to create extended narratives, if you have the space and time, and regular access to the computer room. If each group, rather than trying to produce 40 lines from a play, attempts to write a chapter of a thriller, a long piece will result. The problems of plot construction, style, continuity of characterisation – all of these will emerge in the process and can greatly increase pupils' awareness of the issues.

Limitations are imposed by typing speeds and availability of the equipment, so you might need to do some careful planning and calculation before you embark on anything too ambitious.

You might like to try creating a magazine using this technique, although the function of the editorial group might be more to polish the style of individual articles than to blend texts.

If you have good relationships with neighbouring schools (or even schools on the other side of the world) the internet can be used as the assembly area for the sections of text. This is more difficult to organise and complete, but if you choose a relatively simple idea, it can be an exciting adventure in communal sharing. One word of caution – schools in other parts of the world have very different academic years. Make sure you arrange the activity when both schools can commit to its completion.

Networks allow another supercharged form of collaboration that can involve large numbers and vast distances. Use your imagination. What about a project comparing contemporary slang in your school with that used in the Australian outback? There's nothing to stop you. The connections are all there. You can even find your Aussie partner school using one of the many school-matching websites that exist (try Windows on the World).

Printing

At the end of a typical lesson where computers have been used for writing, a critical point is reached. Each student should make a permanent copy of the work so far, either as a saved electronic file or a hard-copy printout. It is difficult to describe the anguish that students experience when they lose their work, and you should always prepare for, and attempt to avoid, this tragic eventuality.

One way to save work is to print it out. However, printers are problematic in most schools:

- Printer ink is often very expensive.
- Printers can jam easily and need delicate coaxing – there is sometimes a local expert (well worth cultivating) who can rush to the rescue.
- Printer paper runs out – come with a supply.
- Where one printer serves, say, 16 machines, the queue for a printout can seriously throw out your lesson timing. Try to allow for it or arrange for the printing to continue into breaktime.

Whatever the rules on conserving paper and ink, English/ICT lessons should try to retain evidence of drafting. On computers, where all evidence of changes disappears, this is best achieved through the regular discipline of saving drafts or printing out final versions. If you have the flexibility with tables available in the classroom, I recommend the following editing sequence for collaborative writing:

- As a small group, plan a piece of work on paper.
- Write up a first draft on the computer and save as draft 1.
- Print a number of copies.
- Take the copies and edit on paper using coloured pens.
- Return to the file on computer and implement the changes.
- Save the result as draft 2.
- Edit on screen, discussing word, sentence and text level alterations.
- Save the result as final draft.

This sequence (you can vary it as you please) mixes editing and discussion modes. The text looks and feels different on paper; discussion feels quite different around a table as opposed to working in front of a screen. By mixing the modes you can make the experience rich and varied.

The group can then perhaps use a projector to share the various drafts and explain the choices they made to the rest of the class – an ideal conclusion to a drafting session in which you bring conscious reflection to the fore.

Printing is vital in English; it's the outcome of the vast majority of English work, the crisp and beautiful hard copy. But don't make it the focus. Use the process creatively; especially exploit the power of hard copy to map editing decisions, for example all those insertions, deletions and arrows. Electronic editing gives learners a powerful sense of the malleability of text, its infinite flexibility empowered by ICT. And try to capture work in progress to avoid catastrophic losses occasioned by a disc failure or program crash.

Extending and enhancing learning with ICT

If ICT is to make a genuine contribution to the curriculum, it must do more than simply replicate what was done, much more cheaply, using conventional methods. We should expect the technology to offer more – an enhanced or more efficient experience perhaps. Ideally, it should give us capabilities that we did not have before – it should *extend* what we do.

In English, the single most powerful tool is the word processor. It really can allow us to manipulate language, to move things around, to experiment, to sort and sequence, to *play*. Desktop Publishing, similarly, allows a writer to replicate the effects that formerly were the exclusive province of publishers with access to printing machines and typesetters. We take it for granted now, but the plethora of fonts and the subtle adjustments that can be made to layout are relatively new, and they have empowered us all. However, we still need to ask the question, 'How can we make full curriculum use of these facilities to enliven the classroom?'

There are a few basic principles that will help you to distinguish an effective deployment of ICT from an ineffective one.

It must go through the brain

This rule seems self-evident, but there are countless examples of ICT use where the brain is bypassed or where it is possible to complete the task while concentrating on something else (last night's television, for instance). These include:

- Copying up neatly. It's quite possible to type mechanically without too much thought about substance, style, etc. This form of dull, unimaginative application of ICT is the most common bad lesson observed by inspectors in English lessons where computers are used. It's so easy to make the lesson instantly more valuable if you engage the brain. By simply asking the class to perform some transformational task on the text (set a word-length or a new audience, for instance) suddenly the class is obliged to think.
- Drag and drop exercises. If the activities aren't very carefully designed, the computer's limited functionality can be spotted by a pupil. Within seconds,

the task is converted from the one intended to a useless series of actions – if the answer sticks in the right place, it's right. So no thought is required, just drag anywhere and hope. You will find far too many of these hopelessly inadequate activities masquerading as genuine learning objects; they are not. Again, had the designers followed the golden rule, they would have come up with a way of ensuring that thought has to take place.

- Unmediated information. Asking children to do research on a particular topic using computers will inevitably trigger the potentially brainless activity of copy-and-paste. You will receive reams of beautiful-looking, professionally printed and illustrated material. But if you ask the simplest question about the information, you will draw a blank. Pupils will frequently not have read it; it hasn't gone near the brain. This is relatively easy to fix – ask for the information to be re-written for a novel audience (8-year-olds) and it will be impossible to complete the task without thinking about the text.

The 'It must go through the brain' rule should be applied to anything you are planning to do using ICT. If a lesson fails the test, abandon it.

Emphasise collaboration

English teachers use computers to encourage talk, to facilitate collaborative writing (quite hard to manage without a shared writing space like the computer screen) and to stimulate a wide range of cooperative lessons, including whole-class activities using a whiteboard or projector. Look for opportunities for collaboration and teamwork. ICT has immense potential here.

Emphasise pupil-ownership

If you have the time and space to do it, allow students to take ownership of their use of ICT. This approach fits in powerfully with the drive to create autonomous, self-directed learners. ICT offers rich possibilities for autonomous work in English. You need to take some risks, but the rewards can be beyond anything you can imagine.

For example, you might ask groups of students to work on an interpretation of a scene from *Macbeth* using PowerPoint. The PowerPoint slides can act as an ironic backdrop to a reading of the scene, revealing the inner thoughts of the speakers or their moral/spiritual struggle (an image of an angel with a speech bubble and another one of a devil – perhaps the good and bad voices in Macbeth's head as he contemplates murder?). Macbeth says something sweet but subtly menacing to Banquo – on the screen behind the speaker a shark appears . . . Encourage students to break out of the conventional use of PowerPoint (death by a thousand bullets), then wait for their delight.

Emphasise participation

Even with one computer and a projector, participation should be your rule. If image, sound and text are used solely to power-up teacher control, ICT can become an instrument of oppression – passive, gawping spectators watching while teacher has fun, increasingly disenfranchised from the process of their own learning. However, used appropriately, ICT equipment has the potential to allow really exciting participation.

- Don't keep your pupils sitting on the sidelines – let them play an active role.
- Design some lessons where you throw the control over to them. Take the risk.
- Give them the challenge. And even if you are the one at the front, delivering the lesson, lead with questions, draw them into the fray, engage the class.
- Don't use the equipment to mesmerise, passify or subdue, like a parent plonking a child in front of the television (it can so easily be used like that). Aim for active ideas where you practically can.
- Reverse roles – let groups of pupils act as teachers, using the ICT to make presentations to others. Give them creative freedom; trust them – and you will be startled and delighted by the results.

Here is a very brief summary of the sorts of activities enabled by ICT. Each of these techniques is a subject in itself and worth exploring separately. Incidentally, if you can, get hold of the Becta document stating ICT entitlement in English. It summarises the applications of ICT to the subject with a rare elegance and economy.

Word processing

- Text editing – changing, adjusting, correcting – easily and painlessly.
- Text manipulation – ordering, sequencing, rearranging – an endless range of possibilities.
- Combining text or reducing text – using two windows. This technique lends itself to comparisons of text. Blending two texts to a set word-length can be a very demanding editorial task, bringing into play both ICT and English

skills. Comparing two texts is facilitated with this use of ICT (see also text mapping, below).

- Annotating text – with call-outs (speech bubbles etc.), footnotes or embedded notes.
- Processing texts drawn from archives – CD-ROM or the internet.
- Transformations – there are at least eleven kinds of transformation. This is a very popular use of computers in English.
- Text mapping and literacy investigations. Text mapping using ICT, invented by Tony Clifford, involves marking a text with the tools of a word processor (bold, italic, underline, font, font size, colour, highlight) and writing a key at the foot of the text to explain the map.
- Text formatting – awareness of fonts and layout; media studies. You can also use fonts for creative purposes (a special font for each character or a new font chosen to reflect the central character's mood).
- Text mimicking/modelling – to address particular audiences or emulate particular text artefacts – uniquely enabled by ICT. These artefacts can be almost identical to the original model in terms of layout and form; the task of emulating the style is an English skill, of course.

Advantages:

- Control.
- Accuracy.
- Text-marking facilities can reveal properties of language.
- A bread-and-butter use of the computer.

Disadvantages:

- Need for keyboard skills.
- Preferable to use computer suites which might be booked up. If you have a digital projector, however, text mapping can be adapted for whole-class use, the sequencing and organisation of ideas can be illustrated for a whole class, and grammatical points can be made effectively with a word processor.
- Material needs to be well managed – saving and storing work becomes a real issue.

Role play and simulation

Information-stream activities – the computer is programmed to issue bulletins at timed intervals to emulate a teletext machine. The result is a high-pressure context with crushing deadlines that can be used to stimulate: hot-seating, crisis management, newspaper production – Media Studies in action and puzzle solving (the clues are delivered one by one).

Advantages:

- Powerful emotional experiences, often unforgettable.
- Superb team-work opportunities; drama.
- High-level demands on oral skills (ideal for oral assessment).
- Compelling realism.
- Addictive fun because of the adrenalin and sense of real life.
- Can be run using one computer.
- Can be networked to include schools all over the world.

Disadvantages:

- Sometimes takes a whole morning/whole day.
- You need to have a special program to make it realistic.
- Can't be run on a regular basis; these activities are by their nature once-a-term affairs, like a small school play.
- Require preparation and follow-up.

The internet

The internet is famous as a tool for research, and the latest search engines allow you to track down the most obscure information. However, remember that there are three aspects to the internet (frequently called the 3 modes): you can download material, but you can also upload your own information, effectively publishing it to the world; you can also exchange information over the net (the most common use of the system, in fact) through the use of email. The use of experts in the form of professional writers, actors, film-makers, etc. is a well-tried and very rewarding use of this exchange potential. Children feel especially motivated to see their work published on the internet.

Advantages:

- Vast unlimited resources.
- Exciting opportunities for communication projects.
- A growing, evolving medium.
- Highly motivating.
- Classroom-expanding potential.
- Combines well with all other ICT applications for English.
- Generates language uses that are, in themselves, fascinating to study.

Disadvantages:

- Access can sometimes be limited to one node in the school, although with the advent of broadband and wireless networks, this picture is changing rapidly.
- Contains unsuitable material, so care has to be exercised.
- Surfing – is it a waste of time?

Moving around

To keep children static in a computer room rather limits their potential. There are many exciting activities which entail getting up and moving around. Where equipment is limited, this technique gives everyone a fair chance to use the computer and the impoverished technological state of the classroom is disguised. Magic Roundabout is one such technique. It involves moving pupils around a class, from computer to computer, at set intervals. The task is to write stories in a range of genres, using paper and screen as composition media. Magic Roundabout lasts about 40 minutes; it is hilarious, fast-paced and highly productive in generating discussion on genre and the editing process itself.

Jigsaw is another well-established technique, designed to gain the maximum degree of participation and discussion from a group of students. Look up Jigsaw in a search engine and you will find a worldwide community of enthusiastic practitioners generating exemplars, case studies and lesson ideas.

You can also move pupils round to emulate Consequences games – ask all your students to write the opening of a story and press Return until the text disappears from the screen. Move the whole class round one station. Now ask them to write the ending. Move round one. The final task is to bring beginning and ending together and write a suitable passage in the middle to link the two seamlessly. Naturally, there are endless variations on this sort of activity.

Advantages:

- Constant variety and stimulation.
- Wide range of language demands, both written and oral.
- Team-work and collaboration.
- Opportunities for the sugar of humour to sweeten the pill of learning.
- Tasks can be designed to call on a number of skills.
- A way of lifting individual expertise into the public or shared domain.
- Can be used where equipment is limited (i.e. only one computer).

Disadvantages:

- Can be a bitty or fragmented experience.
- May require more than the usual lesson time to be effective.
- Needs strong teaching if the full learning benefit is to be felt.

Extend what can be done so that you and your class explore new territory, or enhance what you already do – this is the ultimate function of ICT. We shouldn't accept applications that simply replicate traditional activities without adding anything. Expect more, demand more. And if you're not offered more from what's available in your school, invent more. Above all, emphasise participation – let your class make videos, present ideas with PowerPoint, research using email and the internet.

Interactive whiteboards

The context is a familiar one for the classroom: you stand in front of the board and use it to illustrate a learning point to the class. However, if the board is in fact the screen of a computer, two things change: the familiar board–teacher–class context and the use of computers as a learning tool.

The problem has been that lessons planned for the new interactive whiteboards have been based either on traditional board use, or on a methodology borrowed from the conventional uses of ICT, where it is seen as a solitary learning device. Combining these two methods demands a fresh approach.

First, we need to look at the potential of this technology to enhance the best aspects of both approaches and then explore where something entirely new is made possible.

If you have an interactive whiteboard in your classroom, there are three ways you can organise the space. Each one has implications for the sort of lesson you can teach and for the design of materials to run on the whiteboard:

1 Teacher stands at the front of the class and teaches the lesson actively using the whiteboard.
2 Teacher stands to one side and encourages members of the class to participate directly, using the whiteboard.
3 Teacher programs the whiteboard to drive the lesson through a stream of information or a series of instructions – teacher can observe speaking and listening activities and note effective teamwork, without being caught up in the machinery of the lesson.

Some lessons will combine elements of all three permutations, others will be characterised by just one. But you need to think flexibly about the resource and explore all of its potential.

This part of the chapter takes you through the implications for each permutation. As is often the case with ICT, there is room for experimentation here, finding what works for you. You can be genuinely innovative. An inspector may step into your classroom, watch you use the board and burst forth into paeans of praise, singing hymns about Best Practice. Be courageous – no one has fully explored the best use of the boards.

As a side note, many English teachers argue that it is not the interactive board that is special; the digital projector that allows the whole class to share the output of one computer is the really magical element, they say. If the board is being used in traditional didactic ways, they may have a point. However, once you allow students to participate in the lesson, their tactile involvement in the process is impossible to replicate fully using a mouse. Watch your own students – you'll see the effect.

Figure 7.5 shows the traditional solitary use of a computer and then compares it to a typical whole-class teaching context. Two points distinguish this latter scenario from the usual computer-based lesson:

1 the whole class can participate;
2 there is a teacher actively operating between the class and the computer screen (in this case the whiteboard).

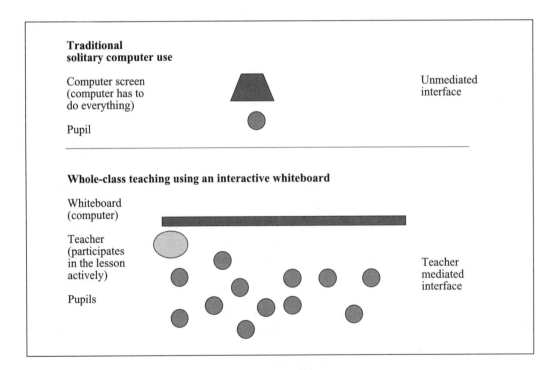

Figure 7.5 Solitary computer use versus whole-class teaching

Teacher stands at the front of the class and teaches the lesson actively using the whiteboard

Let's look at how such a lesson would work:

- **Materials for an interactive whiteboard do not have to indicate right or wrong – they should be left open**
  The material doesn't have to be right or wrong in the usual, restricted, black-or-white, binary way of computers. Nor does the computer need to indicate whether something's correct – you are there to cover that aspect of the lesson and can withhold the answer or allow erroneous lines of thinking to progress, perhaps to allow pupils to develop their own logical approaches.
- **Ideally, deliberate gaps should be introduced into the lesson, creating space for teacher and pupils**
  The materials do not need to be complete – indeed, if the picture is heavily filled-in there will not be as many opportunities for class discussion. Always look for opportunities for gaps or puzzles.
- **Add direct questions in the text on screen that can only be answered by you and the class – an open-ended approach**
  The questions can act as a simple guide to the issues you want to raise at various points in the lesson. The words on screen focus the whole class on the question, but the answer must be supplied through discussion and response – it can't be stumbled upon by random clicking around the screen.
- **Don't design whiteboard materials that 'do everything'**
  If you do, the lesson will have 'failed' in that you are, by definition, excluded from the process, except as a clicker of buttons and driver of the software. Allow for, and celebrate, your own expertise.
- **Design lessons where the use of markers can enhance the learning experience**
  Again, this requires authors to create deliberate gaps. An example might be the use of text mapping, so that the class fills in the information together and the understanding grows from that process.
- **Use links and hypertext creatively**
  Don't think only in linear ways. It is possible to follow a linear path through a subject for part of the lesson, then reach a crossroads where there are several branches. A computer can easily be programmed to provide those alternative routes and make each choice a vivid experience. You can explore alternative takes on a single issue this way, providing the class with dynamic decisions as you proceed.

- **Use loops**

    You can use loops as well as hypertext links so that you design a return to material already covered. This is another break from the linear lesson.

Teacher stands to one side and encourages members of the class to participate directly, using the whiteboard

There are multiple opportunities for enjoyable class participation with white-board technology, but the materials need to be designed consciously for that effect. Ask students near the front to participate.

Figure 7.6 shows the context where pupils take the lesson:

1   the whole class can participate;
2   the whiteboard offers novel and stimulating opportunities to engage pupils in the learning process.

Let's look at the possibilities for involving pupils:

- **Pupils can present to the class**

    This is traditionally done as part of an English oral activity – a talk or speech. With an interactive whiteboard, new potentials emerge. Individual

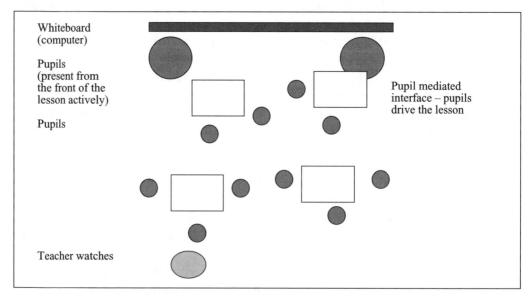

Figure 7.6   Pupils take the lesson

pupils or teams can use ICT presentation tools such as PowerPoint to prepare visually attractive and dynamic presentations for their peers. The strategy provides a strong focus for the team's work. The presentation itself is a dynamic part of the learning process, reinforcing understanding and developing skills of communication and expression. The scaffolding provided by the technology very often counters reticence and timidity, bolstering confidence and supporting the narrative thread of the discourse with timely bullet points. Some excellent work has been done in English using PowerPoint as a counterpoint to a performance (e.g. Macbeth's inner thoughts appear as thought bubbles, at variance to what he actually says).

- **Try semi-competitive activities**

  Two groups in class can compete through representatives at the front of the class. There are a number of puzzle-type activities that can work for a whole class. A classic example is the computer 'snap' game that can be adapted for almost any topic in English.

- **Quizzes**

  Some excellent work has been observed using computer quizzes to stimulate a class's engagement with a subject. Seemingly off-putting features of PowerPoint have proved to be surprisingly effective. Sound effects such as applause, which normally we would recommend you to avoid, make a communal quiz activity much more lively. Some whiteboard companies are keen to sell you voting gadgets, rather like TV remote controls. The application of these toys will inevitably narrow your use of the board in the direction of multiple choice, but they may be worth exploring.

- **Lessons given by the class**

  In the study of a work of literature, for instance, you may wish to divide the class into teams, each concentrating on a particular aspect of the piece. The lesson(s) conclude with each team teaching the whole class. The advantages of this approach are many. The technology makes these mini-lessons much more enjoyable; the whiteboard makes it possible for the whole class to participate (and you may wish to add to the teams' brief that they must ask questions and engage the class) and each team will have a powerful incentive to 'know its stuff' because failure to come to grips with the material will be embarrassing. You may wish to try the well-established Jigsaw technique here. There are a number of excellent websites devoted to it. Try typing 'jigsaw technique' (including the inverted commas) into a search engine, or simply visit www.jigsaw.org/index.html.

- **Whiteboards used to experiment and to focus discussion**

  You may wish to ask groups of pupils at the front of the class to experiment, to try things out in front of their peers, to discuss the outcomes (e.g. the Word Lab activities in English Online).

Teacher programs the whiteboard to drive the lesson, through a stream of information or a series of instructions

When computers first arrived in the classroom there was one problem. It has stayed with us ever since – there are never enough of them. Out of necessity, early users of computers for education used their imaginations and came up with novel solutions. One of the most successful was to make the computer act as an information source, dumped to a printer. Students simply picked up the latest bulletin and acted on that. The result was surprisingly powerful, as anyone who has experienced it will attest. With the advent of the interactive whiteboard, we can utilise again a single information source to drive a lesson. The board will act as a real-time bulletin board, much in the way that NASA's giant displays show the current status of a mission.

Let's see how it works in practice (Figure 7.7):

- Classroom organisation needs to be carefully thought through so that pupils have desk space to work at and the ability to see the screen.
- How will pupils access information from earlier in the lesson? Will it be printed?
- Who will write the script? Are there any scripts in existence? Is there software that will allow you to write your own for the interactive whiteboard?

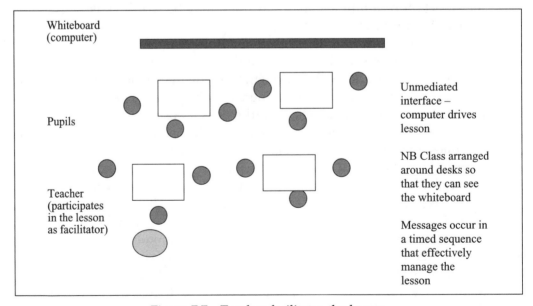

Figure 7.7   Teacher facilitates the lesson

- How will you manage movement around the class if things become excited?
- What rules will you apply for the information?
- How critical is the timing of the bulletins?
- What will be the practical outcomes of the lesson? In the past this technique was used to drive newspaper simulations and there were also experiments with crisis management and puzzle-solving scenarios (Hijack and Murder were favourites).

Ask the whiteboard manufacturers about some of these issues. Often you'll find that the whiteboard software can be adapted for your own purposes.

A whole new pedagogy is evolving in this area and new technologies to match:

- Tablets and wireless connections make it possible for whole classes to be involved with a whiteboard from where they are sitting.
- You will see a proliferation of voting devices. These may have a rather limited use in English.
- The Presenter, a device that combines the flexibility of the old Overhead Projector (OHP) with computer power and digital projector, can lead to some truly remarkable lessons. Children's handwritten class-work can be instantly showcased and discussed.

In conclusion, this is a fast-changing field in which technological change is accelerating – watch out for the innovations.

ICT can play a special role in your classroom, allowing you to prepare powerful lessons at home, enabling you to give your students a stimulating and dynamic learning environment, and allowing them to access highly motivating forms of learning and efficient ways of communicating with others. Its drawbacks are there as challenges to be overcome. The prizes are manifest for those who persist, who won't let small failures put them off, and who engage fully and creatively with the exciting new potential that ICT brings to the classrooms of the future.

8 Inclusion, special needs and differentiation

Leslea Markwick

> An inclusive school is a diverse problem-solving organisation with a common mission that emphasises learning for all students.
>
> (Rouse and Florian, 1997)

Inclusion in education involves the processes of increasing the participation of students in, and reducing their exclusion from, the cultures, curricula and communities of local schools.

Objectives

This chapter will explore:

- the Special Educational Needs (SEN) register and the different levels of special educational needs;
- a brief description of the role of the Special Educational Needs Coordinator (SENCO) within a school;
- catering for the needs of SEN students within the English lesson;
- differentiation;
- managing behaviour.

What does an SEN pupil look like?

Special Educational Needs can cover a huge range of needs from physical, to learning, to emotional, to behavioural, to English as a second language or a combination of all of these. There is no set profile for SEN pupils, so we need to treat each individually. When we think about SEN pupils, we often think of children who experience particular difficulties. However, we must also remember that gifted and able students have special educational needs as well. Teachers can meet the needs of the gifted and able pupil by offering personal support, targeting higher order questions, building in challenging open-ended tasks, and directing supplementary study outside the lesson. The QCA website provides guidance for catering for such students and suggests that schools appoint a gifted and talented coordinator who ideally should not be the Special Educational Needs Coordinator (www.QCA.org.uk/ca/inclusion/). For the majority of this chapter we will be focusing on SEN pupils whose main difficulties are with learning. The following list shows the range of special needs that can be found in a mainstream classroom:

- speech and language;
- Moderate Learning Difficulties (MLD);
- specific learning difficulties such as dyslexia;
- Emotional and Behavioural Difficulties (EBD);
- Asperger syndrome/autism – where the pupil will exhibit the 'triad' of impairment:
  - social behaviour, particularly interpersonal behaviour;
  - language and communication: delayed for both verbal and non-verbal;
  - thought and behaviour: rigid, lacks imagination, absence of 'pretend play' and obsessions with routine.

- hearing impairment;
- visual impairment;
- physical disability;
- gifted children.

Children with special educational needs should be identified as soon as possible after entering the school system, through Early Years Action. The triggers for intervention through Early Years Action could be the practitioner's or parent's concern about a child who, despite receiving appropriate early education experiences:

- makes little or no progress even when teaching approaches are particularly targeted to improve the child's identified area of weakness;

- continues working at levels significantly below those expected for children of a similar age in certain areas;
- presents persistent emotional and/or behavioural difficulties which are not ameliorated by the behaviour management techniques usually employed in the setting;
- has sensory or physical problems, and continues to make little or no progress despite the provision of personal aids and equipment;
- has communication and/or interaction difficulties, and requires specific individual interventions in order to access learning.

(SEN Code of Practice, DfES)

As part of Early Years Action, the SENCO and class teacher, with the consultation of parents, should collect information about the child and then decide on the action needed. The child is then placed on the SEN register which ensures that the individual needs of students are identified and met by the school, and records a student's learning difficulties and the level of support required to address these. Three levels of support are offered by schools:

- School Action (SA): schools monitor progress and implement support to work on identified targets. At this level support is provided solely by the school.
- School Action Plus (SA+): outside agencies are involved with setting up and implementing support within the school environment.
- Statement (ST): this is a legally binding document which sets out the provision required for a pupil and is reviewed annually.

The Special Educational Needs Coordinator takes day-to-day responsibility for coordinating the provisions within a school to raise the achievement of children with SEN. The SENCO should also provide professional guidance and support to colleagues who teach pupils with SEN.

In mainstream schools the key responsibilities of the SENCO may include:

- Overseeing the day-to-day operation of the school's SEN policy.
- Coordinating provision for children with special educational needs.
- Liaising with and advising fellow teachers.
- Managing learning support assistants.
- Overseeing the records of all children with special educational needs.
- Liaising with parents of children with special educational needs.
- Contributing to the in-service training of staff.
- Liaising with external agencies, including the LEA's support and educational psychology services, health and social services, and voluntary bodies.

(SEN Code of Practice, DfES)

Task 8.1: Observation task: meet with school SENCO and observe SEN students

Arrange to speak with the school SENCO to discuss the SEN pupils within the school and observe one or two students closely, for example in a range of lessons in one day. Prepare a one-page summary report on your observations for the SENCO's use and feedback your findings in an English Department meeting or in discussion with your mentor.

When students are on the register they must have an Individual Education Plan (IEP), which is written by the school with the consultation of parents, pupils and any other agency involved. As illustrated in Figure 8.1, an IEP will detail the strengths and weaknesses of the pupil, prioritise the main areas of concern, identify goals and set targets. An effective IEP will include strategies to match targets and share these with the whole school. Any member of staff coming into contact with the pupil should be aware of the IEP and the pupil's targets.

An IEP should include one or two short-term literacy objectives if pupils have difficulties related to language. It is helpful if these objectives are drawn from the Framework for Teaching English. Teachers should evaluate pupils' progress towards the expected outcomes regularly and check that the targets are sufficiently challenging and broken down into appropriately small steps. If necessary, targets can be taken from the primary Framework for Teaching. Some pupils may need time outside English lessons to work on the objectives, but they should also have many opportunities within English. Members of the English team should work closely with the SENCO to ensure that any additional support or particular intervention provided is identified within a pupil's IEP. The English team should also contribute to evaluating pupils' progress in relation to literacy-focused IEP targets.

You will find that the majority of SEN students in a mainstream school are on the register for learning difficulties. Literacy is the most common area for which support is required, especially in the English classroom. Students may experience a general learning difficulty where all aspects of literacy are problematic or have a specific learning difficulty such as dyslexia. Bearing this in mind, English teachers have a significant role to play when supporting SEN pupils.

Positive aspects of pupil's learning and behaviour	Child B likes to be involved in discussions and share his opinions. He likes to explore ideas thoroughly and responds well to high order questions.							

IEP Details	Start date: 05/09/03	Review date: 31/03/04	IEP responsibility:	SATS results:	KS	Eng.	Maths	Sc.
	External agency involvement:							

Priority elements	1 Concentration		2 On Task	
	3 Listening skills	4 Organisation	5 Work rate	

Specific PSS target(s) and strategy(ies)	**Focus all attention on set task** Set times for completion of task **Take file and planner to all classes** *All staff to recognise and reward effort to meet target*	**Child B** **DOB: 29/07/90**
Specific BS target(s) and provision	**Focus attention effectively on task for 20 mins** *In class support by the teacher and TA* **Listen attentively to peers before giving an opinion/ idea** *In class support by the teacher and TA* **Show work to teacher at agreed intervals during lesson** *In class support by the teacher and TA*	Plan:	Stage: SA+

Parental response : Pupil/parent IEP returned ☐ Phone call ☐ Meeting arranged (summary below) ☐
Need for new IEP agreed ☐

Parent contribution:

Parent signature:

Pupil contribution:

Pupil signature:

Meeting summary:

Pupil support team signature:

Figure 8.1 Individual education plan

They need to be aware that their lessons could possibly be the most problematic for SEN students if they are not managed well.

You will often find that younger pupils will have a go at reading and writing even if they find it difficult, but as pupils get older these problems can manifest themselves and create barriers to learning. Your job as a class teacher is to work with the SENCO and the pupil to help break down these barriers and provide access to the curriculum.

In an East Sussex school, as part of a recent school assembly, students and staff were asked to comment on their wishes and goals. One of the questions was 'What three things prevent you from achieving your goals?' A Year 8 SEN student replied, '(1) I am thick, (2) I am thick, (3) I am thick'. This student clearly has a very low self-esteem and needs plenty of nurturing and confidence building to help him to break through this barrier, and both his feelings and attitude towards learning will probably be fairly typical of students on the SEN register. Planning, differentiation and resources are vital to meeting SEN needs, but building confidence and raising self-esteem also have a crucial role to play.

The key to the inclusion of SEN students is to provide a safe environment where they can manage the work, are challenged academically, and are able to ask for help and make mistakes without the feeling of failure. The more you are aware of the students' needs, the more you will be able to address these

Task 8.2: Observation task: putting yourself in their shoes

Put yourself in the shoes of an SEN pupil by attempting the following:

1 Write a short letter with your left hand (or right if you are left-handed). This is what it is like for dyspraxic pupils when asked to write in your lesson.
2 Ask a colleague to guide you around an obstacle course blindfolded. The difficulty you will experience with coordination will be similar to pupils with coordination problems.
3 Read and understand the following text: *kaliMEra. MilAte angliKA. distiHOS, eGO miLO Mono LEEga enliniKA. Den piRAzee. Sas katalaVEno.* Did you understand it? It is a couple of sentences in Greek asking if you speak English. To many pupils with speech and language difficulties, this is what they experience when you present them with a text.
4 Look at the idioms in Figure 8.2 and follow them literally and see how confusing they appear. Idioms are used everyday, but for autistic pupils they add confusion and anxiety to an already very confusing world.

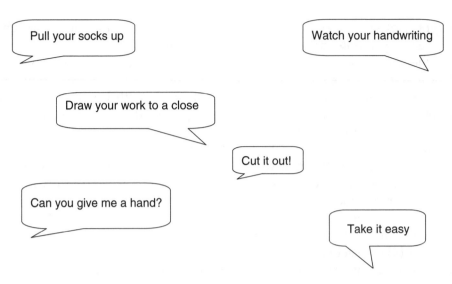

Figure 8.2   Examples of idioms

needs in your lessons. Take time to think what it must be like to be the SEN pupils in your class. Consider the SEN pupils within your class(es) and try to understand how they perceive themselves and how others perceive them. Many of these pupils, especially as they get older, have very low self-esteem. If you can imagine the nature and reality of their school experiences, you will be better able to make their time at school as positive and rewarding as possible.

The English lesson

As is explored in Chapter 2, literacy is the key to achievement in all subjects. During Key Stage 2, the literacy lesson combines teaching explicit skills for literacy with the study of literature. There are a number of literacy-based units within Key Stages 1 and 2 to help boost students working below the national average. At Key Stage 3, pupils' English lessons have a greater emphasis on literature to help teach the Framework's objectives, although literacy is increasingly taught in an explicit way and has also become a whole-school focus through the Key Stage 3 Strategy. Literacy Progress Units (LPUs) are available to help boost Year 7 who are working just below or just on level 4. LPUs consist of five units: phonics, spelling, reading for information, reading between the lines and writing organisation. LPUs are an additional support and, in most schools, are taught outside of the English lesson. Similarly, there are other booster and support programmes, either nationally advocated or individual to schools, which seek to promote students' whole-school literacy abilities.

Nevertheless, the job of the English teacher is at least partially to teach and develop literacy. In the majority of schools, you will be working with mixed ability classes of about 30 students, including those with low levels of literacy, educational behavioural disorders and other special educational needs. How are you going to cater for all their needs? Planning is crucial and is covered fully in Chapter 3. Having first identified your learning intention and outcome from the school scheme of work, you will need to design a learning task to meet this objective to ensure that every student in the class can access the learning. You will find that experienced teachers have a huge repertoire of resources and ideas to draw upon to engage all students in their learning. For Newly Qualified Teachers this may take time, and you should certainly expect to draw on the expertise of other teachers and the SENCO.

You need to be aware of the following challenges that SEN pupils will face in your lessons:

- Difficulty in accessing the reading materials you give out, including instructions.
- Difficulty with expressing ideas on paper.
- Short-term memory difficulties (for example, problems remembering what was learned in previous lessons or a long list of instructions).
- Short concentration span.
- Difficulty with verbal communication.
- Emotional and behaviour difficulties.
- Difficulty with comprehension.

When you are planning, you need to be aware of these difficulties and plan accordingly. You need to consider carefully the pace of your lesson and how you will differentiate the work.

Task 8.3: Observation task: observe teacher managing SEN students

By prior arrangement with a member of the English Department, observe a class which contains SEN students and make notes on the ways the teacher manages the student and has arranged the lesson, seating, support and resources to maximise the student's access to and engagement in the lesson.

Differentiation

'Schools have a responsibility to provide a broad and balanced curriculum for all pupils' (National Curriculum). The National Curriculum is the starting point for planning a school curriculum that meets the specific needs of individuals and groups of pupils. In the National Curriculum document and its website you will find a section on this statutory inclusion statement and ways to provide effective learning opportunities. It sets out three principles:

> A Setting suitable learning challenges.
> B Responding to pupils' diverse learning needs.
> C Overcoming potential barriers to learning and assessment for individuals and groups of pupils.
>
> www.qca.org.uk/ca/inclusion

In relation to the third principle, the National Curriculum states that in many cases, the action necessary to respond to an SEN pupil's requirements for the curriculum access will be met through greater differentiation of tasks and materials. The advantages of designing and delivering differentiated lessons are summarised here:

> Differentiating instruction means creating multiple paths so that students of different abilities, interest or learning needs experience equally appropriate ways to absorb, use, develop and present concepts as a part of the daily learning process. It allows students to take greater responsibility and ownership for their own learning, and provides opportunities for peer teaching and cooperative learning.
>
> (Theroux, 2002)

Differentiation does not necessarily mean working on different tasks. SEN pupils can work on the same or similar tasks as the rest of the class by talking to their friends, as well as with the teacher or assistant. Never underestimate the influence of conversations with pupils of differing abilities. Differentiation can be simply, but effectively, by intervention through very subtle use of praise and comment, through teachers addressing pupils directly and low-level additional help given at the beginning and during a task.

Differentiation can take the following forms:

- differentiating the content/topic;
- differentiating the process/activities, e.g. some more able students would miss out the acquiring stage and go onto extension tasks (compacting the curriculum);
- differentiating the product (outcome);
- differentiation tier by tier;
- differentiating by manipulating the environment or through accommodating individual learning styles, e.g. using laptops, computers, recording in different ways, visual resources.

Planning and preparation is vital to a good lesson but it is also very time-consuming, so you need to find a manageable way of working. If you try to set three different tasks in every lesson to match three levels of ability within your group, it could become unmanageable. Consider the best way of differentiating your lessons to match the objective. For many tasks in English it is perfectly legitimate to use differentiation by outcome. The same piece of writing can be developed on a number of different levels according to the pupil's ability. However, do not rely on this for every lesson. There will be times when you will have to set a different task or adapt the task, but be aware that sometimes 'differentiation by task' can mean students being excluded within their own classroom.

Start your planning by choosing a learning task that will suit the majority of the pupils in your class, i.e. the middle ability pupils.

1   Ask yourself how you can adapt it for the more able and less able.
2   It may be that you just need to provide support in the shape of resources, i.e. a writing frame (see Figure 8.3), vocabulary book, word bank, mind maps, the use of a PC or tape-recorder to record ideas.
3   It may be that support can be offered in the shape of an adult working with an individual or small group; this may be yourself or the Teaching Assistant (TA).
4   If you have a TA in your lesson plan, decide how you are going to use her or him. Plan the use of the TA for the whole lesson, not just the main activity. (Table 8.1 provides a sample lesson plan with clear directions for the TA throughout the lesson and Figure 8.3 illustrates a writing frame to support SEN students.)

Discussion genre

Some people think that

Because

They argue that

Another group who agree with this point of view are ....

They say that

On the other hand ....….......... disagree with the idea that

....…..............................

They claim that

They also say

My opinion is

Because

Figure 8.3　Example of a writing frame

Using learning support staff effectively

The key to success when working with support staff is the relationship between the TA and the class teacher, which enables both to feel comfortable, confident and able to work flexibly within the classroom. If you have a TA working alongside you, shared and thorough planning should facilitate additional support not only for those students with recognised SEN, but for all the members of the class. In particular, TAs are a very good support for the starter and introduction of a lesson if planned well, which sets up a strong and positive learning dynamic to build on. Table 8.1 is a sample lesson plan showing the deployment of a TA. Note that TAs should always be given specific tasks to do, which can range from simple support at a low level of intervention, such as sitting with a student and writing down instructions as they are given for later reference, to more complex activities, such as translating for EAL students.

The benefits of additional support for the pupil and teacher are:

- additional explanation of vocabulary and tasks set;
- keeping a pupil on 'task';
- opportunities for pupils to articulate their thoughts and establish an understanding of tasks;
- preparation of additional resources (as and when necessary);
- continuity for pupils, especially where the one teacher may only see them once a week and the support staff may work with them on several occasions during the week;
- opportunities for follow-up on the teacher's behalf;
- use of various teaching methods: formal / group / individual / technical / practical;
- support in assessment procedures and supervision of practical work within the classroom;
- additional support in the completion and monitoring of homework;
- use of homework support sessions as necessary;
- opportunities to share ideas and understanding.

(Exhall Grange and Southam Technology College, December 2001)

Resources

Students with SEN, low literacy levels and poor concentration are often motivated by the use of a wide range of resources. While it would be a mistake to move too often and too swiftly from one activity and one resource to the next,

Table 8.1 A lesson plan showing the deployment of a Teaching Assistant

	LESSON 1
Whole class, word/ sentence level	**To spell two-syllable words containing double consonants, e.g. bubble, kettle, common.** Ask pairs to find as many two-syllable words with double consonants. They may use a dictionary. Share as a class and discuss spelling strategies. Each pair writes their words on a graffiti sheet. Class challenge to fill up the graffiti sheet by the end of the week. *TA to sit with student with speech and language difficulties.*
Learning intention Whole class, shared text	**To develop personal responses to a fictional text.** Read *The Daydreamer* by Ian McEwan. Each student to have a copy of the text. Use confident readers to help with the reading. *TA to sit with SEN pupil(s) to help them follow the text.* Discuss the main character with the students and how he manages the situation with the bully. *TA quietly discusses the main storyline with the SEN pupil during this time.*
Independent activities	Refer to the learning outcome, which is to make a personal response to the story. Share with the group expectations of what should be included. Students then complete a short review. Support – use writing frame or ICT. Extension – encourage use of paragraphs and a comparison to another story by the same author or a different author.
Teacher's focus	Guided writing – work with a small group of more able students to develop their personal responses and begin to make a comparisons to another story.
Other adult/TA	*Work with a small group, including the SEN student or students. Use an enlarged copy of the writing frame and guide the students through it. Provide support with spellings and sentence structure.*
Plenary	Pass an object around the room to music. When the music stops, ask the student holding the object to share a piece of their work. Provide instant feedback and then play the music to select another student. Repeat. *TA to work with SEN student to model concentration and listening skills.*

a selection of teaching aids used thoughtfully to enhance learning in different parts of a lesson can foster higher attention levels. Paper resources, such as the thinking frame in Figure 8.4, interactive whiteboards, video clips, audio cassettes, digital cameras and visual props, all have their place. Mini-whiteboards are also an excellent resource within the English lesson, as they enable every student to participate at the same time. They can be used effectively to deliver lesson starters, especially if used alongside open questions which encourage a longer or a more diverse answer, rather than a short right or wrong answer,

Name:	Date:

Personal response to *The Daydreamer*
By Ian McEwan

What was the story about?

These words may help you:
bully   victim   pain   hide   telling others
humiliate   stand up to   block things out   disappear

What was Peter's strategy for dealing with bullying and how successful was it?

Peter turned the tables on Barry and made him feel humiliated. Do you think this is right and why?

Why do you think Peter wrote Barry the note at the end?

Do you think this story is useful for people being bullied or the bullies themselves? Explain your view.

Figure 8.4   Example of a thinking frame

and therefore allow more thinking time (and more chance of success) to students who need it. For example, a simple starter might be to give the pupils two minutes to find as many synonyms for 'said' as they can and write them on their mini-boards. In this activity, every student can work to his or her own ability. The speed of the activity gives students little time to worry about hand-writing and presentation, and a TA could be used effectively here, sitting next to an SEN pupil with speech and language difficulty to ensure that the pupil participates and succeeds along with all the others. Mini-whiteboards can be a good motivational resource to be used in the main part of the lesson. Students who lack confidence and find it difficult to write anything down without making a mistake find whiteboards easier to use as they can write down their ideas and erase parts easily without feeling they have ruined their work. This encourages them to see writing as a process rather than worrying about the finished product.

Task 8.4: Planning task: plan a starter and plenary

Plan and deliver a starter and plenary to a lesson that enables every pupil within the class to participate. You may want to think about the resources available and the use of open questions.

Tracking back through key objectives

For some pupils who are working at a significantly lower level than the rest of the class, teachers have to track back through the key objectives of the literacy framework. Often, teachers find that age-related text-level objectives from the Literacy Strategy can be made accessible to all pupils with the aid of differentiation. However, word and sentence level objectives may be more problematic for SEN pupils as it is difficult to progress further until the pupil has a sound understanding of what has been taught before. For example, if a pupil has difficulty writing in simple sentences, he or she will not be able to develop complex sentences. Therefore, the teacher will need to identify the level the pupil is working at, or the corresponding year in the Literacy Strategy, and track back to the relevant objectives. Again, this is where a TA can play a vital role; if the TA is fully aware of the level the pupil is working at, he or she can adapt the word and sentence starter to meet the needs of the individual. Ideally, the TA should be involved in the tracking back and have access to the class planning.

Task **8.5**: Theory task: tracking back through the objectives

Obtain a copy of the Key Stage 1, Key Stage 2 or Key Stage 3 Literacy Framework. Find a word or sentence level objective that you will be teaching and track back to find the objective or objectives that are taught before as a foundation. Use this knowledge to assist your planning.

Working with pupils with Emotional and Behavioural Difficulties

All teachers, both newly qualified and more experienced, find pupils with behavioural and emotional difficulties challenging and wearing. What we must remember is that these pupils' needs should be treated with the same care as pupils with other educational needs. We would not show our frustration or lose our temper when a student has misspelt a word or has not understood the instructions, because we know that would not be productive or help the student to understand what he/she has done wrong. Similarly, we should not resort to losing our temper and shouting at students who behave badly in our lessons. The challenge of working with EBD students is to understand the students' needs and the triggers to poor behaviour.

Poor responses in class are very often a reaction to or a symptom of some other problem. Often such behaviour is linked to learning and self-esteem. If the work is pitched too low, students become demotivated and disaffected. If it is too difficult, they will not want to attempt it because they will be afraid of failure and a public recognition of this. Therefore, many students with SEN will do what ever it takes to avoid the work. EBD students are often very good at avoidance strategies, especially by the time they reach Key Stage 3. As the class teacher you need to be aware of this, and plan activities and provide support to ensure the student can access the work without feeling patronised because the work is too easy. This is a tricky task but essential if you are going to avoid the learning-based triggers to the challenging behaviour. The more you understand the EBD pupil, the easier the task of teaching them becomes. If you have an EBD student in your class, it is essential to talk to the SENCO and any other members of staff working with the pupil. Ask them for strategies that work. Many schools will have systems for sharing strategies and these students may be discussed at regular pastoral or departmental meetings. If you find this information is not available, you could use the ABC approach to behaviour change. First, you keep a record of behaviour patterns using the following format:

Antecedents: what happens before (i.e. what is the trigger and how does it build up)?

Background: where and when does it happen, how long does it last, does it happen at certain times and does it happen with certain people?

Consequences: what happens afterwards (i.e. what is the pay-off)?

It is the adults' responsibility to help change behaviour. Once you have gathered information, you can support the pupil to change the behaviour by changing the antecedents – take away or alleviate the triggers. Look closely at the background to see if you can remove temptation or change the setting, etc. There are several ways of altering the consequence so that undesirable behaviour doesn't pay.

It is important when trying to change behaviour that the teacher models appropriate responses and for the pupil to be given the opportunity to recognise his or her own good behaviour. It is easy sometimes only to notice students' poor behaviour, but we should try to give more attention when the pupil's response is appropriate, through praise which tells pupils that the adult is pleased with their behaviour and gives them attention for behaving well instead of badly. Give praise immediately after the behaviour you want to encourage and be specific; don't just say 'well done'. Instead, say what exactly they did which was good. 'You came into the room very calmly and sensibly then, and now you're showing me you are ready to learn.' Always reward good behaviour in some way, although remember that attention is a powerful reward and may be enough on its own. When it's not, a reward system that leads to concrete rewards, even if used for a short-term period, can promote positive engagement. Involve the student with the setting up of the reward system and choice of reward; this way they will be more motivated to succeed.

Many teachers share some concerns about providing rewards for students who display challenging behaviour as they feel this could give confusing messages to the other pupils in the class or seem unfair to those pupils that behave very well all the time. To overcome this uneasiness you could create a reward system where the EBD pupil works towards a reward for the whole class. This often results in the whole class working to support the pupil and the pupil feeling included rather than excluded. However, if you want to create a reward for the pupil alone, don't feel guilty or bad for the other pupils; we reward pupils' good work everyday to promote engagement and effort in learning, and feel very comfortable with it. There is no reason why rewards shouldn't be similarly used to promote good learning behaviour and bolster students' self-esteem.

If you find a strategy that works (although we must remember that a strategy that works one day may not work every day), share it with other members of staff because probably the most important factor when trying to manage difficult behaviour is the united approach. For further reading on managing behaviour within your classroom, Bill Rogers, a teacher by profession who now lectures on discipline and behaviour management issues, provides a very clear ethos and attitude towards behaviour and gives some very sound advice and strategies to use. He is well known for his commitment to a skills-based approach to discipline and encouraging pupils to take responsibility for their behaviour. See the Further reading list for more details.

Many pupils with Emotional and Behavioural Difficulties have poor literacy skills as a result of their inability to maintain concentration and persevere with tasks. For pupils who have difficulties in concentrating, the four-part lesson structure outlined in the Literacy Strategy provides pace and routine, and opportunities to reinforce learning, offer praise and vary activities. Teachers should invest time in establishing routines of work in the lesson, particularly at the transition between one activity and another. Plenaries at the end of the lesson can be used to review and reward behaviour as well as work.

Pupils with communication difficulties face particular challenges in literacy. Teachers need to provide opportunities for pupils to make progress through clear, effective teaching, which builds confidence and participation. Pupils who have autistic spectrum disorders (ASD) require well-structured lessons with clear routines with predictable parts. There are many very useful reference books available on working with pupils with ASD (see the Further reading list) but two maxims will help to keep you going:

- keep instructions and explanations clear and simple;
- avoid anxieties by making the teaching explicit and ensuring that challenges are direct and well focused.

Often there is confusion between poor behaviour and aspects of the child's special needs and so, as we have mentioned, it is essential to understand these as fully as possible.

The National Curriculum, through its inclusion statement, gives the following examples for managing behaviour and emotions:

- setting realistic demands and stating them explicitly;
- using positive behaviour management, including a clear structure of rewards and sanctions;
- giving pupils every chance and encouragement to develop the skills they need to work well with a partner or a group;
- providing positive feedback to reinforce and encourage learning and build self-esteem;
- selecting tasks and materials sensitively to avoid unnecessary stress for the pupil;

- creating a supportive learning environment in which the pupil feels safe and is able to engage with learning;
- allowing time for the pupil to engage with learning and gradually increasing the range of activities and demands.

Diversity should not be viewed as a problem to be overcome, but as a rich resource to support the learning of all. For example, a popular Year 8 SEN boy who displays attention-seeking behaviour and can be a disruptive influence within the class, wrote a poem after being inspired by the poet John Hegley. His poem was entitled 'I need you like. . . .' and revealed the sensitive side to his personality (see below). He dedicated it to the TA who works closely with him and with whom he has built up a very positive relationship. He was extremely proud of his work and it won a place in the school's weekly newsletter, as well as being published on the official John Hegley website. This open display of sensitivity and enthusiasm helped to engage other boys within the class who may have previously considered it very uncool to write poetry and to express their emotions so publicly. In a well-organised and managed classroom, SEN pupils can make progress both academically and emotionally and offer ideas and inspiration to others.

I need you like a joke needs a clown
I need you like a man needs a frown
I need you like a human needs a home
I need you like a baby needs a clone
I need you like a gnome needs a garden
I need you like every one needs a pardon
I need you like maths needs a school
I need you like people need to be cool
I need you like a car needs some wheels
I need you like dodgy people need a deal
I need you like peace needs a dove
I need you like kids needs lots of love

Aaron, Year 8

Further reading

Attwood, Tony (1993) *Why does Chris do that?*, The National Autistic Society, London.
Grandin, Temple (1996) *Thinking in Pictures*, Vintage Books, New York.

Jackson, Luke (2002) *Freaks, Geeks and Asperger Syndrome*, Jessica Kingsley, London.

Rogers, Bill (1988) *Classroom Behaviour*, Paul Chapman, London.

Rogers, Bill (1995) *Behaviour Management – A Whole School Approach*, Paul Chapman, London.

Taylor, Shirley (2001) *Gifted and Talented Children – A Planning Guide*, Jessica Kingsley, London.

Wing, Lorna (1998) *The Autistic Spectrum: A Guide for Parents and Professionals*, Constable, London.

9 Professionalism and accountability

Andrew Goodwyn

Throughout this book you will find many references to 'the profession' and 'standards', the latter being a level of competence which trainees must reach to enter the profession of teaching. Subsequently, the Newly Qualified Teacher (see Chapter 11) must succeed against a further and more demanding set of NQT standards. Reaching those standards is chiefly the trainee's responsibility, but she or he will also have the support of many other professionals whose judgements will determine whether the trainee's and NQT's progress and performance are reaching the required level. However, these standards are very literal. They are written down and have the status of being part of a national system linked to a legal framework. Much of the time when people talk about standards – usually the media spreading some story about 'how standards are falling' – they are referring to something rather more elusive, but also more fundamental. In this more general sense, people are alluding to some idea about what is essentially right and proper, principally, in the way that people should conduct themselves.

This chapter is more concerned with the concept of standards and the notion of being a 'professional'. So the 'Standards for Initial Teacher Training' and the subsequent NQT Standards inevitably use the term 'professional' very frequently, but they never actually define it. This is revealing in that the anonymous authors therefore imply that their readers will know what they mean. Perhaps it is useful here to consider that the term is applied to 'professional footballers' and 'professional musicians' and in this context it often means no more than that the professional is making a living from their skills, as distinct from the 'pure amateur'. Indeed, both of these groups can also be described as 'semi-professional' – i.e., they are paid, but not enough to make a living. A teacher working part-time will never be described as 'semi-professional'. If they were, it would imply that they were not a 'true' professional and therefore would be suspect. It really is vital, then, for the beginning teacher to have a clear understanding of much more than a set of neat standards in a handbook. Joining the teaching profession provides the new teacher with both status and responsibility, and it is important to stress how demanding this is for every individual, especially, perhaps, because the debate about the exact status of teaching will always be with us. For example, are teachers comparable to doctors or lawyers, often considered 'top professions'?

All teachers working in the maintained sector are joining the profession and one principle of this notion is that therefore they are all equally professional. However, as often stated in this book, English teachers can be considered to be very much in the front line of their profession. This is because they principally deal with subject matter which in itself is confusingly implicated in other ideas of standards such as spelling and literacy, and even the very use of language itself. The popular press never tires of claiming that young people can no longer spell, write or read anything correctly. Unfortunately, we cannot merely dismiss these claims, because they do affect the public consciousness. It is a common moment for an English teacher to have to justify to a parent how they have marked a piece of work or why they are teaching a particular (usually contemporary) novel. Mathematics teachers certainly encounter such challenges far less. Therefore, English teachers, who teach a compulsory subject imbued with national importance, really need to feel confident that they understand the concept of professionalism as it applies to both teaching and their subject. This chapter will therefore explore the concept of the professions and the professional, and will use exemplar which anchor this exploration within the context of English teaching.

The term 'professional'

As indicated above, the term 'professional' has its own debates and the Further reading section at the end of this chapter provides references to much more detailed discussions and analyses. There is a reasonable consensus that professions are typically characterised by a specialist body of knowledge, some initial training without which one cannot practise, defined codes of conduct that are either self- or externally regulated and with a degree of expectation that professionals keep up-to-date. Finally, and especially complex for teachers, professions are client-oriented and therefore bring a duty of care and a form of service ethic. This latter point is neatly illustrated by the way that teachers frequently complain about their relatively low pay, but explain that they are not 'in it for the money'.

Given the above criteria, teaching certainly is a profession, especially if compared to another term – that of a 'worker', someone merely employed to 'do a job'. However, teaching was recently demoted from being a first- to a second-tier profession (on the national census database) because it is now so highly regulated and controlled that it has lost its claim to being a relatively autonomous profession. The introduction of the General Teaching Council (GTC) may, in the long term, restore some of this self-regulation and autonomy. The General Medical Council certainly has enormous status, and respect built up over decades. If a profession is to gain such status, it must also engender a high degree of trust from its clients who give it the power to be self-regulating. Does the public trust teachers? To an extent it does, but perhaps politicians do not. Over the last 15 years education has experienced a number of very high profile interventions that a beginning teacher may simply take for granted, but that would be a fundamental mistake and a few examples will illustrate this point.

The National Curriculum only came into being in 1989; before that, Local Education Authorities and schools had far more power over curriculum design. Whatever the virtues of the National Curriculum, it means that teachers of the past were more skilled at curriculum design and more creative in their daily work, implying that the public then trusted teachers to be experts in curriculum design. The National Curriculum is unlikely to go away, but the degree of influence of teachers and of their own professional bodies such as The National Association for the Teaching of English (NATE) could be much greater and more locally contextualised; this would make teachers more professional, not less so.

Ofsted was introduced in 1992, replacing the much respected system of Her Majesty's Inspectors. The role of Ofsted will always attract controversy, principally because it is still seen by many teachers as a form of policing as opposed to a valuable form of accountability. For many teachers, it is the conduct of Ofsted much more than the actual principle of external inspection that is the issue. Again, an external agency charged with guaranteeing standards of teaching and learning should be a part of education; the public and parents in particular have a right to know how and what teachers do. However, a matrix of examination league tables, high stakes testing, negative inspections and the more recent introduction of performance management have combined to create a great deal of dissatisfaction among teachers, of which Ofsted is the primary dislike. The new Inspection Framework (2003) does appear to be much more dialogic, giving schools far more influence through their self-evaluations than in the past. However, the perception of Ofsted as being targeted against teachers rather than being there to help them improve will take many years to shift.

The new Ofsted Framework is one sign that teachers' professionalism is being revived, in a sense. The idea that teachers should just deliver curricula has made them sound more like workers than professionals and this demotivating terminology has, to some extent, been recognised as such by government and other bodies. This potential improvement can be coupled with the increasing evidence that many teachers are leaving after only a few years, literally because they find much of the current accountability framework to be oppressive. This is where the establishment of the GTC may lead to greater self-regulation and a return to a more trusted and autonomous teaching profession.

Overall, then, teachers' work over the last decade has been made increasingly accountable but also more controlled and restricted. More recently, the damaging effect of this oppressive framework has been recognised and a number of measures suggest a return to more teacher autonomy and professional integrity. This will be discussed further below in relation to the role of teaching assistants.

Teachers' specialised knowledge

But what of the specialised body of knowledge that teachers possess? Can it really be compared to medical or legal knowledge? The answer is 'yes and no'. What is consistent about professionals is that they develop an expertise, something that they can continually improve, which comes about through a combination of experience and reflection, often aided by further training. There is much debate about what teachers actually know about teaching and learning, but it seems more accurate to consider that this knowledge is closer to the understanding of the artist rather than the scientist. In many ways, being a teacher has comparisons with other performance professions such as actors, dancers and musicians, in that the majority of their effective work happens in real time with the equivalent of an audience. Doctors and lawyers typically work one-to-one, although some forms of law do involve courtroom performance. A good metaphor for the teacher may be the conductor. The teacher has a plan and finite resources but cannot ultimately predict every note that each musician (pupil) will produce. A good teacher knows the subject they are teaching, but, even more importantly, knows how to teach it. This can be called 'subject pedagogical knowledge'. This, it is argued, is what makes teaching a distinct profession.

Where is this body of distinctive knowledge? Some of it has been described in ways that mean it can be written down (such as this book) and to some extent learnt, so it is in books and articles from the purely practical to the highly theoretical. But a great deal of knowledge exists in teachers' heads and one reason why teachers so often seem to emphasise the practical is that they feel that is how they have learnt their craft. This can lead them to be dismissive of theory and new fangled ideas. For the beginning teacher, this is not very helpful. How can you learn about teaching if the only real way is through 'doing it'? Also, how can you claim to be a professional if you cannot helpfully describe what you do? Again, it is important to think of how highly developed professional language is in some domains. This language may be off-putting to the non-specialist, but it allows the professionals to communicate in an exact and powerful way. Teaching has very little specialised vocabulary and in this sense it can be argued that teaching remains only a semi-profession.

Teachers, when considering these issues, are likely to argue that their expertise is very real indeed and beginning teachers, struggling to learn their craft, are going to agree. Donald Schön famously characterised the best professionals, including teachers, as 'reflective'. This conceptualisation has been hugely influential. He argues that real expertise is demonstrated in the way that the true professional continually learns from experience, and adapts techniques and methods to improve practice. This is a very attractive notion. However, another mark of the best professions is that they expect and may require their members to seek further professional development (see Chapter 11). It is still the case that very few teachers undertake long-term professional development beyond their initial training, and the profession does not require it. Perhaps the introduction of new roles such as the Advanced Skills teacher hint at other ways to identify and promote professional expertise by generating role models within the teaching force. The introduction of the Fast Track may also add prestige and status to the profession overall.

One reason why teaching does not compare well with professions like law or accountancy or architecture is that it is one of the caring professions. These three professions have a duty to their clients but once the particular contract is completed the relationship is over. 'Caring' sounds like something you either do or don't do, or equally you are a caring person or you are not. In this sense the term 'caring' is somewhat misleading. A great deal of teaching is driven by values and attention to society's values is explicitly part of the job of the trainee and the qualified teacher. Teachers will tell you that much of their motivation comes from their contact with young people and their aspirations for them. Despite the cynics in every staff room, teaching is a truly optimistic profession. However, just like nurses and social workers, an attitude of caring should not be mistaken for sentimentality. Professionalism also requires a degree of toughness and objectivity. This is a form of knowledge as well as an attitude. Good teachers have extensive understanding of the way pupils tend to think and behave. As professionals, they use this knowledge to make quick and effective decisions. What Schön suggests (1983) is that they immediately notice when these generalisations are not working in a specific situation and this brings out their ability to pause and reflect, leading on to a new strategy or approach.

Ultimately, a teacher's professionalism is based much more on knowledge than on some woolly notion of being nice. Having both sympathy and empathy for pupils is important, but it must be a means to insight. This is especially important in a subject like English which is a domain where the personal and issues of identity are in the foreground. English teachers, compared to most subject teachers, have a considerable amount of time with each of their classes. Their pupils regularly talk and write about their actual experiences and English teachers are genuinely interested in their personal reading and viewing habits. In this sense, English teachers can be considered especially close to their pupils. Trainees and NQTs find this proximity part of the excitement of becoming a teacher, but it should come with a health warning. A professional must have high expectations of all pupils equally and needs to preserve a degree of detachment or distance as part of their mode of working. An element in this does relate to health and well-being. In order to give your best, you really need to conserve energy and emotional integrity; being overly vulnerable is not in your own or your pupils' best interests, especially because a teacher has so many roles to operate in any day.

Even social workers and nurses, who are comparable in other ways to teachers, do not operate with such large numbers of clients or have anything like the diversity of roles that the teacher employs on a daily basis. The teacher, for example, has pastoral duties, is *in loco parentis* to all pupils in the school and has a highly specialist function to perform with a range of sets of pupils. It is in the way the teacher carries out these diverse roles that their true professionalism can be demonstrated. This diversity and complexity is unquestionably part of what makes learning to teach so demanding.

Developing a professional approach

There is no question that trainees are constantly evaluated for their professionalism and that these judgements go beyond the specific statements in the Standards. As mentioned earlier, this relates essentially to how each trainee conducts their work in and out of school, with pupils, parents and colleagues.

As teaching is such a public activity, it is inevitable that appearance is a factor. The great majority of schools place insistent demands on pupils to follow a strict dress code. For teachers, there may be nothing written down but this does not reduce the association between professional appearance and professional conduct. Beginning teachers can only help the way they make a positive impression by being scrupulous about fitting in with the school's expectations about dress. If this sounds like a kind of conformity, it is because that is exactly what it is; trainees' individualism is best defined through the excellence of their ideas about teaching.

It is also true to say that no two schools are exactly alike and that each one has a culture of its own. Trainees need to be sensitive to this culture which will include, for example, non-explicit rules about the exact degree of formality in teachers' dress and in the way staff and pupils address each other.

Working relationships

A trainee's first impression is likely to be that getting the right relationship with her or his classes is the absolute key to a successful bid to reach the Standards. However, a careful read of those very Standards will reveal that this is one major domain but not the only one. Paradoxically, teachers spend a great deal of their professional time in front of many pupils but curiously on their own, although this isolationist role is rapidly changing especially with the increase in TAs (see below). This paradox actually highlights how vital professional time is when spent with other teachers, whether formally or informally. It is worth noting here that the combination in the past of teacher isolationism in their own classrooms and the little time devoted by schools to bringing teachers into productive working groups has been one hindrance to making teachers' specialist knowledge explicit and available to others; this is changing but has a long way to go.

The key point for the trainee is that there is nothing more vital than a colleague's time, and that developing effective working relationships with colleagues actually is as important as classroom relationships. It is helpful, if a little humbling, to remember that to the host school the trainee is typically one of many trainees encountered over the years. In other words, you have a short time in which to fit in with their established working practices and methods; they do not have an equivalent time to fit in with you. This is in no way to suggest that trainees do not have entitlements – they do. The greatest step forward for trainees over the last decade has been the establishment of partnerships between schools and training organisations, and the development of trained mentors in schools. Here the level of professional attention to trainees' needs has improved enormously, and the nature of roles and responsibilities is now clearly defined.

One key relationship is thus with the subject mentor in each school. This mentor will be a member of various in-school teams, as will the trainee. It is vital for the trainee to belong to the appropriate school groups and to recognise that they can learn an enormous amount from their membership, and also that they can contribute. Effective teams value new and fresh perspectives. The trainee can act initially as a kind of intelligent stranger by asking the kinds of questions that help the group members to reflect on their thinking and their ways of doing things. As the trainees really become part of a team, they can demonstrate their professionalism by volunteering to go beyond just being there and by seeking to assist the busy team in positive ways.

Trainees need to develop insights into how schools establish and maintain their various groupings. Typically, there will be academic and pastoral groupings, as well as meetings of whole-school staff, senior management, governors and so on, and then more specific working groups perhaps charged with a particular development, such as whole-school literacy or improving target setting etc. In consultation with their mentors, trainees need to identify which groups they belong to and must work with, and which others might be of benefit to their development.

Such identification adds another dimension to the trainee's professionalism – i.e. time management. The public can still perceive teachers as benefiting from short days and long holidays, but a few days in a school will banish that notion for good. Because teachers do all their teaching within a relatively short, intense day, they have to do everything else outside that time and once again this makes time the most precious commodity. Trainees will have to balance their enthusiasm to join in with as many working groups as possible with their need to be a genuine and effective member of only some key groups.

School working groups are often convened to develop or revise a school policy. Over several years schools will have a number of policies at different stages of development, but the majority will be present simply as part of the school's life. These can be very simple and comprehensible, such as policy on uniform, and this may exist as a set of rules. However, it may be a policy on literacy across the curriculum which sets out different levels and types of responsibility and which has yet to be fully implemented by all staff. Trainees need to exercise diplomacy and professional judgement in interpreting the latter kind of policy. Many policies are essentially local versions of national ones and trainees should be introduced to these and helped to understand exactly how they should be applied. Each school will have a policy on discipline and sanctions, and trainees need to be extremely clear on actual procedures as they are almost bound to need its support in their everyday teaching. Finally, all schools are required to have development plans which they revise annually. For most trainees such plans will feel quite remote from their work, but they need to develop a professional understanding of their presence and value. Equally, trainees should be familiar with the school's most recent Ofsted report and especially with the section on English. If the report was critical, they need to know how the school and the department has developed an action plan to respond to the criticisms.

Another seemingly remote part of school life is the governing body. In fact, governors have very real power and influence, and trainees should be very clear about how each school manages their contributions to policies and decision-making. All governing bodies have a teacher–governor who may be an ideal person to talk to about how governing bodies work.

Teaching Assistants

As mentioned above, teaching used to be a relatively isolated activity, but one reason why it is increasingly less so is the rapid increase in the number of teaching assistants. Before discussing the practical implications of this change, it is important to consider some matters of principle.

Primary schools, in particular, have a long tradition of having helpers in the classroom. Typically, these were simply parents willing to muck in and help at a fairly menial level. Since the changes occurred to legislation concerning Special Needs pupils, a number of individual pupils with statements became entitled to adult support. This change led to the evolution of paid specialist assistants who were also trained to varying levels of expertise. Essentially, then, these assistants can be described as 'para-professionals'; they are not trained to teach, but they are developing specialist professional knowledge. Over the last few years a new, more general role of Teaching Assistant has become popular and government policy will lead to a very considerable expansion of this workforce, including, as it will, different levels of TAs such as Higher Level Teaching Assistants. Various professional bodies, and notably the teacher unions, have mixed feelings about this development. They recognise the support that such skilled adults can bring to the teacher's aid, but have some suspicions that this is the government's way of getting extra teachers on the cheap and threatening the very status of the profession as a whole. How do these TAs fit the criteria of a true professional? Trainees need to be aware that the rapid expansion of the TA workforce has implications for the professionalism of teachers in general and that there is a degree of controversy attached.

At a very practical level, however, trainees are now faced with a complex challenge. As well as learning to manage classes of pupils, they also have to manage additional adults. From the point of view of the Standards for QTS, this is a requirement. More fundamentally, these additional adults become part of the working team for each class or even just for one individual lesson in the week. The trainee may have to plan a lesson involving a pupil with SEN who has an attached TA, bearing in mind that there is another TA there to support the whole class. The latter TA may be highly experienced and trained, or new and quite uncertain about how to be effective. The key is to try to know as much as possible about the TAs themselves and about how the deployment of TAs is managed in the school and/or department. There may be other adults also who, under the new working agreement, have support roles outside the classroom, for example organising resources and photocopying, undertaking administrative tasks and so on. These various changes are ongoing and trainees will need to be alert as to how each school is adjusting to the new environment in which para-professionals will increasingly play a significant role.

Informal learning and out-of-after-school activities

Schools in Britain have a long tradition of extra-curricular activities and many teachers join the profession with fond memories of clubs, school plays and musicals, sports and trips – even foreign travel – all organised through their school when they were pupils. These fond memories are useful as long as the nostalgia does not mask the reality of actually organising a club or a school trip. The Standards expect trainees to gain some insight into and experience of these extra-curricular opportunities and there should be no real shortage of opportunities to do this.

English is a subject area with its own longstanding traditions in this area. Taking pupils to the theatre or the cinema, to attend a poetry reading, or to visit a bookshop where a celebrity author is speaking are all very typical activities and enrich children's experiences of language and literature. Similarly, many of these events can be organised in school as special events highlighting pupils' own poetry or drama. English Departments are regularly involved in the school's productions, producing the school magazine and so on. Teachers will usually say that they especially enjoy the opportunity to work with pupils in a more informal way, often seeing a different side to the pupils, as indeed so do the pupils see of them. It can all be great fun, but it does carry with it extra work and responsibilities, and worst case scenarios do happen. The simple theatre trip involves the very real challenge of getting the tickets, the money from the pupils, making sure the coach turns up on time and, most challenging of all, ensuring that pupils behave and do not get lost or sick en route. It is very much to a trainee's advantage, then, to take a modest role in such activities in order to 'learn the ropes' before assuming too much responsibility.

A less traditional area, but of increasing importance, is a new emphasis on informal learning. All the above activities certainly involve very real learning and should be valued as such. However, society generally is growing in awareness that many kinds of valuable learning can take place in a variety of circumstances. The most significant element in all of this is unquestionably the computer and related technologies. It is almost a cliché but nevertheless true that children frequently have at home a computer that is more powerful than any machine at their school. This social change has also dramatised the issue of those pupils who do not have this domestic access, leading to a much-vaunted digital divide. So schools are aware that many of their pupils are learning at home and that others may need special access to school machines out of school hours. Yet it is very hard to prove any direct link between increased computer provision in school and at home with any rise in standards. A good example centres on computer games. Research is divided on whether certain skills are rapidly enhanced by the nature of many games or if they are merely games with the potential to be addictive and harmful. Many adults, including teachers, feel unable to judge, as they have never really engaged with the world of such games.

For the trainee this may all seem a little bewildering. However, one example which connects with English may help. One outcome of the rapid advance of digital technologies has made digital cameras, both still and video, readily available and affordable. Equally, editing software is now more affordable and much easier to use. This combination gives young people access to a powerful means of meaning-making. The crowded English curriculum does not encourage teachers to devote time to extended projects involving cameras and editing. However, the young people in question seem very happy to put in the time and generally learn how to use the technology very readily. What they usually need is an interested adult whose advice and cultural expertise can support them. This example illustrates how the trainee might engage with pupils in this informal way and how all the participants can gain some new knowledge. This kind of model can be especially productive for older pupils who are finding formal schooling increasingly problematic.

Conclusions

The trainee teacher has a complex status. From the moment they begin their training period, they are expected to fit with professional norms and expectations and to be a role model in this respect, while they grapple with learning to teach and a range of highly demanding standards that they may or may not achieve. If they do not achieve these standards then, in the interests of the clients they seek to work with, they are excluded from the profession they have worked hard to join. This latter outcome occurs only rarely, but it must be there to safeguard the quality of the profession. It is useful to reflect here on the care and effort that go into the initial selection of trainees and the stress placed on candidates' need to have an understanding of the true nature of teachers' work unclouded by sentimentality or nostalgia.

Accurate selection to teacher training allows for other professionals to have high expectations of trainees from the outset. High expectations still need to be realistic. Even mature trainees with other forms of professional experience find the transition to becoming an effective teacher extremely demanding. So both the training and induction periods are characterised by high demand but clearly identified support, with an emphasis on a gradual build-up of evidence upon which sound judgements can be made, set against nationally defined standards. Many of these standards focus on being a professional and this chapter has tried to put the term 'professional' into the spotlight and to examine the range of ways in which the teacher exemplifies the true professional. Trainees should therefore be aware from the outset that they have a responsibility to learn about the particular nature of the profession of teachers and that they have a contribution to make to the maintenance and, over time, the improvement of its status.

Further reading

The Standards themselves contain plenty of direction about what is required of trainees and the handbook that accompanies them offers helpful advice. Books about teacher professionalism tend to fall into two categories. Some are like this handbook for English teachers, providing a summary and overview of what is a complex issue with a considerable history. The texts recommended below come from a different category, one which addresses this complexity and draws on research to argue about issues in some depth.

Dillon, J. and Maguire, M. (1997) *Becoming a Teacher: Issues in Secondary Teaching*, Open University Press, Buckingham.

Eraut, M. (1994) *Developing Professional Knowledge and Competence*, Falmer Press, London.

Goodson, I. and Hargreaves, A. (1996) *Teachers' Professional Lives*, Falmer Press, London.

Hoyle, E. and John, P. (1995) *Professional Knowledge and Professional Practice*, Cassell, London.

Schön, D. (1983) *The Reflective Practitioner*, Basic Books, New York.

Tickle, L. (2000) *Teacher Induction: The Way Ahead*, Open University Press, Buckingham.

10 Literacy: whole-school issues and the role of the English specialist

Joanna Haffenden

Introduction

Improving the literacy of school children has long been identified as funda-mental for academic, social and economic success by a range of professionals, including teachers, academics, politicians (from across the ideological range) and employers. This unity of desire perhaps masks, if only briefly, the widely disparate views held by such interested parties in recent decades, first as to the reasons why literacy is not yet deemed to be at a satisfactory level and second how it is to be improved.

A detailed assessment of the range of views on this topic is not for discussion here. Suffice to say that professionals share the view that sound literacy skills are a vital tool for effective learning, and that interventions to improve literacy can be expected to have positive outcomes in all areas of a student's experience, ranging from academic achievement to issues of self-esteem. For trainee teachers embarking on the task of learning to teach, and the vast amount of work that this entails, investigating the wider issue of literacy across the curriculum may not at first seem a high priority. However, developing awareness at an early stage of how your students experience reading and writing elsewhere in the curriculum can offer useful insights into your own teaching practice. And, in time, becoming involved in your own school's management of literacy across the curriculum may offer an excellent opportunity for professional development. In the short term, understanding issues related to cross-curricular literacy will help you to meet some of the Standards that you must meet in order to achieve QTS (Standards 2c, 3.3.2c and 3.3.3, for example).

Furthermore, the English specialist needs rapidly to develop a sensitive appre-ciation of the impact that a strategy for literacy across the curriculum may have on non-English specialist colleagues. You may find in the schools where you work that many colleagues have embraced the whole-school strategy enthusiastically, yet there may be a few who consider literacy-focused tasks in their specialism something of an imposition and an unhelpful diversion from the pressures of their own curriculum. The role of the English specialist and her or his department in this area of whole-school policy needs to be managed with care. The centrality of literacy in the curriculum across the Key Stages of compulsory education (with a focus on the secondary curriculum), and issues arising from a whole-school policy that seeks to underpin this conclusion, are to be the focus of this chapter.

Objectives

This chapter will explore:

- the research background: a case for a cross-curricular Literacy Strategy;
- definitions of literacy;
- putting cross-curricular literacy into practice;
- the role of the English Department.

The research background: a case for a cross-curricular Literacy Strategy

Important studies and research projects, such as Kingman's *Committee of Inquiry into the Teaching of English Language* (1988) and Bullock's *A Language for Life* (1975), have over the years been instigated in response to concerns about falling standards and especially reading standards. The aim of the Bullock Report was to consider all aspects of the use of English, including reading, writing and speech. It is of particular interest here since it hits on a central tension regarding perceptions about the teaching of literacy. The report concluded firmly that all teachers – whether English specialists or not – should be involved in improving students' language skills:

> If standards of achievement are to be improved, all teachers will have to be helped to acquire a deeper understanding of language in education. This includes teachers of other subjects than English, since it is one of our contentions that every school should have an organised policy for language across the curriculum, establishing every teacher's involvement in language and reading development throughout the years of schooling.
>
> (Bullock, 1975)

In other words, the explicit teaching of literacy skills should not be confined to the English classroom only. This may well have come as something of a surprise to non-English specialists – experts in their own area and committed to delivering their own curriculum in ways that they judged to be most appropriate.

Bullock found little evidence of a significant fall in standards of reading, but noted that demands for higher standards of literacy were continually rising. The report's recommendations offered lots of sensible advice, much of which remains relevant now. Many schools acted on the report as best they could, given the practical constraints of time and money. However, it was the introduction of the National Literacy Strategy (NLS) in primary schools in 1997, and the significant funding that accompanied it, that finally saw a truly concerted drive towards specifically addressing literacy skills in all areas of the secondary curriculum. The NLS documentation contained a section on secondary schools:

> Every secondary school should specialise in literacy and set targets for improvement in English. Similarly, every teacher should contribute to promoting it . . . In shaping their plans it is essential that secondary schools do not see work on reading and writing as exclusively the province of a few teachers in the English and learning support departments.
>
> (NLS, 1997)

The exhortation to 'specialise in literacy' placed literacy firmly at the centre of the secondary curriculum, and the role of each and every teacher in 'promoting it' was once again emphasised.

In autumn 1997, when the introduction of daily literacy hours in primary schools was in its infancy, HMI undertook a survey of literacy in secondary schools. Keen to build on and share existing good practice in this area, 49 schools were visited with the aim of identifying what effective strategies were being used by successful schools to improve literacy standards. The short report which was published following this survey set out advice to schools, including 17 specific features of successful management of a whole-school literacy policy, and also listed a range of effective strategies, of which one or more were typically in place in the schools surveyed. The report noted that literacy across the curriculum policy was successful in schools where literacy was seen to be 'the key to improving learning and raising standards' and where the approach adopted was 'relevant to all curriculum areas and pupils of all levels of attainment'. And, as with the Bullock report some years previously, one of the HMI's seven major conclusions placed emphasis on literacy as the responsibility of all teaching staff:

> Approaches that involve curriculum areas other than English, together with work done in English departments, are more likely to be successful than initiatives that are confined to English and/or SEN departments.

In the years since the introduction of the NLS, a new impetus has been behind secondary schools' efforts to raise levels of literacy. Mindful of the literacy hour experiences of their new Key Stage 3 students, and of challenging targets set by LEAs and government, schools have striven to embed a strategy for delivering literacy through all subject specialisms.

Thus, teacher trainees today are likely to find themselves working in schools where there is a policy of delivering literacy across the curriculum, although it may well not yet be fully or evenly implemented. Teachers (trainee or otherwise) are charged with a clear responsibility for fostering literacy skills where appropriate within their subject specialism. Literacy is *not* a discrete range of skills which are specific to the English curriculum; indeed, it has been deemed to be 'too important to leave to English teachers' (HMI Survey, 1997). Literacy, along with other life skills such as numeracy, citizenship and ICT, should be rooted in teaching and learning practices across the curriculum.

Task 10.1: Theory task: researching strategies for an effective literacy policy

Read a copy of the 1997 HMI survey into secondary literacy (your university library should hold a copy – it's only short), noting especially its recommendations about effective strategies for a cross-curricular literacy policy and its observations about barriers to effective practice. Read a copy of your school's policy on literacy. Reflect on issues affecting the practicality of such a policy. If possible, compare the policy of your first placement school with that of your second. Are there significant differences? If so, what might account for these?

Definitions of literacy

During the course of your training, and indeed when in position at your future place of work, you may find yourself engaged in a debate with colleagues about the teaching of literacy. All the experts are agreed on the need to improve literacy. But what does this mean? What is literacy? Literacy may not be a separate set of skills to be developed in English lessons only, but how can such skills be delivered effectively alongside the already heavy demands of other curriculum areas? The questions are valid, and certainly any school will have needed to establish their own answers to them when drawing up their whole-school literacy policy.

Perhaps at first glance the term 'literacy' is unhelpful. Perhaps it is too similar to the words 'literature' or 'literary', leaving a perception that somehow it is to do with books – the domain of the English Department. Of course, literacy embraces talk, reading and writing, regardless of subject matter. It is synonymous with language. A student's ability to access and use language is fundamental to his or her learning, and thus sound literacy skills will foster good learning. Literacy can be defined as 'language for learning'. At the heart of a drive to teach literacy across the curriculum is the desire to equip students to articulate or express their understanding of the ideas, processes and principles explored in the classroom setting.

Perhaps the most fundamental aspect of your teacher training is the part devoted to learning about how children learn. An introduction to key ideas in educational theory can be found in the generic text for this series (Nicholls, 1999). For the purposes of this chapter, however, it is worth noting that while the theories about how children learn and think differ, the idea of effective learning taking place when a child plays an active – not a passive – role is tacitly shared by educationalists. Vygotsky in particular (in *Thought and Language* (1962)) places emphasis on the importance of talk in developing children's thinking and understanding. He identifies the two-way interaction between teacher and student as vital for progress to be made by the learner. In other words, the classroom is not just a place where the teacher teaches and the students receive; rather, students must actively engage and be given the opportunity to express their understanding. Only at this point can both teacher and learner know that learning has taken place. It is how language is used in the communication between teacher and student that is crucial to the development of learning (a view espoused by Bruner too). Thus the teacher must knowingly and thoughtfully deploy – and allow students time to use – language for learning (literacy) in his or her day-to-day dealings with classes. Crucially, wherever appropriate or possible, the nature of text used in the classroom (either to be read or to be generated by the student as a piece of writing) should be explored:

- What is the context of the text?
- What is the purpose of the text?
- Who is the text's intended audience?

This explicit exploration of the meaning of texts encourages students to think about the nature of their reading and writing in a critical and reflective way (of course, this dialogue is as appropriate for ICT and moving image texts as much as it is for book-based texts). Furthermore, if appropriate, such work may usefully evolve into assessment for learning opportunities (see Chapter 4 of this volume for a more in-depth exploration of the value of this type of assessment).

So, to return to the hypothetical question posed by your imagined colleague at the beginning of this section: what is literacy? Certainly, it is more than simply the ability to read and write. Being literate means having the ability to construct meaning from texts and to understand *how* texts of different types are constructed. Being literate means having the ability to produce texts, and being able to understand how context, purpose and intended audience should be taken into account when making decisions about language. Being literate means being able to articulate one's learning in thought, in speech and as written text. Working with students to ensure that they are literate (and, for that matter, numerate, responsible citizens and competent users of ICT) should be the planned outcome of secondary education. The teaching of literacy across the curriculum is not about 'adding on' extra tasks, it is about making the best sense of those tasks that are already in place.

Task 10.2: Observation task: reading and writing experiences across the curriculum

Observe a range of lessons (aim for four or five) experienced by one of your students. How many texts do they read in these lessons? How many texts do they generate? Is there any opportunity for discussion about the structure and organisation of the texts? Does the student know why the text is being used or produced? If possible (perhaps if you are attached to a tutor group), discuss with a small group of students their perceptions about reading and writing. Where do they use these skills the most? Are they aware of all the different sorts of reading and writing that they do? Consider how in your teaching you might refer to students' literacy experiences elsewhere in the curriculum in order to reinforce the cross-curricular nature of talk, reading and writing.

Cross-curricular literacy in practice

Whole-school activities

What sort of literacy-focused activities can you expect to find when you arrive in your placement school? In tandem with all the specific literacy work undertaken in classrooms, you are likely soon to become aware of a number of whole-school strategies or projects designed to enhance students' confidence and pleasure in using their language for learning. Examples of such activities might be:

- a commitment to reading in one or more tutor periods in a week;
- a conscious effort to make display work rich in words as well as visual images;
- a 'spelling pattern of the week', perhaps disseminated via the school bulletin and referred to or displayed in tutor time;
- a paired reading scheme whereby Key Stage 4 or Key Stage 5 students team up with a partners (usually unconfident readers in Years 7 or 8) to hear and help them read;
- regular and structured library or resource centre sessions;
- work on study skills, perhaps specifically for year groups due to take external exams;
- a focus on reading or writing at particular points in the school calendar such as National Poetry Day and World Book Day. Here, all members of staff might be asked to share their favourite poem or read an extract from something they have read recently with their classes, talking about why they have chosen the text. Other events, such as book fairs and visits from writers or perfomance poets, may also be in place;
- extra-curricular activities such as homework clubs or reading, writing and handwriting clinics;
- a reading recovery scheme where selected students are removed from the normal school timetable for a short period of time (perhaps 30 minutes, once or twice a week) to use a programme such as 'Successmaker' in order to improve their reading ability;
- summer literacy schools or schemes;
- focused SEN work with students whose literacy skills are particularly weak, including withdrawal for one-to-one work and in-class support from teaching assistants.

All such activities contribute towards making improvements in participants' literacy levels. They also help to raise the profile of literacy, and continue to chip away at the unhelpful perception that reading and writing that matters only takes place in the English classroom. At their best, these sorts of projects demonstrate that the entire school community values highly and actively promotes the literacy of its members.

Clearly, the effective and regular teaching of literacy in all subject areas acts as the backbone of this whole-school commitment. While each school will have its own unique policy and particular key strategies which suit its particular circumstances, it is likely that many schools will have gone through similar steps when working towards agreement as to how literacy across the curriculum should be delivered.

Steps towards delivery of literacy in all subject areas

1   The case for raising literacy and being explicit about literacy skills in a concerted way across the curriculum is made to staff.
2   Staff in their subject areas identify what sorts of language use they typically ask for from students in terms of talk, reading and writing. For example:

- in Technology, students might use flow diagrams to show a making process as part of a project;
- in History, students might need to explore bias in sources;
- in Mathematics, students might be asked to explain orally how probability works;
- in Dance, Drama and PE, students might need to reflect on their own performances and offer feedback on those of others;
- in Science, students might need to hypothesise about a potential reaction and then articulate the findings once the hypothesis has been tested;
- in Art, students might need to make observations about and evaluate an artist's work;
- in English, students might need to analyse and comment on the presentation of a character in a text.

3   Through INSET, staff are given training and time to consider how specific tasks could be used as opportunities to enhance literacy as well as to cover curriculum content. Common strategies which are designed to promote literacy include:

- display of key words in subject classrooms;
- explicit teaching of the meaning of key words, e.g. 'force' has a range of meanings, depending on whether you are in Science, History or English;
- formalising opportunities for talk, whether it is paired discussion, a group's hypothesis or an individual's evaluation. Recognising talk as the articulation of thought;
- modelling of reading and writing activities such as note-taking from a textbook, taking time to consider why the notes are needed and how to formulate them;
- designing activities where students engage with texts interactively. Ideas in this area could draw on the use of many familiar teaching strategies such as brainstorming, concept mapping, predictive activities, sequencing activities, the use of KWL grids (What do I know?, What do I want to know?, What have I learnt?), and DARTs (Directed Activity Related to Text) such as cloze exercises;

- activating students' existing knowledge about a topic before an activity, and evaluating how learning has progressed at the end of a lesson;
- using writing frames to help structure written work to help students articulate their learning on paper. Maureen Lewis and David Wray have carried out extensive research in this and related areas, and, while their research has focused on primary school children, it is extremely valuable and relevant in the secondary sector (for example, *Extending Literacy* (1997) and *Writing Frames* (1997). See Figure 10.1 for an example of Wray and Lewis' work.

Taken from **Writing Frames** *by Maureen Lewis and David Wray (EXEL Exeter Extending Literacy Project, p. 28). These frames were developed while working with primary school children, but nevertheless offer a very useful basis for writing at more advanced levels. Here's an example of the 'explanation' genre: Lewis and Wray also offer structures for recount, report, procedural, persuasion and discussion genres frames.*

Explanation genre: a model for organising writing which evaluates a variety of explanations for a particular event or phenomenon

There are differing explanations as to why / how / what / when

One explanation is that

The evidence for this is

An alternative explanation is

This explanation is based on

Of the alternative explanations I think the most likely is

Figure 10.1   A writing frame for the explanation genre

Staff may also need to consider how to address objectives set by management as a priority for the whole school. Possible examples might be that staff should discuss and teach explicitly the reading skills to be used (skimming, scanning, receptive or intensive) before approaching a text; or that staff should teach explicitly how to organise pieces of extended writing (when to paragraph, what sort of connectives to use).

Many of the teaching strategies listed at number 3 above are familiar to the majority of staff. In a way, this is what is so exciting about the possible impact of the explicit teaching of literacy across the curriculum: many of the techniques through which literacy can be taught are the same as those through which curriculum content can be delivered. Indeed, this is unsurprising since much learning evolves from the discussion of, the reading of and the production of language-rich texts and, as has been established already, language and learning have an interdependent relationship. Where efforts do need to be made is in ensuring that teachers themselves have the language to teach 'language for learning'.

Task **10.3**: Observation task: teaching literacy in other subject specialisms

If possible, link up with a trainee who is not an English specialist and discuss how literacy is addressed in his or her subject area (alternatively, it might be possible to pursue this discussion as part of your professional studies programme). Be ready to discuss how you yourself might address strategies for numeracy, citizenship and ICT in your own teaching. Identify a lesson where each of you plans to use a text for reading; or ask students to generate a text; or perhaps to discuss their learning in a formalised way. Work together on how each lesson could be enhanced as an opportunity for strengthening literacy. Observe each other's lessons and reflect on the learning that took place.

Task **10.4**: Observation task: maximising the interactive nature of teaching

Revisit the list of teaching strategies at number 3 above. You may well be able to extend the list – it is by no means exhaustive. Consider how you might incorporate one or more of these into a sequence of lessons you are planning to teach. In the classroom, build in time for accessing students' prior knowledge before introducing your activity, and at the end allow for a plenary where learning is evaluated. Perhaps discuss this with your mentor and ask him or her to observe you.

The Key Stage 3 Strategy and cross-curricular literacy

You are no doubt already aware of the Key Stage 3 National Strategy, first introduced for English and Mathematics in September 2001, and with the addition of Frameworks for Science, ICT and TLF (teaching and learning in the foundation subjects) in 2002/3. The implications of the Strategy in terms of your own teaching of English are fully explored in Chapter 2 of this volume. At the heart of the strategy lies the aim of improving teaching and learning. Its key principles are set out in full at the DfES website, but can be summarised thus:

- expectations: establishing high expectations for all pupils and setting challenging targets for progress;
- progression: improving transition between Key Stages and ensuring progression across Key Stage 3;
- engagement: using active approaches to teaching and learning;
- transformation: a commitment to improve teaching and learning through professional development.

The model of teaching that is to be strived for is one that sets out learning objectives explicitly and that engages students as actively as possible, and, as has been demonstrated, this complements the effective teaching and learning of literacy. The Strategy specifically asks schools to 'take part in whole-school initiatives on cross-curricular issues such as literacy and numeracy'. All teaching staff have available to them extensive training materials which demonstrate how to teach in line with the Strategy. Training for the TLF strand includes modules on questioning, explaining and modelling, e.g. ideal strategies for promoting literacy. The ever-growing use of thinking skills in teaching (including specific programmes such as Cognitive Acceleration through Science Education (CASE) and Cognitive Acceleration through Mathematics Education (CAME)) also supports the principles behind an explicit teaching of literacy. The ground, it seems, is fully prepared for the effective teaching of literacy across the curriculum.

However, research shows that, although the majority of teachers when surveyed single out highly interactive teaching strategies as being the most effective for learning, the reality of the classroom can be quite different. Webster, Beveridge and Reed (1996: 132) observed that, in practice, the reading or writing experiences of many secondary school students were 'brief and occurred in fragments . . . Reading or writing events did not occur at all for more than three quarters of the pupils observed.' The researchers further noted that:

> Despite their strong commitment to collaborative styles of working, all of the teachers we observed spent a lot of their time organising and managing learners, giving out information and setting tasks, interacting only briefly with individuals to sustain their involvement and check on progress.
>
> (Webster, Beveridge and Reed, 1996: 132)

This is the ongoing challenge for teachers of all disciplines. The theory and the models of good practice are in place. Ensuring that a policy for cross-curricular literacy is effective is hard work – it requires that each teacher review his or her own practice critically and honestly. So, how might an English specialist contribute to a cross-curricular strategy?

The role of the English Department

The problem of being an 'expert'

As the National Strategy becomes increasingly well established in secondary schools, it is probable (and fortunate) that the frequency with which the English Department hears mutterings from other colleagues about feeling that they are being expected to 'boost English results' is in decline. As an English teacher, you are, however, likely to find yourself viewed as an 'expert' in language and therefore literacy. For the huge number of English teachers who are graduates in literature, this may be quite unnerving. You may well find in schools where you work that a number of departmental colleagues have had to work hard to come to grips with the language of the Framework for Teaching English and indeed several who blanched at first sight of the objectives being delivered by Key Stage 2 colleagues as part of the primary Literacy Strategy. All of this seems doubly difficult when, not unreasonably, non-English specialists may be seeking advice and expertise from the English Department as they strive to deliver literacy across the curriculum. Having all subject areas teaching literacy explicitly is excellent news for English Departments, but this brings with it a significant amount of work in-house ensuring that literacy really is being taught explicitly in our own classrooms. This may be where you, with your experience of a teacher training course rooted in the culture of the National Strategy, may have ideas about good practice to offer your more experienced colleagues.

Playing a part in the whole-school policy

The English specialist clearly has an important contribution to make towards a whole-school policy on literacy, and certainly at least one member of the department is likely to be involved in the management of the policy and any connected INSET (although all recommendations are that it is preferable if not *just* English teachers are seen to be running this). On a minor but important point, this might also involve drawing up a statement about what is *not* good practice: copying at length; setting lines and thereby making writing a punishment; expecting a student with specific literacy difficulties to write at length with ease – but, of course, any competent teacher would be able to contribute in this way.

In some cases, English Departments or the literacy coordinator can be responsible for providing other departments with support materials such as the constituent parts of a particular text type, so that these can in turn be introduced in the appropriate lesson. For example, a list of the techniques that can make either a speech or written text persuasive would enable, say, a History teacher to encourage the use of such techniques in a relevant activity (see Figure 10.2). In the same way, advice about the technical language necessary to describe the structure of a particular text is another way in which English teachers can support other colleagues.

It is worth noting at this point that Webster, Beveridge and Reed express some reservations about an over-reliance on what they call 'genre theory' – the idea that a formula for texts (usually non-fiction) can be created out of a kind of ingredients list of language points – and rightly emphasise the need to place texts in a context in order to strengthen learning about how they work and what they are for. They express the view that 'the generic characteristics of any given text, whilst being linguistically complex, are less powerful determinants of children's literacy development than social interactions around those texts, during reading or writing' (Webster *et al.*, 1996: 24). This is a useful health warning about the use of, for example, writing frames. Remember, it is the interaction with and the discussion of texts that is crucial in developing literacy. That said, the sort of scaffolding that writing frames and other strategies offer students is frequently excellent, and, from the teacher's point of view, they can provide a useful starting point for the explicit delivery of literacy. Further, Wray and Lewis, who have devised highly effective practice around the use of writing frames, also comment emphatically that:

> Children learn to interact critically and purposefully with texts by engaging in critical and purposeful behaviour; that is, the process is not that of practising the 'skills' of being a critical and effective user of text which they then apply to real texts, but rather one of learning through activities which are authentic in their own rights.
>
> (Wray and Lewis, 1997: 6)

1 Involve the audience.

2 Criticise (politely) the other side / opposite argument.

3 Repetition (of impressive points or statistics).

4 Flattery (links with involving the audience: 'I'm sure that responsible people like you...').

5 Bribery (links with involving the audience: 'If you... then ...').

6 Pattern of three (e.g. examples or reasons).

7 Alliteration (use several words with same-sounding first letter in one sentence, e.g. 'Bullying is clearly cruel, but it is also cowardly').

8 Hyperbole (deliberate exaggeration for effect).

9 Humour (helps to involve the audience).

10 Imperative verb (a command or order, e.g. 'Make a stand'! 'Vote for ...!').

11 Rhetorical question (plants an idea in the listener's mind: 'What if...?').

12 Conditional clause ('If no action is taken, then...').

13 Use of statistics ('Over 80 per cent of Year 9 students think that...').

14 Reference to personal experience ('I know how helpful I found it when...').

Figure 10.2   Techniques to make speaking or writing persuasive

Bilateral liaison with other departments

Collaboration with a colleague from another department with a view to making the outcomes of a particular activity or task more 'literate' – a better reflection of learning – can be a developmental and satisfying experience for an English teacher.

An example of such work is where, in one school, an Art teacher worked with an English Department colleague on how to improve guidance (scaffolding) given to GCSE students who needed to compare and evaluate the works of a particular artist. The teacher felt that students were not expressing their learning fully enough in their written work, and indeed the GCSE moderator had highlighted this aspect as having scope for improvement. Informal discussions between the two colleagues resulted in the Art Department's support materials being adapted. In particular, original paragraph prompts which used the question word 'how' were identified as a stumbling block ('How does the style of this painting differ from . . . ?'). Such questions were broken down into smaller, more specific questions, and vocabulary banks were offered at the bottom of the page for additional help. The GCSE moderator noted improvement in the quality of students' responses the following year.

Similarly, as the Science Department began to integrate explicit literacy teaching into its schemes of work, one teacher identified the opportunity for Year 7 students to 'tell the story' of a what happens to a ham sandwich when it is eaten. Again, informal discussion with an English Department colleague led to the task being adapted so that students were expected not only to show their learning about the digestive process, but also to structure their work using paragraphs, each beginning with a temporal connective. Giving the Science teacher the right language to use when introducing this task helped to ensure that the literacy aspect of it was made explicit to the students (see Figure 10.3 for examples of how the Science Department has identified opportunities to teach and reinforce literacy skills).

The challenge for the English teacher

Thus the role of the English specialist in a school where there is a policy for teaching literacy across the curriculum is potentially a complex one. You may find yourself having to work hard to develop confidence in using the terminology of the strategy. You will need to strive to ensure that your lessons provide opportunities for the reading and writing experiences of a developmental quality, reviewing your own practice and sharing ideas and experiences with your colleagues. As your career progresses, you may find that you have the opportunity to work on cross-curricular projects – perhaps working closely with another department or maybe in organising a special one-off event which highlights and celebrates literacy within your school community. Whatever chance for professional development in connection with literacy comes your way, relish it: there really is nothing more important.

Further issues: boys and literacy; other literacies

This chapter has focused on a core consideration of literacy as a mode for expressing learning, and as a tool for engaging with and producing texts. It has

The science schemes of work for KS3 at Heathfield Community College have a common pattern. Opportunities to address literacy, along with ICT and numeracy, are set out on the 'front page' of each scheme. Here is a simplified example:

Year 7: Electricity

From Year 6... (a reminder about what students will have covered at KS2)		
KS3 Content (Attainment targets are set out here)		
Scientific enquiry		
ICT (...)	**Literacy** Lesson 8 – Circuit role play. Use of suggested link works (connectives) with target of using more interesting sentences in their science writing.	**Numeracy** (...)

Year 8: Acids and alkalis

From Year 6... (a reminder about what students will have covered at KS2)		
KS3 Content (Attainment targets are set out here)		
Scientific enquiry		
ICT (...)	**Literacy** Lesson 6 - produce an article describing pollutants and acid rain	**Numeracy** (...)

Figure 10.3   Science schemes of work showing where and how literary skills are addressed

emphasised how central literacy needs to be in the secondary curriculum in order to raise attainment, and it has explored some ways in which language for learning can be built in to teaching across the curriculum. However, during the course of your training, you are likely to come across the description of other literacies such as media literacy, visual literacy and emotional literacy. Each of these deals with distinct and important topics and, as can be inferred from the labels, each offers a 'strand of learning' that can have a significant impact on particular students. It is worth finding out about these and reflecting on how these might feed into your own practice.

Finally, although the role of the English specialist in a cross-curricular literacy policy has been considered, there are additional related issues which warrant further attention but which cannot be explored in sufficient detail here. Most notably, the ongoing need to address boys' attainment in English (which ostensibly acts as some measure of achievement in literacy) is one such issue. Much has been written on this topic and you are well advised to investigate the literature and particular situations of your placement schools.

Further reading

Bruner, J. S. (1966) *The Process of Education*, Vintage, New York.

Millard, Elaine (1997) *Differently Literate: Boys, Girls and the Schooling of Literacy*, Falmer Press, London.

Wray, David and Lewis, Maureen (1997) *Extending Literacy: Children Reading and Writing Non-fiction*, Routledge, London.

QCA (1998) *Can Do Better: Raising Boys' Achievement in English*, QCA, London.

QCA (1999) *Improving Writing at Key Stages 3 and 4*, QCA, London.

QCA (1999) *Not Whether but How: Teaching Grammar in English at Key Stages 3 and 4*, QCA, London.

11 Personal and professional early career development

Liana Coales

Introduction

During teacher training and the NQT year there are many personal and professional development opportunities available. Some are formal events arranged by ITT providers, schools, LEAs, etc., while others are informal and may require the teacher to be proactive in seeking out and creating opportunities. The most important thing is to make the most of these opportunities and to remain positive throughout your career.

> **Objectives**
>
> This chapter will explore:
>
> - personal development from trainee teacher to teacher;
> - how to develop your teaching;
> - early career development options;
> - issues of promotion.

From trainee teacher to teacher

Having completed training and attained QTS, many teachers spend the summer holiday worrying about whether they are actually good enough to be responsible for an entire timetable. Being a trainee teacher is very challenging, but at least there are mentors and tutors assigned to you if you need help. Completing training and becoming a qualified teacher can seem extremely daunting as there seem to be fewer people allocated to your development and you feel solely responsible for teaching your classes for the entire year, but remember you are not alone. You are part of a team – a departmental team and an entire school team who are all working to a common goal – creating the best possible opportunities for the pupils in your school.

There are many positives about becoming a teacher rather than being a trainee teacher: you will have the whole year to build relationships with your classes; you won't be picking up from someone else mid-year, or even halfway through a scheme of work; you won't have to tell the class you are leaving before the end of the year. Furthermore, you won't have to lie when asked the inevitable question: 'Are you a real teacher or just a trainee?' But how will you change from being a trainee teacher to a teacher?

One significant aspect of becoming a qualified teacher is that you will feel differently – you will *feel* like a teacher rather than a trainee – and thus your confidence will automatically increase. Your classes will know you as *their* teacher and will not see you as temporary or doubt your authority in the way they may have done during your training. The early years of a teaching career are when you will develop your personal teaching style and increase your knowledge and understanding of the way children learn.

Developing your teaching

During your training you will have seen and tried out numerous different teaching styles and methods. Your repertoire will have increased dramatically over the year and, hopefully, you will now have a number of tried and tested techniques. You will have had the opportunities to experiment with ideas and probably received a great deal of advice from your college tutors and school-based mentors. However, you may have found you adapted your teaching techniques and style to suit the tastes of whichever teacher happened to be observing you and you may have received conflicting advice from the various mentors, tutors and other teachers you came into contact with. It can be very valuable to hear alternative opinions, but it can also be frustrating. While training, it sometimes feels as if you are teaching in order to satisfy the observer – the tutor or the mentor sitting at the back of the class – but once qualified, the emphasis is placed firmly on teaching the pupils.

The NQT year is the time when you can truly develop your personal teaching style. You can test out new ideas and revisit ones you used during training, and you can also try out the ideas you didn't find time for during training.

It is important to remember that while you were training to become a teacher you did develop your skills, but attaining QTS is not the end, indeed it is just the beginning. Throughout your career you will continue developing and learning. No one expects you to be perfect during your NQT year (or ever) and you should feel that you are able to ask for help and advice from more experienced colleagues. The most useful resource for teachers tends to be other teachers, although there is often a reluctance or hesitation to share ideas in the staff room. Ask questions and ask for help when you need it – remember that generally teachers like helping people. All too often teachers avoid asking questions because they think it will be perceived as a sign of weakness or inability to cope, but this is a very unhelpful attitude and you should get into the habit of sharing ideas with your colleagues early on – just as you will encourage your pupils to ask you questions when they are unsure.

Be reflective

Of course, you will have brilliant lessons and you will also have not-so-brilliant lessons – not just in the NQT year, but throughout your career. Don't dwell on the less successful lessons in a negative way, but reflect on them positively and try to work out what was unsuccessful. Ask yourself which areas of the lesson didn't work. Was it the way you gave instructions or were the resources confusing? Try to pinpoint what it was and then work out how it could have been improved, and during the next lesson try out your new idea. Talk though the lesson with a friend or colleague so that they can offer their perspective on it. Remember that even if the pupils didn't complete the work or there was some unruly behaviour, it doesn't necessarily mean that no learning took place, so don't be too hard on yourself. Similarly, take a few moments to appraise your good lessons and ask the same questions because good lessons aren't a matter of luck.

It is equally important to evaluate successful lessons in order to identify what went well so that you can use the strategies again in the future. This doesn't mean you have to write down a formal evaluation (although sometimes you might want to keep a notebook of ideas for future reference), but at least spend some time thinking through the lesson in objective detail. See Table 11.1 for an example of a lesson evaluation by a trainee English teacher. The sample evaluation shows that the trainee teacher has begun by considering what learning has taken place before noting aspects of the lesson which were particularly effective. Importantly, the evaluation also shows implications for future lessons and refers to both learning and behaviour. When evaluating your lessons, avoid dwelling on behaviour and focus instead on the learning that did, or did not, take place, then use your observations to improve subsequent lessons.

Table 11.1 A trainee English teacher's lesson evaluation

Date: Tuesday 25th March	**Class:** 7.76
Subject: English	**Lesson:** Persuasive letter writing

What did they learn? How do I know?
Although the pupils did all produce letters, not all of them used the specific persuasive devices I had taught during the introduction. The more able pupils showed they were able to use rhetorical questions and emotive language effectively. Less able pupils showed they were able to use a formal letter format correctly but did not use the specified devices.

Teacher: Planning/differentiation/instructions/questioning/feedback/ time management/assessment/
The lesson progressed well and the resources motivated and engaged the pupils. They liked having envelopes to open and letters to read. I could have made more of the explicit teaching moments by slowing the pace down and checking for understanding before moving on. I should also have made it clearer that I expected the pupils to use rhetorical questions and emotive language in their writing. The differentiated resources worked well for the less able, although I should have stretched the most able more by developing an extension activity. The letter is a good extended piece of writing which I can use for formal assessment.

Pupil: Learning/behaviour/interest and involvement/attainment
The pupils were involved, even excited, by the lesson – especially when they received and opened the envelopes. Setting up a task with a real purpose – telling them that the letters would be posted – helped to motivate and engage the class. There were no major behaviour issues as a result, although the excitement did lead to some chatter and sharing of ideas when I had asked for silent individual work. Some of the letters showed real attainment in that they are an improvement on the previous piece of extended writing.

Observations and implications for next lesson
Setting tasks with a purpose really helps to engage the pupils – especially with the use of props. As not all of the pupils grasped the concept of the rhetorical questions and emotive language, I will need to revisit these next lesson. However, for those pupils who demonstrated they could use these forms of language competently, I need an extension – perhaps work on imperatives – or maybe they could write a reply to each other's letters, therefore practising using a formal tone?

Lesson observed? Yes
Written feedback given? Yes

While training you become accustomed to having your lessons observed and receiving almost instant feedback on what went well and how you can improve, but after completing training the observations and feedback from colleagues become far less frequent. This means you will have to be proactive in analysing your lessons and identifying your progress. So who can tell you what works well and what doesn't? Well, although it can seem daunting, you could try asking your pupils. You could do so informally through a chat with a couple of pupils or you could ask the class to write down what they like and don't like in lessons, not just what they like, but how they think they learn best. Ask them what their favourite lesson was and ask them to explain why. Pupils will often give very honest answers and may highlight aspects of your teaching which you had not considered.

Task 11.1: Evaluation task: pupil lesson evaluation plenary

When you have settled into your first school and are at least at the stage of knowing your pupils' names, choose one class to evaluate a lesson for you. Ten minutes before the end of the lesson, ask the pupils to discuss the lesson in groups and to write down two positive and two negative aspects of the lesson – something they enjoyed, something they didn't enjoy and something they learnt. At the end of the lesson collect in the groups' reports and reflect on the pupils' comments. Are there some common comments? Did they think they had learnt what you had intended them to learn? How will this task influence your teaching?

These exercises will give you an indication of what works well from the pupils' point of view – and your lessons should be built around trying to engage your pupils (although you still need to include a variety of approaches, even if they all favour group work). Accept that this exercise may result in some negative feedback and use it as constructive criticism to improve your teaching.

An extension of this approach to improving your teaching is to try to put yourself in the position of the pupils, remember what it was like to be at school and consider how many other things are going on in their lives besides improving their English. In order to teach effectively, you need to engage the pupils and that should be the overarching aim of your lessons. There is no one way of doing this, but the most effective lessons will always have a high degree of engagement. It is extremely difficult to identify engagement – or to understand how it is created – but it would be possible for two teachers to teach the same lesson, one engaging the pupils successfully and the other failing to do so. The lesson in which the pupils were engaged would certainly lead to more effective learning and understanding.

Task 11.2: Observation task: identifying pupil engagement

Observe a lesson and try to identify whether the class is engaged and what it was that the teacher did to achieve this. It is likely to be a combination of elements. Make a list of the effective elements of the lesson and tick off the ones which you think you achieve regularly. Also, make a note of anything you saw which you would like to try and make a point of incorporating it into a lesson in the following week.

See Figure 11.1 for a list of elements which might contribute to achieving engagement in a lesson. Which of these did you see in the lesson you observed? How many of them do you think are required in order to create and deliver an effective lesson?

- High expectations
- Fast pace
- Interactive activities
- Positive classroom atmosphere
- Up-to-date resources
- Appropriately challenging work
- Clear instructions
- Combination of whole class, group and independent learning
- Lots of purposeful oral work
- Several short activities
- Use of support and intervention
- Purposeful activities
- Consistent use of praise and sanctions
- Target setting
- Clearly structured lesson
- Appropriate differentiation
- Variety of teaching approaches
- Reference to pupils' interests

Figure 11.1 Elements of an effective and engaging English lesson

Challenge your pupils and yourself

Focus on what you are doing – don't just think 'I'm a teacher', but remind yourself about the bigger issues involved with the job. You are engaging, motivating, inspiring, challenging, changing, and affecting the pupils you come into contact with. Even when you have been teaching for many years, you should still reflect on what you have achieved and what your pupils have achieved. You may have a good lesson, but if only 28 out of 30 pupils were listening to you, or only 27 did the homework you set, ask yourself why that was. What did you do? How can you improve? A good teacher will never take the easy option of thinking it's just the pupils' fault and nothing you can do can change it/make them listen/force them to do the work. Just as you tell the pupils they can always improve, so can you. Challenge yourself to do better, set yourself targets and aim to reach all the pupils all of the time. Of course, you won't always achieve this and you won't be able to produce all-singing, all-dancing lessons for five hours a day, five days a week, but such lessons aren't necessarily the most effective in any case.

Expectation is the key. You should have high expectations of all your pupils. Don't lower your expectations according to which set you are teaching or because there is a better school up the road. Generally, pupils will rise to the challenge and can often achieve more than we give them credit for. Make sure you give your pupils the opportunity to show you what they are capable of.

Share ideas with colleagues

During your NQT year the school should offer you a structured induction programme providing you with opportunities to go on courses, observe other teachers, visit other schools, and discuss issues with leaders within the school and the LEA and so on. These experiences are valuable in developing your experience and understanding of teaching. Even if some of the courses look like a repeat of something you did during training, it is always a good idea to hear an alternative perspective and you may find some of the ideas more relevant to you now that you have your own classes.

The first few years of teaching are about developing your confidence and your teaching. If you hear of a new teaching method, try it out. If you find it successful, you've added a tool to your tool-box; if not, think about how you can adapt it to make it successful. Share your ideas with your colleagues and ask them what they find successful. It's about building up a repertoire of strategies. One important point to consider here is that teaching activities should not be confined to one year group or even one Key Stage. For example, a successful learning activity can be used with a Key Stage 2 class as well as a Key Stage 4 class and so on. When you get the chance, ask teachers from different Key Stages what approaches they use and try them out in your own classroom. It is quite likely that the novelty of a new activity will stimulate and engage your pupils – this is especially likely at later Key Stages where pupils are often taught in a 'grown-up' lecture style, where teachers often think that activities are no longer appropriate. Think about how you learn. Have you been on courses or to lectures where you are talked to for an hour? Would you prefer to be involved in the learning? To involve your pupils in their learning is the first step towards truly engaging them.

One simple way to develop and extend your teaching skills and strategies is to talk to teachers in other departments as they often have different – and successful – ways of working which you may be able to adapt for use in your own classroom. If you are particularly interested in seeing why your class seem to love French, for example, ask their French teacher if you could observe a lesson in order to see what techniques are being utilised. Then invite the teacher to observe you teach so that together you can reflect on the positive approaches you use. Primary schools tend to be much better at having an open-classroom environment where teachers can see and learn from each other, whereas secondary schools are often closed environments where teachers shut their classroom doors and are very private about what they do and how they do it.

The most important thing to bear in mind here is that as teachers we have to be open to change, to approach new ideas positively and not reject them cynically before we have even tried them.

Think beyond English

Training to teach English is merely a starting point. English is a broad subject which encompasses many different strands, such as literature, literacy, language, drama, theatre studies, media, communication studies, and so on. During your career you may choose to develop your expertise in one or more of these areas. At secondary level, find out which of these subjects are offered at GCSE and A level and perhaps offer to teach the course. You may even want to introduce such a course to your school if there is not one already in existence. There are many different exam boards offering a variety of options, so you will need to research them in order to decide which most suits the interests of you and your potential pupils. A useful starting point would be to ask colleagues in other schools which exam boards they use and what they find positive and negative about them. Likewise, at primary school, you may choose to expand your English or literacy teaching to encompass a wider variety of experience for the pupils.

Mark external exams

Many teachers find it very helpful to act as examiners for SATs, GCSEs and A level exams. Not only are there financial incentives for taking on this type of work, but teachers who take it on almost always comment on how the experience benefits their own teaching. It allows you to develop expertise, to understand exams, to learn exactly how they are marked and therefore what needs to be taught in order to give your pupils the best chance of success; it also means that you can see what pupils in other schools are achieving. Although external exam marking does take a lot of time, the benefits to you and your pupils will be considerable, and you quickly become familiar with the marking criteria and find that you are able to mark very quickly. To become involved in this type of work, keep an eye on the noticeboards in the staff room and check advertisements in the *Times Educational Supplement* (TES).

Career development opportunities

Teaching is a career where there are many options and opportunities for progression. Whatever your goals may be, whatever your reasons for going into teaching, try to continually refresh your enthusiasm in the process of teaching and learning. There are many ways of doing this, some of which are outlined below.

Perhaps the most important piece of advice is simply 'Enjoy the job'. Remember why you chose to become a teacher and focus on the daily positive aspects of your job. Celebrate the successes, the nice comments, the work produced by your classes. Too many teachers dwell on the negative aspects of the job – the lessons that went badly, the disruptive children and so on. Schools tend to have a distinctive personality and atmosphere and if the overriding culture of your school is negative, recognise this and don't get dragged into demotivating conversations at lunchtime. Avoid becoming influenced by the negative culture of the school and seek the people who are enthusiastic about their job. If the school is particularly negative, you might consider moving on in order to refresh your own enthusiasm for the job, or you might try to influence those around you by discussing only the positive, helpful aspects of the day.

Continuing professional development

The first years of teaching are an important time to reflect on and improve your practice. It is also a time to think about the future, to consider what position you might aspire to and how you might go about achieving your goals. Perhaps you have a particular interest in gifted and talented education, for example, and would like to further your knowledge and understanding of this field. Perhaps you recognise early on that you would like to become a head, deputy head or advanced skills teacher. Continuing Professional Development (CPD) is now a major element of the teaching career and every school should have someone who is responsible for this. Keep an eye on the CPD noticeboard in the staff room to see what opportunities are coming up. Ensure you regularly check which courses are being offered by the LEA, exam boards and other agencies as you can use these to develop and extend your understanding and experience of teaching and learning.

Volunteering to be part of a working party or a committee is an excellent way to become more involved in the school and to begin to share in decision-making within the school. Working parties might evaluate and review the school's behaviour policy or investigate the extent to which different learning styles are being catered for across the curriculum. By joining such a group, you will begin to see how management operates and you will become informed about plans that are in the pipeline. As well as being beneficial to you in terms of experience, your interest will be appreciated by the school because unfortunately many teachers do not get involved.

Task 11.3: Preparation task: plan your professional development

When planning your teaching career, you need to be proactive. What do you hope to achieve in the next year? What do you hope to achieve in the next six years? Make a list of your goals and write down how you might go about achieving them. Are there courses you could attend or additional experiences you feel you need? Keep a list and seek opportunities which will allow you to build on your experiences. Find out what is available to you by talking to your colleagues, reading documents relating to CPD and searching the internet. Frequently remind yourself of the bigger picture by referring back to your future goals.

The Fast Track teaching programme

For teachers who aim to reach a position of leadership, such as headteacher, deputy head, assistant head, or advanced skills teacher, there is the Fast Track programme. This is an individually tailored career development programme which supports teachers in achieving their career aspirations and becoming leaders in education. The programme recruits both prospective PGCE students and existing teachers from the primary, secondary and special sectors.

There are currently three stages of assessment, including an assessment centre, which must be passed before a teacher is accepted onto the programme. The stages of assessment are designed so that candidates can demonstrate certain leadership competencies. These include the ability to solve problems; think logically, make decisions, influence and persuade other people, and so on. The assessors look for leadership potential in the ways candidates respond to a series of tasks. Once accepted, there are numerous opportunities available. These include local, regional and national workshops and conferences, personal mentors, equipment, unique CPD opportunities and financial benefits. For further information regarding the Fast Track programme, visit the website at www.fasttrackteaching.gov.uk.

Further academic qualifications

Many universities and colleges, including the Open University, offer qualifications in areas of teaching and education. Some schools will support their teachers in achieving extra qualifications, such as master's degrees, on a part-time basis. Such courses are a formal way to develop your interests in as wide or narrow a field as you choose. Most courses comprise several modules allowing you to increase your knowledge of various educational issues. Academic courses can be a great way to rejuvenate your enthusiasm about teaching, to remind you of the bigger issues and to give you a break from the everyday bureaucracy of the profession. You will learn about the latest theoretical aspects of education, you may produce your own field study and you will be able to put your learning into practice when you return to the classroom. The internet is a good place to start if you want to find out more about higher qualifications in education.

Issues of promotion

Don't get stuck in a rut. Many teachers begin teaching and find themselves in the same position in the same school several years later. The reason is usually that the job has become 'safe and easy'. They have friends on the staff and know the pupils; they are familiar with the systems and feel content. Of course, this may be exactly what the teacher wants, but if it isn't, it's time to consider a change.

Types of promotion

Some teachers will want to take on additional points of responsibility during the early years of their career, while others may choose not to apply for promotions for some time, if at all. Promotion means better pay and will quite often mean less time teaching in the classroom, which is an important consideration. Achieving a promotion with a title also means that you are likely to gain respect from the pupils within the school and this may alter your relationships with the staff. These are all aspects which you must think through before deciding to apply for promotion.

A good thing about teaching is that there are many roles of responsibility at a variety of different levels. The teaching career structure is usually divided into two strands – pastoral and curriculum – although the strands are not entirely separate and teachers do move between them.

Pastoral and curriculum promotion

Pastoral positions, such as head of year, focus on dealing with the pupils, their behaviour and problems and so on, while curriculum positions, such as head of department or head of curriculum area, focus on the effective delivery of the subject within the school. Both types of promotion have rewarding and demanding aspects. In a pastoral role, the teacher will often be required to deal with behavioural problems, which have been passed to them from other teachers. They will also liaise between parents and school, social workers and other outside agencies, often dealing with sensitive issues. It is also worth noting that heads and deputy heads of year/house will often be required to deliver assemblies throughout the year, although in many schools other staff and sometimes students may be involved in these occasions.

The curriculum roles concern themselves more with teaching and learning, planning, assessment, target-setting, evaluating and creating improvement plans. The head of department will also have a budget to allocate to resources within the department. A challenging aspect of the role is dealing with members of staff within the department who may disagree with your ideas or who may show signs of incompetence or reluctance to try new ideas. A curriculum leader will have to deal with such issues sensitively and diplomatically.

There are also other positions of responsibility, such as Gifted and Talented Coordinator, or Literacy Coordinator, which may not be fixed positions and can offer an exciting opportunity for a year or two, as well as preparing you for management later in your career. Such roles enable you to develop an interest in a particular area of education and take on whole-school responsibility. It is likely that these will be internal appointments which you apply for as they become available, rather than changing schools specifically for them.

Promotion leads to better pay and more responsibility, less time spent actually teaching in a classroom, more meetings and more paperwork. The most effective way of finding out whether you want promotion, and if so which position, is to ask people in your school about their roles, to find out what is required of them and how they achieved their position. If and when you decide that promotion is right for you, it will then be a case of deciding whether to stay in your current school and apply for appropriate positions as they arise (i.e. waiting for colleagues to move on) or to look at other schools. Either way, this is a decision which you alone can make. Bear in mind that your school will provide your reference and therefore you won't be able keep your plans secret.

Task 11.4: Preparation task: preparing for promotion

If you are interested in a promotion, talk to colleagues about interviews they have been to and collect a list of questions they have encountered. This will give you a chance to prepare some answers and give you an idea of what to expect from interviews. Make sure you have plenty of examples of your achievements which you can talk about at interview. Although it feels silly, it is a good idea to practise talking about them out loud, perhaps to a friend.

You could also ask people who are currently in the position you aim for how they achieved their job. Make a note of anything you think you might need to do before applying for promotions – for example, do you need more experience of a particular Key Stage?

Be aware of current educational issues

Another important part of your preparation for promotion is to keep abreast of current educational issues and jargon. It is quite likely that you will be asked about your opinions on the most recent educational policies and research. A good source of such information is the TES. Read it regularly and try to implement new teaching theories into your own practice so that you can talk about them with understanding and experience.

Gaining whole-school and extra-curricular experience

At interviews for promotion – whether internal or at a new school – you will be required to demonstrate how you have made a contribution to your school.

One very good way of gaining experience of whole-school issues and of raising your profile within a school is to join working parties. Offering to join such a committee shows that you are enthusiastic and motivated and gives you something to talk about in detail at interview. The experience is likely to make you stand out from other candidates and will prepare you for positions of higher responsibility.

On a wider scale, you could also consider joining cross-curricular and inter-school groups. Don't confine yourself to the English Department, but consider developing cross-curricular links and get involved with other Key Stages. For example, you could join, or begin, a strong working relationship between your school and other local schools, both primary and secondary. Furthermore, there are national and regional groups, such as NATE (National Association for the Teaching of English), which offer CPD events, including workshops and conferences. Details of the opportunities available, as well as teaching resources, can be found on their website at www.nate.org.uk.

Another way of demonstrating your whole-school focus and contribution to the school community is to contribute to extra-curricular activities. You may, for example, help to run the school magazine or create the yearbook. You could also help with producing the school productions – or even produce your own show, with the help of a team. Remember that you don't need to confine yourself to English-based activities; you could become involved with a sports team, for example. There are many benefits to contributing to extra-curricular activities beyond raising your profile and gaining experience. Such involvement shows that you possess skills beyond teaching in the classroom; it shows that you enjoy and can cope with extra responsibility and that you take the initiative. If you are looking towards promotion, you should seek opportunities like these in order to demonstrate and develop your attributes. Furthermore, you will find you develop more positive relationships with the pupils and with members of staff by joining them in reaching a common goal which is outside teaching and learning.

Maintaining a portfolio

Whether or not you are already setting your sights on promotion, it is advisable to keep a record of all your experiences and achievements throughout your career. Such evidence must be referred to when applying to pass through the pay threshold and is an integral part of the Performance Management policies of most schools. When applying for such roles as Advanced Skills Teacher, you will be required to produce a portfolio of evidence. In fact, for most promotions you will need to show what you have achieved and it can be difficult to remember if you have not kept a coherent record. During teacher training you become accustomed to keeping folders of evidence towards meeting the QTS standards and it is a habit worth keeping. From the beginning of your career, you should maintain a portfolio providing examples of your planning and assessment, your involvement at INSET and extra-curricular activities, examples of pupils' work, the results achieved by classes you have taught and so on. A professional portfolio should be a succinct and accessible working document which you regularly update so that it reflects the best work you have produced. It should contain a comprehensive record of your experiences and achievements. Figure 11.2 is a list of items you might include in a professional portfolio in order to demonstrate your achievements.

Teaching is now very much a career, rather than a job. You are able to control your own personal and professional career development and will find that there are many opportunities available to you. Sometimes teachers become engrossed in their daily teaching, ensuring that their pupils progress, and find there is little time to devote to their own progression. During the early years of your teaching career, you are most likely to be enthusiastic and optimistic, so start making your plans early, set yourself goals and have them as a focus which you can return to even when you have a bad day in the classroom. Remember, there are numerous opportunities available to you: make the most of them.

- Page of contents (vital for anyone looking at your portfolio)
- Details of schools you have worked in and classes you have taught
- Details of pastoral experience
- Short-, medium- and long-term plans you have produced
- Examples of assessment – formative and summative
- Performance data: results achieved by classes and value-added information
- Evaluations of your lessons
- Observations of your lessons made by others, including peers and managers
- Examples of pupils' work
- Photographs of displays you have produced or drama productions you have contributed to
- Individual Education Plans (IEP) you have worked on
- Targets you have set pupils and progress towards meeting them
- Reports to parents/carers
- Records of involvement in INSET, workshops and conferences
- Documents relating to contributions to extra-curricular activities (posters, pupil evaluations, photographs, letters to parents)
- Records of involvement in offsite visits
- Feedback from parents
- Learning logs you may have produced
- Evidence of subject knowledge
- Details of how you have collaborated with colleagues
- Articles you have read/been influenced by/written

Figure 11.2   Possible items to include in a professional portfolio

Further reading

Cole, M. (2002) *Professional Values and Practice for Teachers*, David Fulton, London.

Cowley, S. (2003) *How to Survive Your First Year in Teaching*, Continuum, London.

Croft, A. (1996) *Continuing Professional Development: A Practical Guide for Teachers in Schools*, Routledge, London.

Donnelly, J. (2002) *Career Development for Teachers: The TES Handbook*, Kogan Page, London.

Taylor, F. (1996) *Careers in Teaching*, Kogan Page, London.

www.teachernet.gov.uk/professionaldevelopment

12 The future of English

Jane Branson

Introduction

English teachers have always had to, and no doubt always will, balance the old with the new, the classic forms with the emerging forms, the standard and proper with the subversive and challenging. Working within this set of dichotomies, English teachers are well placed to foster traditional skills and highlight the literary gems of the past, although it's likely that few new teachers at the beginning of the twenty-first century would posit themselves merely, or even mainly, as exponents of the Cultural Heritage model (see p. 10). Equally, it is to be hoped that few of us see ourselves solely as deliverers of basic skills, preparing pupils for entry into the world of work. Indeed, if this were the main function of English teaching, we should be spending a lot more time trying to predict the kinds of technological and social change that might shape the working lives of pupils currently in our care. Most English teachers probably occupy the middle ground, recognising the importance of offering students the opportunity to experience and access the literary greats, as well as the more functional nature of our subject and the contribution it makes in creating a skilled, literate workforce of the future. Many of us also want to use our subject to facilitate personal development and engagement among our students, to encourage 'students as participants in, and creators of, culture as opposed to merely inheritors of someone else's' (Goodwyn, 2000: 6). If we add to that the tradition of critical analysis of literature and other texts, and thereby the world they present and represent, we have a broad and fairly enduring definition of English teaching.

However, we live in a constantly modifying world, one in which the rate of change is faster and more visible than ever before. English teachers, somewhat battle-weary perhaps, but nevertheless energetic and passionate, are used to change and will no doubt continue to develop, evolve and adapt, whatever challenges come their way in the current century and beyond.

Objectives

In this chapter, we will consider the future for learners and teachers of English and in particular:

- the importance of maintaining the integrity of the subject of English in a changing world;
- the potential impact of technology on English pedagogy.

The subject of English

English, as Chapter 1 makes clear, is a difficult subject to define, which only makes it more controversial when we try to do so. It is the only one of the core National Curriculum subjects without an obvious discipline to support and inform it. An amalgam of more and less traditional studies, the term 'English' on an academic curriculum includes the study of literature, linguistics, literacy, social science, language, media and grammar. At different stages of education, from reception year to postgraduate level, these and other aspects are given varying degrees of prominence. Perhaps this is why it is a subject whose integrity is under constant attack.

As we cannot predict the future with any certainty, it is even more important that we maintain our defences against these front-line assaults from a range of sources: the basic skills brigade; the pressure to raise literacy levels at all costs; the testing agenda; the persistence of those who hold up the canon as all that is worthy of study; the advance of technology which is changing the very nature of reading, writing and talk; the curriculum writers who are mostly middle-aged non-teachers who inevitably hark back to their own school days for inspiration and decide what's important.

Most English teachers have their own gut instinct about what English teaching is. Defining their subject, they might refer to the importance of promoting critical consumption of the world, of fostering a love of language and the written word, of creating literate and questioning citizens or of nurturing the appreciation of literature. At the heart of all these priorities – and the National Curriculum demands that we engage in them all – lies communication: the ability and process of conveying and appreciating meaning in different forms, for different audiences and for different purposes.

While English remains so indefinable – and, after, all that's what makes it such an exciting subject to teach – English teachers will always have to incorporate new concepts, new text types and new ways of representing, interpreting and creating meaning into their lessons. On a practical day-to-day level, this means that one day we might be discussing Shakespeare and the next be exploring the way that websites are designed to manipulate the reader. On a more fundamental level, it means that we must:

> see the English curriculum *not only* in its traditional role of *preparing students* for that future, but to see the curriculum, and the people who experience it, as *making and shaping* that future through the competent and confident action.
>
> (Kress, 1995: 3)

Kress sums up both the challenge and the possibilities of English teaching. Because we know only that the future will be different, we must be open to change, and embrace newness and the unfamiliar. At the same time, we cannot allow the amorphous nature of our subject to be an excuse for those with ulterior motives to undermine and hijack its breadth and scope.

The impact of technology on English pedagogy

Coping with change

As with all the subjects of the curriculum, both traditional and emerging, the practice of teaching English is undergoing a period of far-reaching change. English teachers need to be at the forefront of the technological developments that are affecting communication, and which, after all, are at the heart of our subject (see Chapter 7). This is perhaps the greatest challenge facing English teachers today. Apart from dealing with the inadequacies of funds and resources that make it so hard to keep up with – let alone be ahead of – such developments within schools, the challenge for most us is to incorporate these technologies in a seamless way into our lessons. English must not become a slave to ICT. Rather, it should be the opposite: new technology must be exploited in order to enhance teaching and learning in English classrooms. At the same time, English teachers must be aware of the ways in which the very acts and arts of communication are evolving as a result of technological development. They must embed this awareness within their lessons; to learn English in the modern world is necessarily to learn about the social and economic power of language manipulation.

School life is changing in general terms under the influence of technological possibility and the computerisation of administration, and hastened by union calls for the reduction of teaching workload. Table 12.1 presents an overview of a small selection of whole-school and English situations to summarise how they

Table 12.1   Changes in schools

The past	The present	The future?
Annual reports written by hand	Termly reports word-processed, facilitated by mail-merging tools or generated by specially written software	Data and comments electronically stored and emailed to parents on request
Lesson notes copied from blackboard	Notes and activities electronically stored and reproduced by the teacher	Lesson notes and interactive exercises published on school website, for access by all students and parents
Head teachers' communications with staff and parents typed and posted/delivered to staff pigeonholes	School newsletter produced and distributed weekly; email used for day-to-day communication	In-school announcements made via computer screens around school building updated hourly and by email/text message to all staff, parents and students
External and internal exams written and marked by hand	Some internal exams electronically delivered and assessed, designed in-house or by designated web-based providers	Students sit external and internal exams online
'Chalk and talk' teaching methods dominate English classrooms, complemented by 'reading around the class' and learning by rote	Increasing use of interactive whiteboards to present information and engage students actively in their learning; use of video, audio and digital technology to bring texts to life	Individual palm-top technology allows students to work independently with frequent one-to-one teacher intervention
Students produce handwritten essays, stories and exercises for their teacher, or sometimes for display purposes	Students' writing in a wide variety of forms can be published to a professional standard using DTP packages and communicated to a range of audiences, via the internet and school website	Students' work sent directly to teacher within electronic learning environment for developmental feedback, with comments and progress stored for later reference and monitoring purposes

have developed in recent times and how they might realistically evolve in the near future. One of the difficulties of predicting such developments is that schools around Britain may currently find themselves at any one of the points described here, very loosely, as 'past', 'present' and 'future'. National attempts to move schools on and to widen access to technology, such as the creation of the National Grid for Learning, have been partially successful, yet the variation of provision is wide. To a great extent, the progress of schools in making full and exploitative use of technology depends on the vision, energy and determination of their staff. Some things never change!

The classroom of the future

Chapter 7 of this volume deals in detail with methods of enhancing learning in English with ICT tools, and also with the logistical and secretarial implications of easy (and sometimes not so easy) access to ICT in schools. Here, it is important to consider the ways in which a typical English classroom might change in the foreseeable future. The rate of change in last 20 or so years has been extreme and, visiting any school today, it is to be hoped that you will notice huge differences between what you find there and your memories of your own English classroom. And the rate of change will only accelerate. In a 1997 survey of trainee teachers' experience of and attitudes to IT, less than 4 per cent had made 'considerable use' of computers in their own school experiences (Goodwyn *et al.*, 1997: 6). We can be sure, at least, that the vast majority of school leavers today will have been exposed to a range of ICT experiences, even under the mantle of the English curriculum, from preparing a PowerPoint presentation to contributing to the school website or taking part in a video conference.

Of course, one of the most significant obstacles to change and development in schools is that their infrastructure is very inflexible. Many schools have been designed and built in a piecemeal fashion, over decades and even centuries, with financial corner-cutting and in a culture in which the learning environment is paid little heed. Even new schools are not necessarily designed or constructed with a teacher on hand. Frustratingly, pupil numbers dictate funding, but only in retrospect; an over-populated school will be seen as a sign of success, yet such schools are often desperate for more accommodation.

But we can all dream. Let us for a moment imagine an ideal English classroom, designed by English teachers for English teachers.

Space and furniture

The room would be two to three times the size of an average classroom in a typical school, with enough PCs or laptops for each individual use, as well as sufficient space for a range of seating arrangements – individual desks, grouped tables for collaborative work, a horseshoe for presentations. Pupil desks and chairs would be flexible in height and angle to provide for the smallest to the tallest of students, and for comfortable positioning for different tasks, as well as being free of graffiti and nubs of hardening chewing-gum. They would be easily moved to facilitate collaborative pair or group work, or to clear a space for a drama activity. Chairs would also be padded and supportive of good posture. There would be sufficient shelving for a classroom library of fiction and reference books, together with adequate secure cupboard space for a wide range of gadgets. In a teacher's area, a comfortably sized and lockable desk would be complemented by an area of soft seating for small group interactions, pastoral interventions and assessment feedback.

Resources and equipment

In addition to the full set of individual computers, we might expect to find a digital camera, recording and editing equipment, a music/audio system with headsets, a TV with DVD/video player, a telephone, an interactive whiteboard and projector, and an OHP. A set of basic drama tools (some props and pieces of costume, a sponge ball, a set of beanbags) would also be available. Paper in a range of sizes, lined, plain and coloured, is a prerequisite, as well as a full range of stationery items – hole-punches, staplers, sticky tape, Blu Tac, rulers, pens, pencils, and so on.

Physical environment

The classroom would be light and airy, but with the capacity for total black-out to facilitate drama and media work. Display boards would cover all walls and be properly maintained, providing sample work to inspire students as well as practical information, advice and reminders about English skills. Carpet to limit the noise of students and teacher moving around the room, fresh paint on the walls and a comfortable working temperature would enhance the teaching and learning atmosphere.

Some of these requirements may not seem excessive. Indeed, in a few years many of them will seem passé as the classroom experience evolves to incorporate new generations of technological advance. Yet head teachers, governing bodies and local authorities do not have the resources to create even one of these classrooms, let alone a suite of them. And, despite scarcity of equipment, poor quality furniture, shoddy and uninspiring decor, and when even the departmental hole-punch is a jealously guarded tool, excellent English lessons are being taught every day. Many English teachers succeed in creating a pleasant and welcoming learning environment against all the odds, deploying their organisational and presentational skills to great effect. Perhaps more than anything, the future of English – i.e. its integrity, its diversity, its ability to evolve and assimilate – depends on the enthusiasm, passion and imagination of its teachers. And we can at least depend on those.

Further reading

Bloom, Lynn Z. (ed.) *et al.* (2003) *Composition Studies in the Millennium: Rereading the Past, Rewriting the Future*, Southern Illinois Press, Carbondale, IL.

Hodges, Cliff G. with Moss, John and Shreeve, Ann (2000) 'The Future of English', *English in Education*, 34 (1), Spring.

Popcorn, Faith and Hanft, Adam (2002) *Dictionary of the Future: The Words, Terms and Trends That Define the Way We'll Live, Work and Talk*, Hyperion, New York.

References

Abbs, P. (1982) *English within the Arts: A Radical Alternative for English and the Arts in the Curriculum*, Hodder & Stoughton, London.

ALITE (Accelerated Learning in Training and Education) 'What are brain breaks?', available at www.alite.co.uk (accessed 31 July 2003).

Andrews, R. (ed.) (2003) *The Impact of ICT on Literacy Education*, RoutledgeFalmer, London.

Applebee, A. (1974) *Tradition and Reform in the Teaching of English: A History*, NCTE, Urbana.

Bazalgette, C. (1989) *Primary Media Education: A Curriculum Statement*, BFI, London.

Bazalgette, C., Earle, W., Grahame, J., Reid, M. and West, A. (eds) (2000) *Moving Images in the Classroom*, BFI, London.

BBC Skillswise, available at www.bbc.co.uk/skillswise (accessed 31 July 2003).

Beavis, C. (2001) 'Digital Cultures: Digital Literacies', in *P(ICT)ures of English: Teachers Learners and Pedagogy*, C. Durrant and C. Beavis (eds), AATE/ Wakefield Press, Kent Town, South Australia.

Benton, P. (1996) 'Children's Reading and Viewing in the Nineties' in *What is English Teaching?*, C. Davies (ed.), Open University Press, Buckingham.

BFI (1999) *Making Movies Matter: Report of the Film Education Working Group*, BFI, London.

BFI (2000) *Moving Images in the Classroom: A Secondary Teacher's Guide to Using Film and Television*, BFI, London.

Black, P. and Wiliam, D. (1998) *Inside the Black Box: Raising Standards Through Classroom Assessment*, King's College London, available at www.kcl.ac.uk/ education/publications/Black%20Box.pdf (accessed 6 September 2003).

Bowker, J. (1989) *Secondary Media Education: A Curriculum Statement*, BFI, London.

Britton, J. (1970) *Language and Learning*, Penguin, London.

Britton, J., Shafer, R. and Watson, K. (1990) *Teaching and Learning English World-wide*, Multilingual Matters, Clevedon.

Bryson, B (1990) *Mother Tongue: The English Language*, Hamish Hamilton, London.

Buckingham, D. (ed.) (1993a) *Reading Audiences: Young People and the Media*, Manchester University Press, Manchester.

Buckingham, D. (1993b) *Children Talking Television: The Making of Television Literacy*, Falmer Press, London.

Buckingham, D. (1996) *Moving Images: Understanding Children's Emotional Responses to Television*, Manchester University Press, Manchester.

Buckingham, D. (2000) *The Making of Citizens: Young People, News and Politics*, Routledge, London.

Buckingham, D. (2002) *After the Death of Childhood: Growing Up in the Age of Electronic Media*, Open University Press, Buckingham.

Buckingham, D. (2003) *Media Education: Literacy, Learning and Contemporary Culture*, Blackwell, London.

Buckingham, D., Grahame, J. and Sefton-Green, J. (1995) *Making Media: Practical Production in Media Education*, The English and Media Centre, London.

Burn, A. (2000) 'Creativity with Moving Images' in *Moving Images in the Classroom*, C. Bazalgette, W. Earle, J. Grahame, M. Reid and A. West (eds), BFI, London.

Burn, A. (2003) 'ICT and Moving Image Literacies', in *The Impact of ICT on Literacy Education*, R. Andrews (ed.), RoutledgeFalmer, London.

Burn, A. and Reed, K. (1999) 'Digi-teens: Media Literacies and Digital Technologies in the Secondary Classroom', *English in Education*, 33 (3), Autumn 1999, NATE, Sheffield.

Burn, A. and Parker, D. (2001) 'Making your Mark: Digital Inscription, Animation, and a New Visual Semiotic', *Education, Communication and Information*, 1: 155–179.

Burn, A. and Schott, G. (2003) 'Heavy Hero or Digital Dummy: Multi-modal Player-avatar Relations in Final Fantasy 7', *Visual Communication*, 3 (2), pp. 213–233.

Burn, A., Brindley, S., Durran, J., Kelsall, K., Sweetlove, J. and Tuohey, C. (2001) 'The Rush of Images: A Research Report into Digital Editing and the Moving Image', *English in Education*, 35 (2), NATE, Sheffield.

Burton, G. (2000) *Talking Television: An Introduction to the Study of Television*, Arnold, London.

Cope, B. and Kalantzis, M. (eds) (1993) *The Powers of Literacy: A Genre Approach to Teaching Writing*, Falmer Press, London.

Cope, B. and Kalantzis, M. (2000) *Multiliteracies: Literacy Learning and the Design of Social Futures*, Routledge, London.

Crystal, D. (1987) *The Cambridge Encyclopedia of Language*, Cambridge University Press, Cambridge.

Crystal, D. (2001) *Rediscover Grammar with David Crystal*, Longman, London.

DES (1975) *A Language for Life* (The Bullock Report), HMSO, London.

DES (1989) *English for Ages 5–16* (The Cox Report), HMSO, London.

DES (1990) *English in the National Curriculum*, HMSO, London.

DES (1995) *English for Ages 5–16* (First major revision to the National Curriculum for English), HMSO, London.

DfEE (2001) *Framework for Teaching English: Years 7, 8 and 9*, DfEE, London.

DfEE and QCA (2001) *Key Stage 3 National Strategy*, DfEE, London.

DfEE (1999) *English National Curriculum*, DfEE, London.

DfEE (2000) *English National Curriculum*, DfEE, London.

DfES (2002a) (accessed 20 August 2002) DfEE A–Z available at www.teachernet.gov.uk/a-z/HOMEWORK%5FPOLICY.html.

DfES (2002b) *ImpaCT 2: The Impact of Information and Communication Technologies on Pupil Learning and Attainment*, HMSO, London.

Doughty, P., Pearce, J. and Thornton G. (1971) *Language in Use* (Schools Council Programme in Linguistics and English teaching), Heinemann, London.

Durrant, C. and Beavis, C. (eds) (2001) *P(ICT)ures of English: Teachers Learners and Pedagogy*, AATE/Wakefield Press, Kent Town, South Australia.

Eagleton, T. (1983) *An Introduction to Literary Theory*, Basil Blackwell, Oxford.

Ellis, V and Robinson, M (2000) 'Writing in English and Responding to Writing' in *Evaluating Creativity: Making and Learning by Young People*, J. Sefton-Green and R. Sinker (eds), Routledge, London.

Exhall Grange and Southam Technology College (December 2001) 'Inclusion Issues' for SEN, available at www.standards.dfes.gov.uk/ (accessed June 2003, via Standards Site).

Goodson, I (ed.) (1993) *School Subjects and Curriculum Change*, Falmer Press, London.

Goodson, I. and Medway, P. (1990) *Bringing English to Order*, Falmer Press, London.

Goodwyn, A. (1992a) *English Teaching and Media Education*, Open University Press, Buckingham.

Goodwyn, A. (1992b) 'Theoretical Models of English Teaching', *English in Education*, 26 (3), NATE, Sheffield.

Goodwyn, A. (1997a) *Developing English Teachers: The Role of Mentorship in a Reflective Profession*, Open University Press, Buckingham.

Goodwyn, A. (1997b) 'Mother Tongue or Mother Media', paper given at the International Association for The Improvement of Mother Tongue Education, International Conference, University of Amsterdam, July 1997.

Goodwyn, A. (1997c) 'English Teachers' Theories of Teaching', paper given at the International Association for The Improvement of Mother Tongue Education, International Conference, University of Amsterdam, July 1997.

Goodwyn, A (ed.) (1998) *Literary and Media Texts in Secondary English*, Cassells, London.

Goodwyn, A. (ed.) (2000) *English in the Digital Age*, Continuum, London.

Goodwyn, A. (ed.) (2002a) *Improving Literacy at KS2 and KS3*, Sage, London.

Goodwyn, A. (2002b) 'Breaking up is Hard to Do: English Teachers and that LOVE of Reading', *English Teaching, Practice and Critique*, 1 (1), pp. 66–78.

Goodwyn, A. (2003) 'Literacy or English: the Struggle for the Professional Identity of English Teachers in England', in *English Teachers at Work: Narratives, Counter-narratives and Arguments*, AATE/Interface and Wakefield Press, Kent Town, South Australia.

Goodwyn, A. (2004) *English Teaching and the Moving Image*, RoutledgeFalmer, London

Goodwyn, A. and Findlay, K. (2001) 'Media Studies and the Establishment', *The International Journal of Media Education*, 1 (1), pp. 23–40.

Goodwyn, A. and Zancanella, D. (2003) 'How Pre-service Teachers in England and the United States View Media Literacy', paper given at the American Educational Research Association Conference, Chicago.

Goodwyn, A., Adams, A. and Clarke, S. (1997) 'The Great God of the Future: English Teachers and Information Technology', *English in Education*, 30 (2), NATE, Sheffield.

Goodwyn, A., Clarke, S. and Adams, A. (1997) 'The Future Curriculum in English and IT: How Teachers and Student-teachers View the Relationship' in *The Future Curriculum Journal of Information Technology for Teacher Education*, 6 (3), Triangle Journals.

Green, B. (ed.) (1993) *The Insistence of the Letter: Literacy Studies and Curriculum Theorizing*, Falmer Press, London.

Haas-Dyson, A. (1997) *Writing Superheroes: Contemporary Childhood, Popular Culture and Classroom Literacy*, Teachers College Press, Columbia.

Hannan, G. (1999) *Improving Boys' Performance*, Folens, Dunstable.

Hart, A. and Benson, T. (1992) *Models of Media Education: A Study of Secondary English Teachers Teaching Media, Part 1, Overview, Occasional Papers, 11*, Centre for Language in Education, University of Southampton, Southampton.

Hart, A. and Benson, T. (1993) *Models of Media Education: A Study of Secondary English Teachers Teaching Media, Part 2, Profiles and Lessons, Occasional Papers, 12*, Centre for Language in Education, University of Southampton, Southampton.

Hart, A. and Hicks, A. (2002) *Teaching Media in the English Curriculum*, Trentham Books, London.

Harvey, I., Skinner, M. and Parker, D. (2002) *Being Seen, Being Heard: Young People and Moving Image Production*, BFI/National Youth Agency, London.

Hay Group (accessed 5 August 2002) 'Transforming Learning', available at www.transforminglearning.co.uk/default.cfm?pagename=homepage%2F aboutus%2Ecfm&uid=147FBE7C-A884-11D6-8AEC00508B668278.

Higgins, C. (2002) 'Using Film Text to Support Reluctant Writers', *English in Education*, 36 (1), NATE, Sheffield.

Jeffcoate, R. (1992) *Starting English Teaching*, Routledge, London.

Kar2ouche® www.kar2ouche.com.

Kenway, J. and Bullen, E. (2001) *Consuming Children: Education, Entertainment, Advertising*, Open University Press, Buckingham.

King, S. (2001) *On Writing: A Memoir of the Craft*, Hodder & Stoughton: New English Library, London.

Kress, G. (1995) *Writing the Future: English and the Making of a Culture of Innovation*, NATE, Sheffield.

Kress, G. (2002) 'English for an Era of Instability: Aesthetics, Ethics, Creativity and Design', *English in Australia*, 134: 15–24.

Kress, G. (2003) *Literacy in the New Media Age*, Routledge, London.

Kress, G. and Van Leeuwen, T. (1996), *Reading Images: a Grammar of Visual Design*, Routledge, London.

Lankshear, C. (1997) *Changing Literacies*, Open University Press, Buckingham.

Leavis, F. R. and Thompson, D. (1933) *Culture and Environment*, Chatto & Windus, London.

Lee, C. and Smagorinsky, P. (2000) *Vygotskian Perspectives on Literacy: Constructing Meaning through Collaborative Inquiry*, Cambridge University Press, London.

Lemin, K. (2001) 'Practical Production Work within an Integrated English and Media Curriculum: Acquisition of Theory or Creative Exploration?', *English in Education*, 35 (1), NATE, Sheffield.

Livingstone, S. (2002) *Young People and New Media: Childhood and the Changing Media Environment*, Sage, London.

Marland, M. (ed.) (1977) *Language Across the Curriculum*, Heinemann Educational, London.

Masterman, L. (1980) *Teaching about Television*, Macmillan, London.

Mathieson, M. (1975) *The Preachers of Culture*, Allen & Unwin, London.

Morgan, W. (1997) *Critical Literacy in the English Classroom: The Art of the Possible*, Routledge, London.

Myers, M. (1996) *Changing our Minds: Negotiating English and Literacy*, NCTE, Urbana.

National Advisory Committee on Creative and Cultural Education (1999) *All our Futures: Creativity, Culture and Education*, DfEE, London.

The National Curriculum, DfES, www.nc.net (accessed 2003).

Nicholls, G. (1999) *Learning to Teach*, Kogan Page, London.

Noble, C. and Bradford, W. (2000) *Getting it Right for Boys . . . and Girls*, Routledge, London.

Pirie, B. (1997) *Reshaping High School English*, NCTE, Urbana.

QCA (2002) *Changes to Assessment 2003: Guidance for Teachers of Key Stage 3 English*, QCA, London.

QCA 'Inclusion: Providing Effective Learning Opportunities for all Pupils', available at www.qca.org.uk/ca/inclusion/index.asp?fp_clk (accessed July 2003).

QCA 'Guidance on Teaching Gifted and Talented Pupils', available at www.qca.org.uk/ca/inclusion/index.asp?fp_clk (accessed July 2003).

Rogers, B. (2000) *Classroom Behaviour: A Practical Guide to Effective Teaching, Behaviour Management and Colleague Support*, Books Education, London.

Rouse M. and Florian L. (1997) 'Inclusive Education in the Marketplace', *International Journal of Inclusive Education* 1, pp. 323–336.

Scholes, R. (1985) *Textual Power: Literary Theory and the Teaching of English*, Yale University Press, London.

Sefton-Green, J. and Sinker, R. (eds) (2000), *Evaluating Creativity: Making and Learning by Young People*, Routledge, London.

Smith, A. (1998) *Accelerated Learning in Practice: Brain-based Methods for Accelerating Motivation and Achievement*, Network Educational Press, Stafford.

Special Educational Needs Code of Practice (2001) DfES, London.

Standards Site Individual Education Plans (IEP), available at www.standards.dfes.gov.uk/ (accessed June 2003).

Teachit (1999) 'Teachit Planning Aids', available at www.teachit.co.uk (accessed 31 July 2003).

Theroux, P. (2002) 'Enhance Learning with Technology–Differentiating Instruction', available at www.enhancelearning.ca (accessed November 2002).

TTA (2003) *Qualifying to Teach Professional Standards for Qualified Teacher Status and Requirements for Initial Teacher Training*, TTA, London.

Tuman, M. (1992) *Word Perfect: Literacy in the Computer Age*, Falmer Press, London.

Tweddle. S., Adams, A., Clarke, S., Scrimshaw, P. and Walton, S. (1997) *English for Tomorrow*, Open University Press, Buckingham.

Watkins, C. (2001) 'Learning about Learning Enhances Performance' in *National School Improvement Network Research Matters 13*, Institute of Education, London.

Webster, Alec, Beveridge, Michael and Reed, Malcolm (1996) *Managing the Literacy Curriculum – How Schools Can Become Communities of Readers and Writers*, Routledge, London.

Wray, David and Lewis, Maureen (1997) *Extending Literacy: Children Reading and Writing Non-fiction*, Routledge, London.

Zancanella, D., Hall, L. and Pence, P. (2000) 'Treating Computer Games as Literature', in *English in the Digital Age*, A. Goodwyn (ed.), Continuum, London, pp. 87–102.

Index